BENJAMIN FRANKLIN

His Contribution to the American Tradition

I. BERNARD COHEN

Makers of the American Tradition

THE BOBBS-MERRILL COMPANY, INC.
Publishers

INDIANAPOLIS   NEW YORK

E
302.6
F8
C67

First Edition

BENJAMIN FRANKLIN

Makers of the American Tradition Series

General Editors

HIRAM HAYDN
DONALD BIGELOW

Volumes Ready:

Volumes in Preparation:

Volumes Planned:

THOMAS JEFFERSON
COTTON MATHER
JOHN C. CALHOUN
RALPH WALDO EMERSON
WILLIAM JAMES
and others

To

FRANCES

GENERAL INTRODUCTION

FOR THE

Makers of the American Tradition Series

THE PURPOSE of this series is to present in a fresh and challenging way the great figures of the American tradition—those individuals who have been most influential throughout the history of the American people in forging that strong and yet complex phenomenon that constitutes what we call the American tradition or the American way of life.

Countless books have been written about these men; a good many books containing their writings and speeches have been published; many biographies of them have appeared. But the *Makers of the American Tradition* Series is a genuinely new approach to the story of our heritage. These books are not biographies; they are not anthologies. They are a combination of original text and interpretation. They embody a new and fresh approach because they combine the best and most characteristic of the original written and recorded spoken words of outstanding American figures with thoughtful and incisive interpretations by the distinguished scholars chosen to put these books together.

In each volume the focus is upon those elements in the contributions of these Americans—whether in terms of original thought or articulate and decisive leadership—

which best characterize the *particular* quality, in each case, of the contribution. All other aspects of, say, Benjamin Franklin or Andrew Jackson or Roger Williams are in these books subordinated to what each had most peculiarly to contribute to the shaping of the American tradition.

When we speak of the American tradition, we are, of course, referring to a complex of various and sometimes opposing traditions, but if there is any single outstanding American principle, I suppose that it is that of the finding of unity through multiplicity and diversity. The American tradition, a composite in itself, is analogous to the United States and the American people, each being a complex of many simples.

Similarly, when we speak of the *makers* of this tradition, we are, of course, aware that no ten or twenty or fifty men, however talented, however able, really *made* this tradition. Nevertheless, the individuals we have chosen as the subjects for these books seem to us to have been outstandingly important in shaping the way of life that is our heritage today. Hence, just as we welcome in the American tradition its superficially strange mixture of radical idealism and plain horse sense, of a general love of liberty and a sober sense of social responsibility, of honest conservatism and honest dissidence, so we welcome in this series such conflicting disparate figures as Thomas Jefferson and Alexander Hamilton, Roger Williams and John C. Calhoun, Cotton Mather and John Dewey.

For whom is this series intended? It is our hope and belief that it is intended for every literate American of whatever age and description. For we are firmly convinced that the books in this series will leave their readers with a far more concise and exact idea of what the great leaders of the American people have thought, said and stood for than they have ever had before.

Much has been made and is being made of the confusion and anxiety under which all of us labor today. Much has been said in various ways of the extent to which all people, and among them notably Americans, are searching for their souls. Much has been said about both the external and internal threats to our American way of life—threats that many Americans, with whatever different interpretations, feel surround us on all sides. We are faced unquestionably with the challenge of building a free and confident America, for ourselves and for the free world in our time.

In a time of crisis, how may we find that strength and that confidence? It seems to me that it is a constant in human nature at such times to turn inward, to return to one's roots, one's origins, to find such resources. I believe this to be as true for peoples as for individuals. The ideal of self-knowledge as a source of strength and confidence does not imply a selfish or extravagant preoccupation with self. Rather, a time of crisis calls for an examination and appraisal of one's own resources in order to turn one's attention outward again, freshened and fortified by a new inner sureness. As Americans, we can best effect this self-examination, we can best find our true origins, by returning to the words and thoughts of those individuals who have contributed most mightily to our enduring strength. And since most of us lack the special training that would enable us to move unaided with ease in the social and intellectual context of another time, we solicit the help of such people as those who are making the books in this series—individual author-editors whom we have chosen for breadth and depth of knowledge and for generosity of mind and spirit—that they may the better guide us, through these books, in our self-examination.

HIRAM HAYDN

Foreword

ONE of the outstanding needs in Franklin scholarship is a study of his humorous writings and satires; many of them, created as "space-fillers" for his newspaper, have never been identified as his and collected. I am certain that when such a job will have been done, Franklin will emerge as America's first humorist, in the tradition of Mark Twain, Mr. Dooley and Will Rogers. So it is with a sense of regret that we learn that Mark Twain never found in Benjamin Franklin a kindred iconoclastic spirit and that apparently he never knew the gay and witty Franklin—master of the hoax and practical joke, writer of "tall stories," author of joyous drinking songs and lover of puns, who also wrote a few "broad" and earthy pieces that his editors have not thought fit to be reprinted. Mark Twain's generation was acquainted with Franklin chiefly as a moralizer about daily life, presented in the *Autobiography* and Poor Richard's maxims on thrift, industry, good health and the way to become wealthy. Throughout most of the nineteenth century Franklin was never grasped in his full stature; his scientific research which had caused scientists throughout the world to call him the Newton of their age was reduced to the single experiment of the lightning kite, and he became known as an inventor of stoves, lightning rods and all manner of useful gadgets,

rather than as a pure scientist; men forgot that Franklin
had been referred to as the father of his country and knew
this title only as it was applied (later) to George Washington; and, in general, Franklin's delightful genius which
had made him one of the outstanding men of his day was
reduced to a collection of commonly admired middle-class
virtues.

It was just these virtues which Mark Twain could not
stomach and they were the occasion of some of his most
wicked and hilarious creations. A wonderful essay in *The
Golden Era* (for July 3, 1864) began with a display of
Poor Richard's most famous saying and a reply invented
by Mark Twain for the occasion:

> *Early to bed, and early to rise,*
> *Makes a man healthy, wealthy and wise.*
> —Benjamin Franklin.

> *I don't see it.*—George Washington.

Now both of these are high authorities—very high and
respectable authorities—but I am with General Washington first, last, and all the time on this proposition.
Because I don't see it, either. . . .

The lightning rod and the Franklin stove equally inspired
Mark Twain; most readers will remember how hard they
laughed at the lightning-rod salesman in "Political Economy." In "The late Benjamin Franklin," Mark Twain announced his intention "to snub those pretentious maxims"
of Poor Richard and also to snub Benjamin Franklin's
"stove, and his military inspirations, his unseemly endeavor to make himself conspicuous when he entered
Philadelphia, and his flying his kite and fooling away his

time in all sorts of such ways when he ought to have been foraging for soap-fat, or constructing candles."

To judge by the accounts in American history books, the image of Franklin that aroused Mark Twain's heroic irritation persists; to this day Franklin is not appreciated in all his mighty dimensions, and we may observe that certain common misconceptions about Benjamin Franklin are related to erroneous ideas about the American character. Scholars are aware of his patriotic services in his country's cause, but they often tend to stress unduly what they mistakenly call the pragmatic aspect of his character. Furthermore, Franklin's concern for success in business, expressed in the sayings of Poor Richard and a guide called *The Way to Wealth,* has become almost universally accepted as his dominant trait, just as a zeal for making money has become the distinguishing mark—in the eyes of writers throughout the world—of the American national character. The sociologist Max Weber chose Franklin (in his maxims on how to obtain wealth) as the major example to illustrate the thesis that the "Protestant ethic" was particularly adapted to the rise of capitalism, and scholars have generally approved the choice. Calvin Coolidge's famous saying, "The business of the American people is business," has evoked approval as a description of the major aspect of our national life, and many Europeans and Americans would agree that Franklin's formulation of rules for getting rich is symbolic of the American materialist concentration on acquisition of the world's goods.

Those who quote Calvin Coolidge on business do not usually repeat what Coolidge added to that sentence: "The chief ideal of the American people is idealism. I cannot repeat too often that America is a nation of idealists." Americans are supposed to place a higher value on

making money than Europeans, but they are also noted
for their generosity, for spending their money freely and
giving it away. In America, as Harriet Martineau observed
in the nineteenth century, "the eager pursuit of wealth
does not necessarily indicate a love of wealth for its own
sake." Making money has had a special significance to a
nation made up of men and women who could recall "how
hungry and ill-clad their ancestors had been through the
centuries in the Old World," A. M. Schlesinger has written. "It was the means of living a life of human dignity.
In other words, for the great majority of Americans it was
a symbol of idealism rather than materialism." The American "had an instinctive sympathy for the underdog, and
even persons of moderate wealth gratefully shared it with
the less fortunate, helping to endow charities, schools, hospitals and art galleries and providing the wherewithal to
nourish movements for humanitarian reform. . . ."

Any view of the American character which is based on
a concentration on how Americans make money is bound
to be a distortion unless an equal consideration is given
to what Americans do with the money they make; so our
conception of Franklin as an individual, and as a pioneer
of the American personality, must suffer if we do not keep
uppermost in our minds his constant injunctions against
miserliness, if we do not emphasize the ideals to which he
devoted himself while making money and after he had
acquired a moderate fortune. Franklin, in other words,
was more typical of America than his *Way to Wealth*,
taken by itself, would indicate. Defender of the rights of
man, he demanded that men help one another to live better lives. Patron of the arts, sciences and higher learning,
he taught by precept and by example that men must endow and maintain schools and colleges to serve men's

minds as well as hospitals to care for their bodies. The American blend of practicality and idealism is exemplified by the very combination of his activities: subscriptions in support of churches and a synagogue, and a college library; inventions to produce comfortable homes that were well heated and ventilated and protected from the lightning; support of the movement for the abolition of slavery and sponsorship of a school so that those Negroes who had been freed could learn trades and earn a standard of living equal to that of whites; organization of a fire company and a regular constabulary and also a subscription library; and a proposal for a more direct democracy than we know today.

Selections from the writings of Benjamin Franklin have appealed to the reading public ever since the first one was put together by Peter Collinson and published in London in 1751. That volume was devoted entirely to Franklin's scientific work, chiefly his research on electricity, and supplements were issued in 1753 and 1754. By the time of the American Revolution, it had been enlarged into an American miscellany of natural philosophy, and five editions had been published in England, while translations had appeared in French, German and Italian. In 1779, Benjamin Vaughan brought out a volume of selections containing political and "philosophical pieces"—the only edition of Franklin's nonscientific writings to be printed during his lifetime. During the 202 years from 1751 to 1953, collected editions of Franklin's writings and new volumes of selections have appeared with great regularity. Most of the latter have been intended to show Franklin as a "man of letters" or the preacher of homely maxims on frugality, but others have presented his "autobiographical" writings, "letters to the press" or scientific communications; a large number of them have simply displayed the "many-sided" Franklin. The present work differs from these in its aim of showing to Americans in the mid-twentieth century how Franklin expresses some of our most cherished ideals. The nature of the series for which it was compiled has precluded any attempt to tell the reader what Franklin *did;* he is presented here in terms of what he *said,* exhibiting qualities of belief that we esteem in our American tradition. Thus, for example, his services to his country as diplomat have not been treated, nor his trade as printer.

David Hume called Franklin "the first philosopher" and "indeed the first great man of letters" for whom Europe was "beholden" to America. Franklin was considered by his contemporaries to be the foremost experimental physicist of the age, not for his kite experiment or his invention of the lightning rod, but for his research in pure science and his theory of electrical action; honors for achievement in pure science included the Copley Gold Medal of the Royal Society of London in 1753 and his designation, in 1772, by the French Academy of Sciences as one of the eight greatest living scientists who were not Frenchmen. In his scientific work Franklin displayed a far greater originality than in those many other activities which occupied his full life; but, curiously enough, his scientific research had little direct influence on his countrymen—at least a century or more passed before America produced another pure scientist of his stature, and during all that time research in pure science did not hold a high place in American life nor did it call forth support on a large scale. But Americans did follow Franklin's lead in making mechanical inventions and in finding new applications of scientific discoveries, and so I have included in this book a section on inventions and applications of science although there is none on his fundamental research in pure science. I have also omitted Franklin's writings on education and on economics, which are readily available in separate monographs; the former did not have the influence Franklin would have wished and the latter are difficult for the non-specialist to understand; both subjects would require editorial discussion much longer than the quotations from Franklin.

The selections have been chosen so that they may be intelligible to the reader without too much commentary. For the sake of greater readability in the twentieth century, I have dropped the upper-case letters, often used by Franklin for common nouns, to lower case and I have romanized the italics Franklin usually employed to display names of persons and of places. Deletions are indicated in customary fashion by suspension points (. . .). Although I have kept Franklin's spelling throughout, I have spelled out conventional abbreviations of the eighteenth century (chiefly the omission of the *e* in the past tenses of verbs), using the modern convention of *etc.* in place of Franklin's customary *&c.* In the first long extract from the *Autobiography*, the bulk of chapter two, I have—for the ease of the reader—spelled out Franklin's ubiquitous *&* as *and*, but in all other selections I have left the combination of *and* and ampersand in the same, apparently random, fashion used by Franklin. At times I have altered the punctuation to produce greater readability, but such alterations have been introduced sparingly, and I have not attempted to force Franklin's eighteenth-century prose into consistent modern punctuation rules, just as I have in no case tried to make his spelling uniform. In one selection, "The Drinker's Dictionary," I have presented the text essentially as Franklin did, so that the reader might savor the full-bodied flavor of the original. Franklin thus appears in this book in a "modern" but by no means a "modernized" text.

This is the sense of the distinction made by Samuel Eliot Morison in his edition of William Bradford's *Of Plymouth Plantation,* the first time that that venerable classic has been published in a form that enabled the modern reader to enjoy it and to appreciate its virtues; I have followed the example and wise counsel of America's foremost colonial historian in presenting Benjamin Franklin so that he might easily be read, but without compromise to his own expression.

The selections from Franklin's *Autobiography* have been based on the text recently published from Franklin's manuscript version, reprinted with the permission of the University of California Press; several letters written by Franklin for the British press have been taken from the edition of those letters made by Verner W. Crane and are reprinted with the permission of the University of North Carolina Press; the greater part of the other selections printed in this book is based on Albert H. Smyth's edition of *The Writings of Benjamin Franklin* (10 vols.; New York: The Macmillan Co., 1910), and are reprinted with the permission of The Pennsylvania Company for Banking and Trusts, executor and trustee under the will of Howard C. Myers, who was executor and beneficiary of the estate of Albert H. Smyth. A number of selections, some reprinted for the first time in a book made up of Franklin's writings, others never reprinted since the eighteenth century, have been included; in each case, the source is clearly indicated.

All students of Benjamin Franklin will recognize how

much this volume owes to the scholarly researches of the late Carl Van Doren, with whom on many occasions I had the privilege of discussing the many aspects of Franklin's career and thought. I should like to acknowledge my debt to the members of the Harvard History Department who have influenced my views on the eighteenth century and the growth of America: Professors Crane Brinton, Paul H. Buck, Samuel Eliot Morison and Arthur M. Schlesinger. It is especially fitting to express my gratitude to two institutions: the Harvard College Library and the American Philosophical Society, where my research on Franklin has been conducted. Harvard gave Franklin his first honorary degree (in characteristic American fashion, Franklin picked up two others in America, and also two in England), the first major edition of Franklin's works was prepared by Professor Jared Sparks of Harvard, and Franklin —ever the patron of higher learning—planned an annual "subscription" to "increase and improve" the Harvard College Library as a token of his "hearty good will and respect to the College." The American Philosophical Society, the first American scientific or "learned" society, was founded by Benjamin Franklin and is the chief repository of manuscripts and books by or relating to Franklin.

Professor Perry Miller of Harvard University kindly read the whole work in manuscript to the reader's profit. My wife, Frances Parsons Davis, shared every aspect of the editing and proofreading. The good fortune of having a faithful secretary, Mrs. Marion Van Aman, simplified the whole job of preparing the book for publication.

I. B. C.

Cambridge, Massachusetts
1953

CONTENTS

CHRONOLOGY

1706—Born in Boston

1718—Apprenticed as a printer to his brother James

1723—Left Boston for Philadelphia

1724-26—First visit to London

1727—Founded the Junto in Philadelphia

1728—Opened his printing shop in partnership with Meredith

1729—Took over publication of the *Pennsylvania Gazette*

1730—Took Deborah Read to wife

1731—Founded first American subscription library

1732—Began publishing *Poor Richard's Almanack*

1743—Proposed the founding of an American Philosophical Society

1744—Published account of his new stove, the "Pennsylvania fire-place"; met Dr. A. Spencer in Boston and became acquainted with subject of electricity

1747—Formulated the Franklinian theory of electrical action

1748—Retired from business as printer

1749—Invented the lightning rod

1751—His book on electricity published in England

1752—Franklin's lightning experiments performed in Europe; Franklin carried out kite experiment in Philadelphia and erected first lightning rods

1753—Awarded Copley Medal of Royal Society of London for his research in electricity; appointed Deputy Postmaster for continental British America

1754—Drafted Albany Plan of Union

1756—Elected a Fellow of the Royal Society of London

1757-62—In England to present case of Pennsylvania Assembly against the Proprietors

1762—Chosen representative in Pennsylvania Assembly

1764-75—In England as chief advocate of American cause; colonial agent for Pennsylvania, Georgia, New Jersey and Massachusetts; witness in Parliament against Stamp Act; lost postmastership and agencies after Hutchinson affair; presented petition to king from First Continental Congress

1775—Chosen delegate to Second Continental Congress; proposed Articles of Confederation; member of committee to draft Declaration of Independence; first American Postmaster General

1776—Sent to France to represent America

1777—Negotiated treaty of alliance with France

1778—Appointed Minister Plenipotentiary to Court of France

1782-83—Negotiated treaty of peace with England

1785—Returned to Philadelphia; elected President of Pennsylvania

1787—Delegate to Constitutional Convention

1790—Died in Philadelphia

BENJAMIN FRANKLIN

I · Introduction

I. Benjamin Franklin and the American Tradition

In the American tradition Benjamin Franklin is the living symbol that America is the land of opportunity: he is the original boy who made good. The facts of his rise to wealth and to fame are more impressive than any story written by Horatio Alger and, being the stuff of life itself, more representative of the American character. "Franklin is claimed by more groups than any other person in our history," as Calvin Coolidge described his reputation in 1927, and admiration for what Franklin did transcends the bounds of color, religion or political party.

Author of *The Way to Wealth*, Franklin has become a patron saint of businessmen, and the club he founded and called the "Junto" has been claimed as the original "Rotary"; but he is also the hero of the men who work with their hands and it was as artisan—printer and mechanic—that he made his way in the world. "A penny saved is a penny earned" may be found engraved on the walls of savings banks throughout the land, but printers remember that at the height of his national prestige and international fame he still described himself as a craftsman: "Benjamin Franklin, of Philadelphia, printer," adding in a lesser place that he was also "late Minister Plenipotentiary from the

United States of America to the Court of France" and
"now President of the State of Pennsylvania." He has been
called the "father of American vulgarity," but he is also
known as the patron of American art, letters and sciences,
and was convinced that "the Arts have always travelled
westward, and there is no doubt of their flourishing on
our side of the Atlantic." His college was the printing
shop and his university the newspaper; and so he sym-
bolizes the aspirations of ordinary men, the tradition that
in America high place does not depend on the material
advantages in youth, including a college education. But
Franklin is also the founder of schools and libraries and
the advocate of the doctrine that a man needs a sound
education to prepare him for the trials of life, success in
affairs, and the defense of his rights.

Mechanic, man of the people, spokesman for plain
Americans, Franklin satirized titles of honor in his youth
by showing that the Bible did not refer to "Master Adam"
or "the Right Honourable Abraham, Viscount Mesopo-
tamia, Baron of Canaan," and in old age he ridiculed the
suggestion of an American hereditary aristocracy by saying he would prefer "hereditary professors of mathematics"; yet in his *Autobiography* he took a childish pride in
boasting that he had known five kings and that one of
them had even asked him to sit down in his presence.

It is part of the paradox of Benjamin Franklin that he
lends himself so easily to opposing currents of American
life. Prohibitionists have numbered him as one of them
because he ridiculed drunkenness. In his *Autobiography*
he related that he could carry "a large form of types in
each hand" while the other workmen, "great guzzlers of
beer," could carry "but one in both hands"; he earned their
respect for his muscular prowess and the title of "the

Water-American." But Franklin is also the patron of the vintners and the drinkers—although not the drunkards!— and said that God made the joints of a man's arms just long enough to carry a glass to the mouth; invoking the argument from design, he concluded: "Let us adore, then, glass in hand, this benevolent wisdom; let us adore and drink."

The homely maxims of Poor Richard on thrift, virtue, sobriety and industry are better known to Americans than his robust drinking songs or his off-color bagatelles, and Americans are more familiar with the practical moralizing of the *Autobiography* than with the facts of his life and the quality of his thought.

Americans, by and large, have not taken Franklin at his own full measure; we have chosen to preserve only those sayings of Poor Richard that seemed to represent our own American virtues of success and the way of achieving it: "Early to bed, early to rise, makes a man healthy, wealthy, and wise"; "God helps them that help themselves"; "God gives all things to industry"; "One today is worth two to-morrows"; "Little strokes fell great oaks"; "Keep thy shop and thy shop will keep thee." We have tended to forget or have ignored those others which gave a somewhat different philosophy of life and conduct, as: "An egg today is better than a hen tomorrow"; "Be temperate in wine, in eating, girls, and sloth, Or the gout will seize you and plague you both."

Franklin had decided to confine his autobiography to his early years to make it "of more general use to young readers, as exemplifying strongly the effects of prudent and imprudent conduct in the commencement of a life of business." But the familiar versions of the *Autobiography* (often prepared for children) were edited to show the struggle of virtue over adversity without the "errata"—that is, to show "the effects of prudent . . . conduct" without bothering with the "imprudent," such as Franklin's attempt to seduce the milliner who was a friend of that Ralph who figures so largely in the *Autobiography*. If Franklin has become a kind of prig, a man whose virtue saved him from every imprudence, the fault is not his but rather lies in those editors who never really agreed with Franklin that experience is the best teacher. The intention of the *Autobiography* was to permit others to learn from Franklin's experience and so be saved the price of paying for errors they might otherwise commit.

Although he was an idealist, Franklin appreciated the limitations of human frailty and in *Father Abraham's Speech* (a collection of Poor Richard's best maxims put into the mouth of an old man haranguing a crowd in Franklin's presence), Franklin noted that after the multitude had listened intently to the old man quote Poor Richard, the people—having "heard . . . and approved the doctrine"—"immediately practised the contrary, just as if it had been a common sermon; for the vendue opened, and they began to buy extravagantly, notwithstanding his cautions and their own fear of taxes." Franklin himself admitted "to the reader" that he had forgot his own counsel and "had at first determined to buy stuff for a new coat," but having heard the "echo" of his own preaching, he "went away resolved to wear my old one a little longer. Reader, if thou wilt do the same, thy profit will be as great as mine."

Franklin doubted that his maxims would affect all of those who needed them most, since that same "Experience" who "keeps a dear school" had shown him his own weaknesses. He preached the gospel of thrift but was too generous to practice it consistently himself. In later life he admitted, "Frugality is an enriching virtue: a virtue I never could acquire in myself; but I was lucky enough to find it in a wife, who thereby became a fortune to me." Poor Richard knew that Benjamin Franklin was so generous as to be lavish: "Avarice and happiness never saw each other," he said, "how then should they become acquainted?"

We trust Franklin as a preacher because what Poor Richard said was based on the actual experiences of Benjamin Franklin: the *Autobiography* is thus a proof or witness in experiment of his worth as a guide through life. Hawthorne spoke for many Americans in 1842 in the evaluation of Franklin's popularity that he had a Boston father give to his son. "I doubt," the father said, "whether Franklin's philosophical discoveries, important as they were, or even his vast political services, would have given him all the fame he acquired. It appears to me that Poor Richard's Almanac did more than anything else, towards making him familiarly known to the public. As the writer of those proverbs, which Poor Richard was supposed to utter, Franklin became the counsellor and household friend of almost every family in America. Thus, it was the humblest of his labors that has done the most for his fame."

Americans are always interested in the recollections and reflections of the men who have done something in the world, particularly those who achieved success by their own efforts and without material advantages. What we particularly want to know is whether the great man has some key to success: a formula, a rule of conduct, a method which we in turn may use or teach our children. Thus Franklin stands four square in the American tradition of making one's own way through life to the highest

pinnacle of fame and fortune, and also as a man who
gladly told others how he had done it.

I think there can be no doubt of Franklin's sincerity,
but plainly there is a problem as to whether he was always
serious. On occasions that commanded an exaltation of
spirit, as in the final speech at the Constitutional Convention, there was apt to be a joke, a pun or at least a
witticism that often may seem out of keeping with the
occasion. Moving the unanimous acceptance of the Constitution, he could not help telling the delegates about "a
certain French lady, who, in a dispute with her sister, said:
'But I meet with nobody but myself that is always in the
right.'" It has been said that the writing of the Declaration of Independence was not entrusted to Franklin because of fear that a joke would be concealed in it; we know
that he wrote an early draft which climaxed in burlesque
by apostrophizing Britain for her ingratitude "to Saxony,
her mother country . . . an example we hope no provoca-
tion will induce us to imitate." He may not have actually
uttered that pun attributed to him on the signing of the
Declaration—"We had better hang together or we'll all
hang separately"—but it certainly would have been in
character. In the tradition of politics in America in the
late nineteenth and early twentieth centuries, humor was
not considered to be in keeping with serious occasions of
state; can anyone imagine Harding, Taft or Coolidge, or
even Wilson, making a pun in public? But Franklin D.
Roosevelt, who certainly thought of himself as a representative of a Franklin-Jefferson tradition, and who called
Franklin "an inspiration to every American citizen," restored a sense of humor to the dignity of serious address,
reminding us that an American trait exemplified by Franklin is not to take ourselves too seriously on every occasion.

Benjamin Franklin is as complex and as difficult to pin down or describe in a few words as our American way of life, of which he is a foremost representative—and perhaps for that very reason a perfect symbol of it. Benjamin Franklin has never been a hero of the American people in the sense that George Washington has been; he was made of too common a clay, the only one of the founding fathers of our republic with whom we can conceive ourselves shaking hands, sharing a jug of beer or a glass of port or madeira, listening to a good joke, and departing with the feeling of having made a good friend. We seem to know Franklin, while Washington remains aloof and unknowable. Parson Weems was at a loss to understand why his life of Washington was a best seller and his life of Franklin a failure. The reason is that there was no way of telling whether the anecdotes he invented about Washington were true or false or even in keeping with his character, but Franklin was an old friend and Americans could learn from his own lips the stories of his youth: how he and his friends built a wharf of stones they stole, how they played at being pirates, how young Benjamin misappropriated Mr. Vernon's money and suffered remorse about it for the rest of his life. These are real-life stories and they conjure up in each reader's mind the events of his own youth. As familiar to Americans as the picture of Abe Lincoln splitting logs is the one of "Ben" Franklin walking down the streets of Philadelphia munching a roll.

But for all that we seem to know Benjamin Franklin as a human being as contrasted to the statuelike Washington, we are usually ignorant of Franklin's stature in the world and his role as one of the architects of our American traditions. Because of the inherent paradox in all great men— perhaps as a result of the many-sidedness that has allowed

Franklin to seem the archetype of such different strains in
Americanism—or possibly because America is an amalgam
of so many kinds of traditions and therefore so difficult to
interpret—for any of these reasons, an account of Franklin
in relation to "the" American way of life is apt to be a
personal testament of the commentator concerning the
America he most admires. Even so, it is possible to study
what Franklin said and thought and did and to see him
a defender of the rights and principles that were upheld
by the founders of our country: as a representative of
the high ideals of the eighteenth century—the freedom to
think, write and publish without jeopardy; the dignity of
labor; the liberty of representative government; equality
of opportunity for all; the obligation of being a good neighbor; and, in general, the doctrines of the rights and dignity
of man written into the Declaration of Independence and
the Bill of Rights of the Constitution. In esteeming Franklin, the men of the age were, therefore, only honoring
themselves. Yet the ideals of the eighteenth century were
modified in Franklin in a particular way by his American
heritage and environment and so, by honoring Franklin,
the men of the eighteenth century were also saluting the
coming greatness of America, recognizing that in producing Benjamin Franklin America had given to the world an
earnest of her future.

His associates saw him as an exponent of great ideals
which they shared in common and imparted to the republic they founded. Franklin did not invent any radically
new political or social doctrines and was never the advocate of a successful policy uniquely his. Since Franklin's
ideas on political and economic matters and social justice
were a product of his environment, there is always a risk
in attempting to project his views into our present cir-

cumstances. In accordance with the thought of the eighteenth century and the conditions of life in a primarily agricultural milieu before the era of industrialization, Franklin was a believer in a *laissez-faire* economics—but how can we tell whether he would continue in such a view as applied to twentieth-century industrial society or whether his concern for the condition of the ordinary man would lead him to a different position? In an address at the bicentennial celebration of the University of Pennsylvania, Franklin D. Roosevelt said:

. . . Benjamin Franklin, to whom this University owes so much, realized too that while basic principles of natural science, of morality and of the science of society were eternal and immutable, the application of these principles necessarily changes with the patterns of living conditions from generation to generation. I am certain that he would insist, were he with us today, that it is the whole duty of the philosopher and the educator to apply the eternal ideals of truth and goodness and justice in terms of the present and not in terms of the past. Growth and change are the law of all life. Yesterday's answers are inadequate for today's problems—just as the solutions of today will not fill the needs of tomorrow.

Eternal truths will be neither true nor eternal unless they have fresh meaning for every new social situation. . . .

I believe that Franklin would have sympathized with much of the "New Deal." A case might be made out that he too had attacked the "economic royalists": those of 1789 who, he feared, wanted to establish an aristocracy of the rich by basing representation on wealth. "Is it supposed," he asked, "that wisdom is the necessary concomitant of riches, and that one man worth a thousand pounds must have as much wisdom as twenty who have each only

999; and why is property to be represented at all?" He
held that "private property . . . is a creature of society, and
is subject to the calls of that society, whenever its necessities shall require it, even to its last farthing" and he
regretted "a disposition among some of our people to
commence an aristocracy by giving the rich a predominancy in government."

But we can also select quotations from Franklin that
might seem to imply a hostility to aspects of the New
Deal, and not only the spending that was in opposition
to his principles of thrift, or the rise of executive power
against which he constantly warned his countrymen. "It
is contrary to the nature of commerce," he wrote, "for
government to interfere in the prices of commodities," and
he once maintained that "a dependence on somewhat else
than a careful accumulation during youth and health for
support in age and sickness" would take away from the
poor "the greatest of all inducements to industry, frugality, and sobriety" and would offer "a premium for the
encouragement of idleness."

So it is that we cannot interpret Franklin for our times
merely by rudely lifting things he said or wrote from their
context of the eighteenth century and reading them as if
they were intended to illuminate the particular issues of
our own day. Yet Franklin has a meaning for the twentieth century which will reward our exploration and which
is the measure of his worth and enduring fame. This
meaning may be found in the broad principles that motivated his love of country and of liberty and his passionate
defense of human rights: the principles that made him, as
he described himself when sixteen years of age, "an enemy
to vice, and friend to vertue . . . a mortal enemy to arbitrary government and unlimited power."

II. What Franklin Stood for

Among the problems facing the interpreter of Benjamin Franklin is the paradox that although he seems to us a modern man, he actually lived a long time ago. He was a contemporary of Cotton and Increase Mather and was born less than a century after the death of Shakespeare. That he was also a contemporary of Jefferson, Washington, Hamilton and Madison was a result of his longevity; he was old enough to have been the father of any of them. In contrast to Jefferson or John Adams—at the time of the Revolution, and before we had begun our national existence—Franklin seemed already to have completed a longer life of service to his country than is vouchsafed to most men. As the oldest member of the Second Continental Congress in 1776 and again the oldest delegate to the Constitutional Convention in 1787, he had been the advocate of a united America when the other American leaders were boys. Madison had been but three years old, John Adams nine, Jefferson eleven and Washington twenty-two when Franklin in middle age had drafted the Albany Plan of Union in 1754, the first major endeavor to organize the colonies for their general welfare. Even in the '60s Franklin's political opponents had referred to him as "Pappy," using Debbie Franklin's favorite nickname for her husband; in terms of age and service the founders of our republic could not help thinking of Franklin as the father of his country, a title only later transferred to George Washington. Jefferson was speaking for all his countrymen when he referred to "Franklin, our Patriarch, whom Philosophy and Philanthropy announced the first of men, and whose name will be like a

star of the first magnitude in the firmament of heaven,
when the memory of those who have surrounded and ob-
scured him, will be lost in the abyss of time."

In 1776 Franklin's reputation was more universal in his
own country than that of any other American, and he was
the only member of the Continental Congress to be known
and admired throughout the world. To the British and the
French, Franklin seemed to be Mr. American; Jefferson,
succeeding Franklin as ambassador in France, wrote warn-
ings to his countrymen that "Europe fixes an attentive eye
on your reception of Doctor Franklin" and, again, "The
reception of the Doctor is an object of very general attention, and will weigh in Europe as an evidence of the
satisfaction or dissatisfaction of America[ns] with their
Revolution." Patriot John Adams might well have been
annoyed to discover how many people in France believed
Franklin to have been personally responsible for the Revolution and the author of all the state constitutions.

Even in the nineteenth century Balzac could still call
Franklin the inventor of the American republic, along
with the lightning rod and the hoax, and Carlyle referred
to him as father of all the Yankees. Horace Greeley, in a
lecture on self-made men in 1862, concluded that Franklin was "the consummate type and flowering of human nature under the skies of colonial America." Over the years,
Franklin has continued to be cherished as one of the most
characteristic Americans we have ever produced, a pioneer of the American personality.

George Washington merely voiced the sentiments of
all Americans when he wrote to the aged and ailing Franklin in 1789: "If to be venerated for benevolence: if to be
admired for talents: if to be esteemed for patriotism: if to
be beloved for philanthropy, can gratify the human mind,

you must have the pleasing consolation to know that you have not lived in vain." We may take this quadrivium of benevolence, talents, patriotism and philanthrophy and the trivium of life, liberty, and the pursuit of happiness as the measure of Franklin in the American tradition.

As we examine the record to discover in more detail why Franklin is a great American, one of the exemplars of our American way of life, we must keep in mind that he was a man of action as well as reflection and that his deeds show him to us as a symbol more often than his words reveal a prophet. Franklin had no talent whatever for speaking in public, for exhortation, or for those noble statements of principle or appeals to sentiment that have characterized the great leaders of our country. His views are usually found in statements advocating some particular course of action rather than setting forth or defending a theory or general policy; often we come closest to an understanding of his beliefs by examining the attitudes or statements he found it necessary to attack or satirize. Franklin could never have written the Declaration of Independence, as Carl Becker observed, because though Franklin was a master of a clarity, simplicity, precision and felicity equal to Jefferson's, whatever he wrote had in it "something homely and intimate and confidential, some smell of homespun, some air of the tavern or the print shop." Franklin could have marshaled the evidence against the king as well as Jefferson, but he certainly could not have set forth principles of conduct with that "high seriousness [and] a kind of lofty pathos which . . . lift the Declaration to the level of a great occasion."

The comparison between Jefferson and Franklin is instructive, because it draws our attention to Franklin's quality as the kind of American who is more successful in

addressing himself to each problem as it arises than in
mastering the abstractions that would enable him to explain the philosophy motivating him. Franklin appears
to us as a man who became embarrassed by the naked
expression of lofty aims and high purpose, which may
explain why his writings on major public issues were apt
to end up in a pun or a story; but possibly he simply had
that trait of modesty Americans have admired in many of
our great men. The American character appears as much
in men who simply see their duty and perform it as in
those whose stirring words call forth the deeds of others.
Poor Richard said, "Well done is better than well said,"
and "Great talkers, little doers," but he admitted, "If you
would not be forgotten, as soon as you are dead and rotten, either write things worth reading, or do things worth
the writing."

Because the record of Franklin's concern for public affairs encompasses a span of almost seventy years, he more
than once found himself obliged "to change opinions . . .
which I once thought right but found to be otherwise."
Thus the interpreter of Franklin encounters many vexing
problems when he tries to uncover the axioms of his
conduct. "Franklin's principles"—abstracted from his actions and the pamphlets, editorials, articles or letters to
the press which were calculated to produce action—reveal
inconsistencies as well as examples of genuine growth or
revision of fundamental concepts. But Americans have always admired the quality of open-mindedness and courage that enables our leaders to change their views and
adopt new positions that are more correct than old ones.
We appreciate Franklin's efforts to abolish slavery all the
more when we learn that in early life he was a slave-
owner and bought and sold Negroes in trade. Consistency

—"the hobgoblin of little minds," according to Emerson— or power or even high place have always been worth less to many Americans than being right; Henry Clay's statement that he would rather be right than president is as familiar to Americans as if it had been said by Poor Richard.

In the American tradition Franklin stands foremost as a man who loved his country, his state (or colony), his city, his friends, his neighbors and his family. Viewing him as the idol of the world, we are apt to forget how intensely American he was: in his person, his manners, his speech, his humor and his literary style. As a boy writing for his brother's newspaper, he described himself as "naturally very jealous for the rights and liberties of my country." As a colonial agent in England he defended these rights and liberties, but was also a passionate upholder of everything American—including the American breakfast! Philadelphia he described as "the city I love," and once, when in the midst of one of those political "altercations" he so intensely abhorred, he wrote that "if I did not love the country [Pennsylvania] and the people [I] would remove immediately into a more quiet government, Connecticutt, where I am also happy enough to have many friends."

Men who willingly go into the wilderness to hew out a nation must necessarily have a certain amount of optimism and in various forms this optimism has been one of the characteristics of America ever since. Franklin displayed a confidence in the future that was equal to all obstacles. He was the original "booster." Soon after he had opened his new printing house in Philadelphia, an old gentleman came a-calling and predicted failure for the enterprise and prophesied that the city as a whole was

going to ruin, and he did so with "such a detail of mis-
fortunes now existing, or that were soon to exist, that he
left me half melancholy," as Franklin described the meeting. He was a "croaker," said Franklin, and there "are
croakers in every country, always boding its ruin," but
men of industry, hope and courage are never deterred by
them.

On the eve of the Revolution, Franklin faced up to
the distresses and inconveniences ahead "with fortitude,"
secure in the belief of "better times expected." While "ambassador" to France he greeted bad news of the war with
a cheerful use of the colloquial phrase "*Ça ira,*" which
helped to maintain faith in the American cause and was
a declaration of confidence of the highest order.

Franklin's own way through life was assurance to himself and to generations of Americans that there were no
barriers to a man of virtue and integrity, that in America
the future was unlimited. America provided the natural
conditions under which a man might achieve dignity and
independence—the means necessary to a good life: "a
good climate, fertile soil, wholesome air, free governments,
wise laws, liberty, a good people to live among, and a
hearty welcome." He took fierce pride in the achievements of his country and was certain that England and
France and eventually the whole world would follow in
her footsteps to promote equality, liberty and justice for
all. Convinced that the winning of independence was a
mark of the favor of divine Providence, he believed in
America's mission in the world: to provide the example
that men might follow everywhere. The success of the
Constitutional Convention in establishing a new government in America, he hoped, might serve as an inspiration
and guide to Europe to unite in "a federal union and one

true citizen on America + the world

grand republick of all its different states and kingdoms, by means of a like convention; for we had many interests to reconcile."

Our history provides many other examples of the conviction that America would lead the world to a system of government like hers and to a belief in freedom, justice and equality. "God grant," Franklin wrote, "that not only the love of liberty, but a thorough knowledge of the rights of man, may pervade all the nations of the earth, so that a philosopher may set his foot anywhere on its surface, and say, 'This is my country.'"

Over and over again, Franklin expressed his conviction that "Serving God is doing good to man." Abstractions like "man" or "the people" were collective names for the men and women he had known. When he wrote about the poor or the needy he had in mind his neighbors and friends who were less well off than he was; these were no "little people" or "common men" viewed from towered isolation but the flesh and blood of his acquaintance. He did not write of "laborers" and "artisans" as if they were only the primitive concepts in terms of which the postulates of a social philosophy might be framed; for him laborers and artisans were the chaps who had worked beside him in printing houses in England and in America, men he knew by name. "Having been poor is no shame," according to Poor Richard, "but being ashamed of it, is." Franklin never forgot that he had once been poor, just as he was always proud of having been a man who worked with his hands. Remembering the needs of his own early days, and seeing the conditions of men and women whom he knew and liked, he acted in their behalf to make their lives easier, better and more secure. His humanitarianism was in keeping with the age, but it was based on the experi-

ence of knowing men more than on reflections about the
nature of man. Since education gives men advantages
over the uneducated, he organized his friends into a
mutual improvement club (possibly the first instance of
adult education in America), instituted a library and
founded schools so that his friends' and neighbors' children could be prepared for life's hazards and ardors. The
same spirit marked his efforts in founding the first permanent American hospital. A good neighbor and a good
friend, Franklin exemplifies the great American tradition
of lending one's helping hand to the oppressed and needy,
and the spirit of philanthropy and benevolence that does
not stop with a "cash contribution" but requires personal
effort in raising funds from others in Community Chest
drives and the labor of organizing and supervising institutions of public trust and benefit.

The exponents of the "Enlightenment" in France were
probably more eloquent than Franklin in their assertions
of the dignity of man and their attacks on the deplorable
living conditions of most men in that time, but neither
Voltaire nor Diderot ever worked as Franklin did to establish a hospital or to found a school to teach trades to
orphans and free Negroes. This is the practical Franklin
being benevolent, if you wish, a familiar type of American
who implements his ideals in applications to the improvement of living and working conditions in a methodical
progression to the never-complete architecture of the better world.

 Another American trait that was strongly marked in
Franklin may be seen in his efforts to increase the comforts of daily life and reduce its hazards. His "public improvements" indicate a perception of what needed to be
done, what was possible. The fire company, insurance

system and regular constabulary for which he was responsible in his community are examples of Franklin's activity in increasing domestic security, as was his invention of the lightning rod. Actual living was made pleasanter or easier by his introduction of improved heating and ventilating of homes and the introduction of all sorts of useful gadgets, like the one he invented to take down books from a high shelf (the prototype of the tool grocers use to get down packaged goods), or the chair that opened into a stepladder (similar to the stools found in many American kitchens to this day). Franklin probably did not invent the rocking chair, although it has been attributed to him, but he did contrive a special one for the summer days which fanned him while he rocked. The original Rube Goldberg, Franklin as a household gadgeteer is as characteristically American as Franklin the inventor who could not resist making practical innovations in the printing art. Considering his inventions improvements for the public good, he refused to take out patents, asserting: "That, as we enjoy great advantages from the inventions of others, we should be glad of an opportunity to serve others by any invention of ours; and this we should do freely and generously."

Franklin's concern for man's estate was based on a recognition of what men actually are as well as their potentialities. His associates and friends were representative of many types and many religions. Knowing man for what he is made Franklin tolerant of man's weaknesses, and he assessed his own faults as readily as those of others. "The brave and the wise," Poor Richard observed, "can both pity and excuse; when cowards and fools shew no mercy."

A tolerance of individuals led naturally to tolerance of groups. Although Franklin's personal religion was unorthodox, he respected all religions and was ever their friend. Of which other Founding Father of the Republic can it be said, as of Franklin, that he contributed to the support of Protestant churches and a Hebrew synagogue, helped to establish the Catholic Church in America (using his friendship with the Papal Nuncio in Paris to have his patriot friend John Carrol made the first American bishop), and declared himself ready to welcome a Mohammedan preacher sent by the Grand Mufti in Constantinople? His behavior may be contrasted with the *philosophes* or *encyclopédistes* who preached religious tolerance in attack on the official religion of the state but were intolerant of Roman Catholicism. Franklin, of course, welcomed the unorthodox as well as the orthodox, helping to provide a pulpit for the revivalist Whitefield and defending the privileges of freethinkers.

Franklin is thus a symbol of American religious liberty, and he stands for the equality of all men despite their color or their creed. His *Narrative of the Late Massacres*, deploring the unprovoked and brutal murder of Christian Indian families, contained an eloquent attack on race prejudices:

If an Indian injures me, does it follow that I may revenge that injury on all Indians? It is well known that Indians are of different tribes, nations and languages, as well as the white people. In Europe, if the French, who are white people, should injure the Dutch, are they to revenge it on the English because they too are white people? The only crime of these poor wretches seems to have been that they had a reddish-brown skin and black hair; and some people of that sort, it seems, had murdered some of our relations. If it be right to kill men for such a reason, then, should any man with a freckled face and red hair kill a wife or child of mine, it would be right for me to revenge it by killing all the freckled red-haired men, women and children I could afterwards anywhere meet with.

The logic of his beliefs led him to accept the presidency of the Pennsylvania Society for Promoting the Abolition of Slavery, and the Relief of Free Negroes, Unlawfully Held in Bondage. The Society appealed in his name to the public and presented a memorial to the first Congress in 1789 urging the new government to "step to the very verge of the power vested in you for discouraging every species of traffic in the persons of our fellow-men." James Jackson of Georgia rose to defend slavery in the light of religion and history, and Franklin, aged and infirm, replied in a spirited hoax printed in the *Federal Gazette:* it took the form of a defense by Sidi Mehemet Ibrahim of Algiers of the right and duty of Algerians to own and to sell Christian slaves, despite "the petition of the sect called Erika or Purists, who prayed for the abolition of piracy and slavery as unjust."

There was nothing unique in opposing Negro slavery, or even in being an abolitionist, but Franklin stands apart from other humanitarians in recognizing that the free Negroes of his day were badly off and that they should be taught trades in order to be able to support themselves and raise their living standards. Franklin is, therefore, an exemplar of that philanthropic realism Americans admire and practice, which recognizes the importance of a continued address to the day-to-day problems of our unfortunate neighbors, the needs of the "here" and "now" which require immediate attention.

III. The Empirical Temper

As an expression of the American character, Franklin spoke with the personality of his own genius, but the particular qualities of the American character that he represented were also the results of the time and place in which he lived. He was a product of the philosophies of the eighteenth century, but he also came out of an American background—in Boston and Philadelphia—that conditioned the way he thought and that gave him a view of man and nature that stamped his contributions to our American way of life with a mark of its own. To define exactly what Franklin was, and to grasp in its full integrity what it is that Franklin stands for, we must pause to examine the wellsprings of that blend of idealism and practicality that he displayed.

It is true, of course, that even when we emulate Franklin, or address ourselves to problems of business, government and society in the Franklinian manner, we do so from a motivation that is apt to be somewhat different from his. Yet, even though two centuries of time and culture intervene between him and us, there are elements in his general approach to the world that have appeared again and again in Americans from his day to ours. Franklin's orientation is most easily discernible in the field of action in which he made the most original contribution—science—and so we may best see him in his own terms by first exploring the qualities of mind he displayed in studying nature and only then seeing how these qualities illuminate his way through life.

It has become commonplace to say that Benjamin Franklin was a practical man and to imply that his standard of value was always the working usefulness of the end result rather than the means of obtaining it or the motivation. We think of Franklin as having been primarily a practical man because so many of his enterprises were successful and because he had a doctrine of "usefulness" that seems akin to practicality. But in thus limiting Benjamin Franklin, we fail to grasp his full dimensions and may even slight our own national character. For there is a sense in which practicality implies expediency, and its ascription to the American character would rob our history of the lofty ideals and high purposes which have motivated so many of our leaders and our ordinary citizens; it would make a parody of Franklin as a guide through life.

As a man of the eighteenth century and an American, Benjamin Franklin was an empiricist. The America of his day was a young country in which a man's courage, faith, optimism or ability counted for nothing if he could not recognize and face up to the raw facts of life and nature. Franklin was not a product of the frontier in that he was an urban American, spending his boyhood in the city of Boston and his young manhood in the city of Philadelphia; he did not grow up in a log cabin in the wilderness, tilling fields with a flintlock by his side. But the spirit of the frontier certainly made its presence known in Philadelphia: the city itself was rough, unfinished and growing; there were Indian alarms not far away and a threat of pirates; and, in general, a spirit of building and material creation produced an atmosphere of close contact with the real world.

Nature, as Franklin realized, is both man's enemy and friend, providing fertile soil and rain and also plagues of insects and droughts. The only way to master nature is

to understand her laws and to operate within her frame-
work. Shaking a fist at the skies will neither make it rain
nor stop the locusts, although in Franklin's day men believed that prayer and fasting might do both. But the
men who had braved the wilderness, although placing
their reliance on their prayer book and Bible, knew that
their faith in God needed to be buttressed by hard work
and skill in shooting muskets. The Old World patterns of
life, in which a man lived like his father and his father's
father before him, could not long survive in the New
World, where a man had to adapt himself to the realities
of the situation in which he found himself, to find a way
of life consistent with the data of experience that made
up the external environment. It is this last quality which
is the primary ingredient of empiricism: a respect for the
data of experience and the application of reason to them.

    In Benjamin Franklin this strain of empiricism enabled
him to become a foremost scientist of that age, and it was
a major factor in producing that special view of man, his
needs, his rights and his works which has become so precious an element in our American heritage. Franklin stands
in the American tradition for the proposition that reflections about society should produce useful institutions for
the improvement of the conditions of life; considerations
about the estate of man should yield more than eternal
principles and noble concepts, and must be fruitful of a
system of government and laws to safeguard man's rights;
an understanding of the nature and character of man
should lead to conduct that respects a man for what he
is without regard to color or religion or economic and
social origin. Many Americans have acted in accordance
with these principles simply because they have become a

part of our American pattern of behavior, but in Franklin they were a result of the brand of empiricism that marked his thought and conduct. To see Franklin's particular contribution to America, therefore, we must try to understand how being a good scientist and being a good neighbor, friend and citizen were but different aspects of a single fundamental quality of mind.

Empiricism is a philosophy which is of the eighteenth century and may be studied in Locke, whom Franklin respected, and Hume, whom Franklin knew and admired. One of its major tenets was the theory of how ideas originate in the mind by the action of sensations. Skeptical of any sort of metaphysics, Franklin was not a systematic philosopher, and doctrines of the origin of ideas held no great interest for him. Even so, throughout his writings we find a tendency to regard experience as the grand source of values and doctrines. He was certainly an empiricist in the sense that he considered an experiential test more important in evaluating the worth of concepts than their logical consistency or their mutual relatedness in a system.

Franklin's outlook demanded that concepts be founded on experience, whether that experience was the data of experiment in the laboratory or the observation of man's behavior. Reason, operating on these concepts, discovers laws of nature or rules of conduct, which must meet two important tests. First, these laws or rules or principles must be true—that is, they must be testable against that same experience of the laboratory or the world. But even if such an experiential test reveals the validity of the discovered generalization, the whole effort is not worth while unless it is productive of something new. It is this quality of productivity that gives man the final measure of the way in which the initial data and the reasoning process have led to the final conclusions.

Real works are thus, as Bacon put it, the fruits of knowledge and it is in this sense that he wrote that the roads to knowledge and to power are the same. For in the empiricist philosophy the end product can be no more divorced from real experience than the original concepts. In science, then, an empiricist begins by making experiments with his own hands, then constructing concepts that are related to the actual operations or manipulations he performs; next he applies his reason to generalize what he has observed into ground principles on which a logical theory can be built; then the final result is a new form of experience or at least a new view of some segment of experience.

One result of empirical science is a prediction, such as Newton made, of the tides; the time of tides was observable to anyone, but up until the time of Newton no one had understood the attractions of the sun and moon sufficiently well to explain how they might control the seas. Newton's predictions agreed so well with observation that the validity of his theory was assured. Newton's work led to predictions which were testable by experience and it contributed to an enlarged view of the world that we observe around us, thus being doubly productive. Sometimes the end product of empirical science is a new effect or phenomenon that the scientist can produce with his own hands in the laboratory, but often it is a new instrument or device which is itself the new experience that is the product or fruit of investigation.

As a scientist Franklin knew that the life of ideas in science is always controlled by experiment and observation and that a new theory such as he created is valuable in correlating phenomena that had not been thought related or in predicting new phenomena which, on being discovered, would prove the theory's usefulness. Applying his new concepts of electrical equilibrium and the states of electrification he called "plus" or "positive" and "minus" or "negative," Franklin discovered the first exact law of electricity: the law of conservation of charge. This occurred in the course of his experiments to analyze the charge in a condenser—the Leyden jar, consisting of a glass bottle coated on the outside with metal foil and filled with water or bird shot. Such an instrument, when charged, was capable of giving a noticeable shock to seven hundred men, but Franklin stated that there was no more "electricity" in a charged jar than an uncharged one and he proved it by the experiment of "electrical convection." He also found that the charge "resided" in the nonconducting glass rather than the metal coat or water. But this led immediately to the production of new experience, because if charge "resides" in glass because glass is a special kind of nonconductor, then a condenser need not have the shape of a bottle, but could be made of glass plates with metal sheets affixed to either side. To the nonscientist this example may appear trivial, but it marked the beginning of condenser design and the condenser is one of the vital organs of every piece of electronic equipment ever made.

Furthermore, one of Franklin's greatest achievements was to show which electrical properties of bodies depend on their shape and which do not. Franklin never saw any practical use in the condenser, by which I mean that in his day the Leyden jar was never embodied in an instrument to serve man's needs or increase his fortune. Franklin's explanation of the condenser's action, we may note, was considered by his contemporaries to have been one of his major contributions to science; this discovery was useful because it increased man's understanding of nature's operations and it was productive because it led to new principles or laws of nature.

The distinction between productive usefulness and practicality may best be illustrated by Franklin's research on the lightning discharge. Having discovered that a pointed conductor will "draw off" the charge from an electrified body at a considerable distance, and having at last understood the role of grounding and insulation in electrostatic experiments, Franklin was in a position to make the grand experiment. If clouds are (as he thought) electrified, then an elevated vertical metal rod ending in a point will "draw off" some of the charge from low clouds though they are far away. This original experiment, described by Franklin and performed according to his specifications before he had thought of the kite experiment, established as an empirical fact the phenomenon that clouds are electrically charged and that lightning is therefore an electrical discharge. So the facts of experience and a theory based on correct reasoning had been productive of new experience; nature's artillery had been shown to be only a large-scale instance of a common laboratory phenomenon: the spark discharge. In this case, however, the research was not only productive, it was useful; it revealed the function of electricity in the "economy of nature" and it was applied by Franklin in an attempt to throw light on the whole process of cloud formation and rain.

But Franklin's research had led him to another conclusion, that a long vertical rod of metal, pointed at the top and set deep into the earth, would protect buildings from a stroke of lightning; the empirical test was to construct lightning rods in order to discover whether they would afford such protection (which Franklin, as an empiricist, never doubted), which is only another way of saying that the result of Franklin's research was a predicted new element of experience—a lightning rod—which had to be put to the trial of lightning.

This whole process of empirical science was beautifully described in the seventeenth century by Robert Hooke, who wrote:

So many are the links upon which the true philosophy depends, of which, if any one be loose, or weak, the whole chain is in danger of being dissolved; it is to begin with the hands and eyes, and to proceed on through the memory, to be continued by the reason; nor is it to stop there, but to come about to the hands and eyes again, and so, by a continual passage round from one faculty to another, it is to be maintained in life and strength, as much as the body of man is by the circulation of the blood through the several parts of the body. . . .

This is the sense in which Franklin's scientific research was productive and useful and fruitful. It was productive in that it led to a new theory of electrical action which was the source of a more profound understanding of nature, one which enabled men to predict (and for the first time) what would happen in many of their common electrical experiments in the laboratory, and it also led to many new physical phenomena that had never before been observed. It was useful in that it produced an instrument that enabled men (again for the first time) to protect their homes, barns, churches and ships from destruction by lightning. And the rod itself was fruitful in that it became an instrument that in Franklin's hands and ours has led to a deeper knowledge of the electrification of clouds and of the earth itself and the mechanism of the lightning discharge.

The doctrine of empiricism was always hospitable to the view of Bacon that "fruits and works" are "sponsors and sureties" for the truths of science. But we must keep in mind that Bacon had added that "works themselves are of greater value as pledges of truth than as contributing to the comforts of life." As an empirical scientist Franklin would have agreed, although, being Franklin, he might have questioned the word "greater." The empirical view of the scientist would be satisfied equally by the production of new experience, whether a phenomenon of importance or a device that embodied the newly discovered principles.

Franklin did not pursue the science of electricity because of a particular practical aim; had this been his intent he would hardly have chosen electricity as his major area of inquiry: in his day electricity was not a practical subject. The only supposedly practical application of electricity then was in a kind of medical therapy, but Franklin was convinced that the "cures" arose from the patient's desire to get well rather than from the electric shock. But once Franklin had reached the stage in his investigations where the new knowledge could be put to use in the service of man, he was quick to see an application. I believe that Franklin was convinced that pure science would always produce useful innovations, and here we may see him in the great scientific tradition that has only recently become a major feature of American civilization.

Throughout the nineteenth century, America was noted more for the applications of scientific discoveries that had been made in other lands than for the production of that fundamental scientific knowledge we applied so fruitfully. It is only in the last fifty years or so that America has risen to be a foremost scientific nation of the world. During the nineteenth century Franklin was considered by Americans to be an "applied scientist," the inventor of the lightning rod and the Franklin stove, and his whole contribution to pure science was reduced to the kite experiment. The great laboratory discoveries, the first unitary theory of electrical action—the research in pure science that made his contemporaries call him the Newton of their age—were ignored.

Today we are beginning to recognize that the applications of scientific discovery to the cure of disease, the improvement of our living conditions and the safeguarding of our national existence must depend on fundamental discoveries to apply. We may, therefore, in this new tradition look back on Franklin as our first scientist. We may see him as one of those pioneers who understood that empirical science must *always* produce new experience which enlarges our view of nature and our understanding of the processes going on in the world around us, and that it *sometimes* produces (along the way) practical innovations of inestimable value for our health and our economic security. Characteristically, Franklin's most eloquent defense of that research in science that has no particular practical consequence in view took the form of a witticism. Watching the first balloon ascent in Paris, he overheard the usual question: What good is it? His reply has never been equaled: "What good is a newborn baby?" Discussing the new element chlorine, discovered in 1810, and applied to the bleaching of cloth, Michael Faraday said in 1816:

Before leaving this substance, chlorine, I will point out
its history, as an answer to those who are in the habit of
saying to every new fact, "What is its use?" Dr. Franklin
says to such, "What is the use of an infant?" The answer
of the experimentalist would be, "Endeavor to make it useful." When Scheele discovered this substance it appeared
to have no use, it was in its infantine and useless state; but
having grown up to maturity, witness its powers, and see
what endeavors to make it useful have done.

Franklin's scientific ideas and his conception of the potentialities of science have influenced Americans only
indirectly, through the nineteenth-century European masters under whom our scientists studied. But, wholly apart
from his personal influence or the effect of his discoveries
and theories on the development of science as such, his
empirical approach to the world of man produced qualities of concept and action that are embodied in great
American institutions and that have become a precious
American heritage.

Franklin was not a true philosopher in the sense that
Jonathan Edwards was, but he was a natural philosopher—
in that larger sense in which scientific learning and a general outlook on God, man, nature and the world were included within a single expression in a day when scientists
were not merely physicists or chemists or astronomers or
biologists. Franklin may be fairly described as an empirical Newtonian in the realms of science and of human
affairs. In both realms, the principles and conclusions of
reason applied to experiential data—the facts of nature
and the facts of man—had to be embodied in experience
or they were meaningless and irrelevant. Franklin's understanding of nature led him to control nature's operations just as his knowledge of men's actions made him a

master of men and the affairs of the world. And just as in science his conclusions became elements of experience in new phenomena to be observed or new instruments to be put in use, so in society new elements of experience were created and put to the trial of use: new institutions (a hospital, school and fire company), new rules of conduct, a new form of government, a tax, or a simple act of kindness.

It is well known that the original rough draft of the Declaration of Independence contained Jefferson's statement that principles such as that all men are created equal were held to be "sacred and undeniable," and that in the manuscript these words are changed in Franklin's handwriting to make the statement read: "We hold these principles to be self-evident." Now historians usually interpret this alteration simply as a literary improvement and certainly Franklin's cadence has a wonderful ring to it and is much more effective than Jefferson's. But the difference between the two phrases is much more profound than mere literary quality. Jefferson implied that the principles in question were holy, of divine origin, and were to be respected and guarded with reverence for that reason: to deny them would be sacrilege. But "self-evident" was a technical or scientific term applied to axioms, as John Harris' popular eighteenth-century *Dictionary of Arts and Sciences* defined it, and was exemplified in such propositions as: "That nothing can act where it is not; That a thing cannot be and not be at the same time; That the whole is greater than a part; That where there is no law, there is no transgression; etc." Such an axiom is "a generally received ground principle or rule in any art or science," and "it cannot be made more plain and evident by demonstration, because 'tis its self much better known than any thing that can be brought to prove it." This is the sense in which Franklin's phrase represents the summit of effectiveness.

Axioms or postulates are considered in our contemporary scientific language (mathematics, logic) to be propositions which are assumed without proof solely for the purpose of exploring the consequences or logical deductions which follow from them. But in Newtonian science, consequences were deduced from axioms because the axioms were true, which should imply that if the reasoning process or deduction were correct, the results would be equally true or verifiable in experience. In the *Principia Mathematica* Newton explored the logical or mathematical consequences of certain laws of force, notably the famous three laws of motion and the law of universal gravitation. Now, as Newton explained the matter in 1713, "experimental philosophy" or empirical science "proceeds only from phenomena" or the data provided by experience, and it "deduces general propositions from them only by induction." Thus anyone who wanted to take exception to the *Principia* would have to "draw his objection from some experiment or phenomenon." In this "experimental philosophy," Newton added, the "first principles or axiomes which I call the laws of motion" are "deduced from phenomena and made general by induction: which is the highest evidence that a proposition can have in this philosophy."

In other words, Newton's scientific outlook in the *Principia Mathematica* was that the whole system of dynamics was derived by reason (*i.e.*, mathematics) from self-evident principles, which were "self-evident" because they were based on phenomena or experience; the test of the reasoning process and the correctness of interpretation of the evidence from which these principles were "deduced" (we would rather say "induced") lay in the conformity of the final results with phenomena or further experience.

Franklin's revision of the Declaration of Independence placed the principle that all men are created equal in the category of an axiom, self-evident; like the laws of motion, it was a principle "deduced" from experience. Now the particular experience that Franklin had in mind was probably his own and that of his fellow Americans. The inequalities in men's material circumstances or position that could be observed in Europe must have been a product of the artificial circumstances of society, continued by the system of class structure and hereditary rights. Proof lay in America, where land was plentiful and where a man's fortune was apt to be determined by his industry, so that the differences between rich and poor tended to be less than in Europe. Franklin once compared American conditions to those in Ireland and Scotland, observing:

In those countries a small part of society are landlords, great noblemen, and gentlemen, extremely opulent, living in the highest affluence and magnificence; the bulk of the people tenants, living in the most sordid wretchedness in dirty hovels of mud and straw and clothed only in rags. I thought often of the happiness of New England, where every man is a freeholder, has a vote in public affairs, lives in a tidy, warm house, has plenty of good food and fuel, with whole clothes from head to foot, the manufacture perhaps of his own family. Long may they continue in this situation!

The absence of great differences between rich and poor in a land of opportunity, America, surely was empirical justification that such inequality was not a result of man's innate character. Of course, some men are better endowed than others, just as some men are more virtuous than others. As Poor Richard put the matter in "How to get riches"—"The art of getting riches consists very much in thrift. All men are not equally qualified for getting money, but it is in the power of every one alike to practise this virtue." This led to the conclusion that "Useful attainments in your minority will procure riches in maturity, of which writing and accounts are not the meanest." Hence the need for education: "Learning, whether speculative or practical, is, in popular or mixt governments, the natural source of wealth and honor."

We have already mentioned that Franklin was a confirmed abolitionist, but could he believe that Negroes were in any sense the equal of whites? Experience certainly showed that they were not, because anyone could observe that "negroes, who are free [and] live among the white people, . . . are generally improvident and poor." But experience must always be interpreted by reason, and in this case reason, said Franklin, tells us that free Negroes are not by nature "deficient in natural understanding," but simply that Negroes "have not the advantage of education." Here we may see more than an example of the application of reason to explain the data of experience, the condition of free Negroes. In considering society, ideas must be just as productive as in the study of nature. Thus Franklin's analysis was fruitful in creating a new form of experience, a trade school for Negroes, and by its means the whole doctrine was put to the test: if Negroes are inferior because they lack education, he said in effect, let us educate them and see whether they will not then be able to do the work of whites.

Franklin was secure in his convictions about the natural equality of men despite their color, and so he had no fear about the outcome of the proposed test in experience. As a matter of fact, Franklin firmly believed that truth could, by his definition, survive every experiential test which falsehood would necessarily fail; so it is very much in keeping with his character of empiricist that he maintained the freedom of the press, the right of the printer to publish all views and to let truth combat error publicly and vanquish her on the field of experience. Over and over we see Franklin embodying his conclusions in acts rather than concepts. It is misleading to think of him as the enemy of the abstract and master of the concrete, however, because this description would rob his empiricism of the role of reason.

Reason produces concepts out of experience and these concepts are always abstract, like the mutually repelling invisible particles in the electric fluid which he supposed was transferred from one body to another in electrostatic experiments; or abstract generalizations about matter, like its inability to act where it is not, or about man, like equality or rights. But a wide gulf separated Franklin from those who professed equality, for example, but did not practice it universally. He was not necessarily more sincere than they were; he was motivated by a different philosophy which made each abstraction live in its productive effect upon society rather than live a life of its own. This may not be the dominant philosophy in our history, but Americans have often acted as if it were. Like Franklin we have worked to found and support schools, hospitals, orphanages, homes for the aged, and we too have tried to improve our cities and towns and generally to make our habitation on earth pleasanter.

Next to the scientist the businessman is probably the

greatest empiricist the world knows. Dealing with facts
and with figures, he too contrives theories and applies
reason to the facts of experience. A businessman, be he
a manufacturer, merchant or shopkeeper, who finds his
theories killed by ugly facts will probably be a failure.
To make money requires predictions about trends and
events which are verified. To earn a fortune demands
qualities of initiative, shrewdness, observation and judgment but also an empirical temper of mind. Franklin's
rise to fortune came from his industry and thrift, but also
from his ability to see opportunities and to make the most
of them and to gauge the public needs and desires.

Franklin's major contribution to political thought was
a theory of population growth, based on the data available to him in America. He had observed that "the natural livelyhood of the thin inhabitants of a forest country
is hunting; that of a greater number, pasturage; that of
a middling population, agriculture; and that of the greatest, manufactures; which last must subsist the bulk of the
people in a full country or they must be subsisted by
charity, or perish." He claimed that the American population was increasing so as to double every twenty or
twenty-five years and would continue to do so (it did
up to about 1860) and that cheap and plentiful land, one
of the principal causes of American population increase,
would maintain high wages in America (as it did for at
least a century).

Franklin's essay had two consequences. It influenced
Malthus (in the second edition of his work) and it was
embodied in action, in accordance with the empiricist
philosophy. Franklin's observations on population growth
produced his influential pamphlet advocating the annex-
ing of Canada rather than Guadeloupe; America needed

room for expansion. Furthermore, it led him to a view based on simple calculation that America would eventually become more populous than Britain. America in the 1750s and '60s was, he said, "to be considered as the frontier of the British empire," but in 1760 he wrote that he had "long been of opinion that the *foundations of the future grandeur and stability of the British empire lie in America;* and though, like other foundations, they are low and little seen, they are, nevertheless, broad and strong enough to support the greatest political structure human wisdom ever yet erected." Franklin's concern for the empire thus became, in a real sense, the interest of the future major partner. Franklin's political thinking was based always on his study of society—or societies—through history books he had read and firsthand observation.

The empirical scientist may wrestle with the facts revealed by his laboratory experiments, but as an empiricist he cannot deny them. Franklin's theory of electrical action was generally satisfactory even though it could not adequately explain the repulsion between two negatively charged bodies, and yet he could not deny that such repulsion existed—despite his theory. Experience, as every scientist knows, is a hard taskmaster and it often makes the investigator abandon or alter cherished ideas by presenting an ugly little fact that does not fit. Early in his electrical research, Franklin had such an experience and "observed a phenomenon or two" that he could not account for on the principles he had set forth. "In going on with these experiments," he commented, "how many pretty systems do we build, which we soon find ourselves obliged to destroy! If there is no other use discovered of electricity, this, however, is something considerable, that it may *help to make a vain man humble.*" This facing up to facts, so natural to scientists in their laboratories, was a valuable asset to Franklin in ordinary life. The *Autobiography* shows how easy it was for him to accept the realities of experience and to learn from them how to be effective in achieving his aims.

The inflexible facts of nature constantly remind the experimental scientist that he is human enough to err and they induce a kind of humility and honesty that are always concomitants of an empiricist outlook on nature, man or society. The successful investigator is familiar with the need of altering his most cherished theories to make them fit the realities of experiment, the only way in which he can save the phenomena without jeopardizing the fundamental axioms of his science. In many ways this quality of integrity and adaptability in the scientist reminds us of the statesman whose code permits him to effect a compromise on matters of detail and mechanism and even degree without sacrifice of his fundamental principles. Whether Franklin's outstanding performance as the representative of America in France during the Revolution arose from such qualities, or whether nothing more was required than a native shrewdness and the bargaining skill of a businessman, he was certainly a master of the conference table. His major contribution to the Constitution was that compromise between the large and small states on the question of representation in the Congress.

Carl Van Doren, Franklin's greatest biographer, has written that this compromise "was Franklin's great victory in the Convention." He was author of "the compromise which held the delegates together at a time when they were ready to break up without forming any new Federal agreement. The Constitution was not his document. But without the weight of his prestige and the influence of his temper there might have been no document at all."

One of the features of the Constitution that most appealed to Franklin was the provision for amendment on trial, the possibility for alterations to be made in the light of actual experience. I am convinced that in Franklin's mind the greatest experiment was not the test of the electrification of clouds but the test of whether a democratic form of government could be established in the world and whether it could survive the trials of experience and function as its framers had intended.

II · The Lessons of Experience

BENJAMIN FRANKLIN's *Autobiography* is one of the most widely read documents in American literature. Americans have cherished this story for its bold and joyous style and because of a genuine affection for its author. It is a moral tale about the rewards of a good life, and an adventure in self-improvement and in selfless devotion to the needs of others. Americans have respected Franklin's *Autobiography* because of the frank admission of faults, weaknesses and mistakes—as a good printer Franklin called them "errata." It offers proof that there is no limit to what a man of virtue can achieve in a land of opportunity: America.

The introductory section printed below is taken from the first part of Franklin's autobiography, written in about two weeks during the summer of 1771. It is addressed to Franklin's son William, and was first written as a kind of family document. As the years went by, Franklin revised the text and made additions to it and showed the manuscript to a number of friends. Thus the *Autobiography* was transformed into a public document for his countrymen as well as his posterity, and for the whole world, although the manuscript still bore (at the time of the author's death) the salutation, "Dear son." Known universally as Franklin's *Autobiography*, this account of his life was called by Franklin his "Memoirs." Although the eighteenth century produced many notable autobiogra-

phies—Franklin's, and those of Jean Jacques Rousseau,
Edward Gibbon, David Hume and others—the word "autobiography" was not applied to them and was a novelty
introduced in the last century. The text is based on Franklin's original manuscript, first published by the University
of California Press in 1949.

Twyford, at the Bishop of St.
Asaph's 1771.

Dear Son,

I have ever had a pleasure in obtaining any little anecdotes of my ancestors. You may remember the enquiries
I made among the remains of my relations when you were
with me in England; and the journey I took for that purpose. Now imagining it may be equally agreable to you
to know the circumstances of *my* life, many of which you
are yet unacquainted with; and expecting a week's unin-
terrupted leisure in my present country retirement, I sit
down to write them for you. To which I have besides
some other inducements. Having emerged from the poverty and obscurity in which I was born and bred, to a
state of affluence and some degree of reputation in the
world, and having gone so far thro' life with a considerable share of felicity, the conducing means I made use
of, which, with the blessing of God, so well succeeded,
my posterity may like to know, as they may find some
of them suitable to their own situations, and therefore
fit to be imitated. That felicity, when I reflected on it,
has induced me sometimes to say, that were it offered to
my choice, I should have no objection to a repetition of
the same life from its beginning, only asking the advantages authors have in a second edition to correct some
faults of the first. So would I if I might, besides cor-

r[ectin]g the faults, change some sinister accidents and events of it for others more favourable, but tho' this were denied, I should still accept the offer. However, since such a repetition is not to be expected, the next thing most like living one's life over again, seems to be a *recollection* of that life; and to make that recollection as durable as possible, the putting it down in writing. Hereby, too, I shall indulge the inclination so natural in old men, to be talking of themselves and their own past actions, and I shall indulge it, without being troublesome to others who thro' respect to age might think themselves obliged to give me a hearing, since this may be read or not as any one pleases. And lastly, (I may as well confess it, since my denial of it will be believed by no body) perhaps I shall a good deal gratify my own *vanity*. Indeed I scarce ever heard or saw the introductory words, *Without vanity I may say,* etc., but some vain thing immediately followed. Most people dislike vanity in others whatever share they have of it themselves, but I give it fair quarter wherever I meet with it, being persuaded that it is often productive of good to the possessor and to others that are within his sphere of action: and therefore in many cases it would not be quite absurd if a man were to thank God for his vanity among the other comforts of life.

And now I speak of thanking God, I desire with all humility to acknowledge that I owe the mentioned happiness of my past life to His kind Providence, which led me to the means I used and gave them success. My belief of this induces me to *hope*, tho' I must not *presume*, that the same goodness will still be exercised towards me in continuing that happiness, or in enabling me to bear a fatal reverse, which I may experience as others have done, the complexion of my future fortune being known to Him only: and in whose power it is to bless to us even our afflictions.

. . . Josiah, my father, married young, and carried his wife with three children unto New England, about 1682. The Conventicles having been forbidden by law, and frequently disturbed, induced some considerable men of his acquaintance to remove to that country, and he was prevailed with to accompany them thither, where they expected to enjoy their mode of religion with freedom. By the same wife he had 4 children more born there, and by a second wife ten more, in all 17, of which I remember 13 sitting at one time at his table, who all grew up to be men and women, and married. I was the youngest son, and the youngest child but two, and was born in Boston, N.England. My mother the 2d wife was Abiah Folger, a daughter of Peter Folger, one of the first settlers of New England, of whom honourable mention is made by Cotton Mather, in his church history of that country, (entitled *Magnalia Christi Americana*) as a *godly learned Englishman*, if I remember the words rightly. . . .

My elder brothers were all put apprentices to different trades. I was put to the grammar school at eight years of age, my father intending to devote me as the tithe of his sons to the service of the church. My early readiness in learning to read (which must have been very early, as I do not remember when I could not read) and the opinion of all his friends that I should certainly make a good scholar, encouraged him in this purpose of his. My Uncle Benjamin too approved of it, and proposed to give me all his shorthand volumes of sermons, I suppose as a stock to set up with, if I would learn his character. I continued however at the grammar school not quite one

year, tho' in that time I had risen gradually from the
middle of the class of that year to be the head of it, and
farther was removed into the next class above it, in order
to go with that into the third at the end of the year. But
my father in the mean time, from a view of the expence
of a college education which, having so large a family,
he could not well afford, and the mean living many so
educated were afterwards able to obtain, (reasons that
he gave to his friends in my hearing) altered his first intention, took me from the grammar school, and sent me
to a school for writing and arithmetic kept by a then
famous man, Mr. Geo. Brownell, very successful in his
profession generally, and that by mild encouraging methods. Under him I acquired fair writing pretty soon, but
I failed in the arithmetic, and made no progress in it. At
ten years old, I was taken home to assist my father in his
business, which was that of a tallow chandler and sope
boiler. A business he was not bred to, but had assumed
on his arrival in New England and on finding his dying
trade would not maintain his family, being in little request. Accordingly I was employed in cutting wick for
the candles, filling the dipping mold, and the molds for
cast candles, attending the shop, going of errands, etc.
I disliked the trade and had a strong inclination for the
sea; but my father declared against it; however, living
near the water, I was much in and about it, learnt early
to swim well, and to manage boats, and when in a boat
or canoe with other boys I was commonly allowed to gov-
ern, especially in any case of difficulty; and upon other
occasions I was generally a leader among the boys, and
sometimes led them into scrapes, of which I will mention
one instance, as it shows an early projecting public spirit,
tho' not then justly conducted. There was a salt marsh

that bounded part of the mill pond, on the edge of which at highwater, we used to stand to fish for minews. By much trampling, we had made it a mere quagmire. My proposal was to build a wharf there fit for us to stand upon, and I showed my comrades a large heap of stones which were intended for a new house near the marsh, and which would very well suit our purpose. Accordingly in the evening when the workmen were gone, I assembled a number of my playfellows, and working with them diligently like so many emmets, sometimes two or three to a stone, we brought them all away and built our little wharff. The next morning the workmen were surprized at missing the stones, which were found in our wharff; enquiry was made after the removers; we were discovered and complained of; several of us were corrected by our fathers; and tho' I pleaded the usefulness of the work, mine convinced me that nothing was useful which was not honest.

. . . I continued thus employed in my father's business for two years, that is till I was 12 years old; and my brother John, who was bred to that business, having left my father, married and set up for himself at Rhode Island, there was all appearance that I was destined to supply his place and be a tallow chandler. But my dislike to the trade continuing, my father was under apprehensions that if he did not find one for me more agreable, I should break away and get to sea, as his son Josiah had done to his great vexation. He therefore sometimes took me to walk with him, and see joiners, bricklayers, turners, braziers, etc., at their work, that he might observe my inclination, and endeavor to fix it on some trade or other on land. It has ever since been a pleasure to me to see good workmen handle their tools; and it has been useful

to me, having learnt so much by it, as to be able to do
little jobs my self in my house, when a workman could
not readily be got; and to construct little machines for
my experiments while the intention of making the experiment was fresh and warm in my mind. My father
at last fixed upon the cutler's trade, and my Uncle Benjamin's son Samuel, who was bred to that business in
London, being about that time established in Boston, I
was sent to be with him some time on liking. But his
expectations of a fee with me displeasing my father, I was
taken home again.

From a child I was fond of reading, and all the little
money that came into my hands was ever laid out in
books. Pleased with the *Pilgrim's Progress,* my first collection was of John Bunyan's works, in separate little
volumes. I afterwards sold them to enable me to buy .
R. Burton's *Historical Collections;* they were small chapmen's books and cheap, 40 or 50 in all. My father's little
library consisted chiefly of books in polemic divinity,
most of which I read, and have since often regretted that
at a time when I had such a thirst for knowledge, more
proper books had not fallen in my way, since it was now
resolved I should not be a clergyman. Plutarch's *Lives*
there was, in which I read abundantly, and I still think
that time spent to great advantage. There was also a
book of Defoe's, called an *Essay on Projects,* and another
of Dr. Mather's, called *Essays to do Good,* which perhaps
gave me a turn of thinking that had an influence on some
of the principal future events of my life.

This bookish inclination at length determined my father
to make me a printer, tho' he had already one son (James)
of that profession. In 1717 my brother James returned
from England with a press and letters to set up his busi-

ness in Boston. I liked it much better than that of my father, but still had a hankering for the sea. To prevent the apprehended effect of such an inclination, my father was impatient to have me bound to my brother. I stood out some time, but at last was persuaded and signed the indentures, when I was yet but 12 years old. I was to serve as an apprentice till I was 21 years of age, only I was to be allowed journeyman's wages during the last year. In a little time I made great proficiency in the business, and became a useful hand to my brother. I now had access to better books. An acquaintance with the apprentices of booksellers enabled me sometimes to borrow a small one, which I was careful to return soon and clean. Often I sat up in my room reading the greatest part of the night, when the book was borrowed in the evening and to be returned early in the morning lest it should be missed or wanted. And after some time an ingenious tradesman Mr. Matthew Adams, who had a pretty collection of books, and who frequented our printing house, took notice of me, invited me to his library, and very kindly lent me such books as I chose to read. I now took a fancy to poetry, and made some little pieces. My brother, thinking it might turn to account, encouraged me, and put me on composing two occasional ballads. One was called the *Light House Tragedy*, and contained an account of the drowning of Capt. Worthilake with his two daughters; the other was a sailor song on the taking of Teach or Blackbeard the pirate. They were wretched stuff, in the Grubstreet ballad stile, and when they were printed he sent me about the town to sell them. The first sold wonderfully, the event being recent, having made a great noise. This flattered my vanity. But my father discouraged me, by ridiculing my performances,

and telling me verse-makers were always beggars; so I
escaped being a poet, most probably a very bad one. But
as prose writing has been of great use to me in the course
of my life, and was a principal means of my advancement,
I shall tell you how in such a situation I acquired what
little ability I have in that way.

. . . About this time I met with an odd volume of the
Spectator. It was the third. I had never before seen any
of them. I bought it, read it over and over, and was
much delighted with it. I thought the writing excellent,
and wished if possible to imitate it. With that view, I
took some of the papers, and making short hints of the
sentiment in each sentence, laid them by a few days, and
then without looking at the book, tried to compleat the
papers again, by expressing each hinted sentiment at
length and as fully as it had been expressed before, in
any suitable words that should come to hand.

Then I compared my *Spectator* with the original, discovered some of my faults and corrected them. But I
found I wanted a stock of words or a readiness in recollecting and using them, which I thought I should have
acquired before that time, if I had gone on making verses,
since the continual occasion for words of the same import
but of different length, to suit the measure, or of different
sound for the rhyme, would have laid me under a constant
necessity of searching for variety, and also have tended
to fix that variety in my mind, and make me master of
it. Therefore I took some of the tales and turned them
into verse: and after a time, when I had pretty well forgotten the prose, turned them back again. I also sometimes jumbled my collections of hints into confusion, and
after some weeks, endeavoured to reduce them into the
best order, before I began to form the full sentences, and

compleat the paper. This was to teach me method in
the arrangement of thoughts. By comparing my work
afterwards with the original, I discovered many faults
and amended them; but I sometimes had the pleasure
of fancying that in certain particulars of small import,
I had been lucky enough to improve the method or the
language and this encouraged me to think I might possibly in time come to be a tolerable English writer, of
which I was extreamly ambitious.

My time for the exercises and for reading was at night,
after work or before work began in the morning; or on
Sundays, when I contrived to be in the printing house
alone, evading as much as I could the common attendance
on publick worship, which my father used to exact of
me when I was under his care: and which indeed I still
thought a duty; tho' I could not, as it seemed to me,
afford the time to practise it.

. . . And now it was that being on some occasion made
ashamed of my ignorance in figures, which I had twice
failed in learning when at school, I took Cocker's book
of arithmetick, and went thro' the whole by my self with
great ease. I also read Seller's and Sturmy's books of
navigation, and became acquainted with the little geom-
etry they contain, but never proceeded far in that science.
And I read about this time Locke, *On Human Understanding*, and the *Art of Thinking* by Messrs. du Port Royal.

While I was intent on improving my language, I met
with an English grammar (I think it was Greenwood's)
at the end of which there were two little sketches of
the arts of rhetoric and logic, the latter finishing with
a specimen of a dispute in the Socratic method. And
soon after I procured Xenophon's *Memorable Things of
Socrates,* wherein there are many instances of the same

method. I was charmed with it, adopted it, dropt my
abrupt contradiction, and positive argumentation, and
put on the humble enquirer and doubter. And being
then, from reading Shaftsbury and Collins, become a real
doubter in many points of our religious doctrine, I found
this method safest for my self and very embarassing to
those against whom I used it; therefore I took a delight
in it, practised it continually and grew very artful and
expert in drawing people even of superior knowledge into
concessions the consequences of which they did not foresee, entangling them in difficulties out of which they
could not extricate themselves, and so obtaining victories
that neither my self nor my cause always deserved. I
continued this method some few years, but gradually
left it, retaining only the habit of expressing my self in
terms of modest diffidence, never using when I advance
any thing that may possibly be disputed, the words, *certainly, undoubtedly,* or any others that give the air of
positiveness to an opinion; but rather say, *I conceive,* or
I apprehend a thing to be so or so, *it appears to me,* or
I should think it so or so for such and such reasons, or
I imagine it to be so, or *it is so if I am not mistaken.* This
habit I believe has been of great advantage to me, when
I have had occasion to inculcate my opinions and persuade men into measures that I have been from time to
time engaged in promoting. And as the chief ends of
conversation are to *inform,* or to be *informed,* to *please*
or to *persuade,* I wish wellmeaning sensible men would
not lessen their power of doing good by a positive as-
suming manner that seldom fails to disgust, tends to create opposition, and to defeat every one of those purposes
for which speech was given us, to wit, giving or receiving
information, or pleasure: for if you would *inform,* a positive dogmatical manner in advancing your sentiments

may provoke contradiction and prevent a candid attention. If you wish information and improvement from
the knowledge of others and yet at the same time express
your self as firmly fixed in your present opinions, modest
sensible men, who do not love disputation, will probably
leave you undisturbed in the possession of your error;
and by such a manner you can seldom hope to recommend
your self in *pleasing* your hearers, or to persuade those
whose concurrence you desire. . . .

My brother had in 1720 or 21, begun to print a newspaper. It was the second that appeared in America, and
was called *The New England Courant*. The only one before it was *The Boston News Letter*. I remember his being
dissuaded by some of his friends from the undertaking,
as not likely to succeed, one newspaper being in their
judgment enough for America. At this time 1771 there
are not less than five and twenty. He went on however
with the undertaking, and after having worked in composing the types and printing off the sheets I was employed to carry the papers thro' the streets to the customers. He had some ingenious men among his friends
who amused themselves by writing little pieces for this
paper, which gained it credit, and made it more in demand; and these gentlemen often visited us. Hearing
their conversations, and their accounts of the approbation their papers were received with, I was excited to try
my hand among them. But being still a boy, and suspect-
ing that my brother would object to printing any thing
of mine in his paper if he knew it to be mine, I contrived
to disguise my hand, and writing an anonymous paper
I put it in at night under the door of the printing house.
It was found in the morning and communicated to his
writing friends when they called in as usual. They read
it, commented on it in my hearing, and I had the ex-

quisite pleasure of finding it met with their approbation,
and that in their different guesses at the author none
were named but men of some character among us for
learning and ingenuity. I suppose now that I was rather
lucky in my judges: and that perhaps they were not
really so very good ones as I then esteemed them. Encouraged however by this, I wrote and conveyed in the
same way to the press several more papers, which were
equally approved, and I kept my secret till my small
fund of sense for such performances was pretty well exhausted, and then I discovered it; when I began to be
considered a little more by my brother's acquaintance,
and in a manner that did not quite please him, as he
thought, probably with reason, that it tended to make
me too vain. And perhaps this might be one occasion
of the differences that we frequently had about this time.
Tho' a brother, he considered himself as my master, and
me as his apprentice; and accordingly expected the same
services from me as he would from another; while I
thought he demeaned me too much in some he required of
me, who from a brother expected more indulgence. Our
disputes were often brought before our father, and I fancy
I was either generally in the right, or else a better pleader,
because the judgment was generally in my favour: but
my brother was passionate and had often beaten me,
which I took extreamly amiss; and thinking my apprenticeship very tedious, I was continually wishing for some
opportunity of shortening it, which at length offered in
a manner unexpected.*

One of the pieces in our news-paper, on some political

---

* I fancy his harsh and tyrannical treatment of me might be a means
of impressing me with that aversion to arbitrary power that has stuck to
me thro' my whole life. [Franklin's note.]

point which I have now forgotten, gave offence to the Assembly. He was taken up, censured and imprisoned for a month by the Speaker's warrant, I suppose because he would not discover his author. . . . My brother's discharge was accompanied with an order of the House (a very odd one) *that James Franklin should no longer print the paper called the New England Courant.* There was a consultation held in our printing house among his friends what he should do in this case. Some proposed to evade the order by changing the name of the paper; but my brother seeing inconveniences in that, it was finally concluded on as a better way, to let it be printed for the future under the name of Benjamin Franklin. And to avoid the censure of the Assembly that might fall on him, as still printing it by his apprentice, the contrivance was that my old indenture should be returned to me with a full discharge on the back of it, to be shown on occasion; but to secure to him the benefit of my service I was to sign new indentures for the remainder of the term, which were to be kept private. A very flimsy scheme it was, but however it was immediately executed, and the paper went on accordingly under my name for several months. At length a fresh difference arising between my brother and me, I took upon me to assert my freedom, presuming that he would not venture to produce the new indentures. It was not fair in me to take this advantage, and this I therefore reckon one of the first errata of my life: but the unfairness of it weighed little with me, when under the impressions of resentment, for the blows his passion too often urged him to bestow upon me. Tho' he was otherwise not an ill-natured man: perhaps I was too saucy and provoking.

When he found I would leave him, he took care to prevent my getting employment in any other printing-house of the town, by going round and speaking to every master, who accordingly refused to give me work. I then thought of going to New York as the nearest place where there was a printer: and I was the rather inclined to leave Boston, when I reflected that I had already made myself a little obnoxious to the governing party; and from the arbitrary proceedings of the Assembly in my brother's case it was likely I might if I stayed soon bring myself into scrapes; and farther that my indiscrete disputations about religion begun to make me pointed at with horror by good people, as an infidel or atheist. I determined on the point: but my father now siding with my brother, I was sensible that if I attempted to go openly, means would be used to prevent me. My friend Collins therefore undertook to manage a little for me. He agreed with the captain of a New York sloop for my passage, under the notion of my being a young acquaintance of his that had got a naughty girl with child, whose friends would compel me to marry her, and therefore I could not appear or come away publickly. So I sold some of my books to raise a little money, was taken on board privately, and as we had a fair wind in three days I found my self in New York near 300 miles from home, a boy of but 17, without the least recommendation to or knowledge of any person in the place, and with very little money in my pocket.

My inclinations for the sea were by this time worne out, or I might now have gratified them. But having a trade, and supposing my self a pretty good workman, I offered my service to the printer of the place, old Mr. Wm. Bradford, (who had been the first printer in Pennsylvania, but removed from thence upon the quarrel of Geo. Keith). He could give me no employment, having little to do, and

help enough already: but, says he, my son at Philadelphia
has lately lost his principal hand, Aquila Rose, by death.
If you go thither I believe he may employ you. Philadelphia was 100 miles farther. I set out, however, in a boat
for Amboy, leaving my chest and things to follow me
round by sea. . . .

I have been the more particular in this description of
. . . my first entry into that city [Philadelphia] that you
may in your mind compare such unlikely beginnings with
the figure I have since made there. I was in my working
dress, my best cloaths being to come round by sea. I was
dirty from my journey; my pockets were stuffed out with
shirts and stockings; I knew no soul, nor where to look
for lodging. I was fatigued with travelling, rowing and
want of rest. I was very hungry, and my whole stock of
cash consisted of a Dutch dollar and about a shilling in
copper. The latter I gave the people of the boat for my
passage, who at first refused it on account of my rowing;
but I insisted on their taking it, a man being sometimes
more generous when he has but a little money than when
he has plenty, perhaps thro' fear of being thought to have
but little. Then I walked up the street, gazing about, till
near the market house I met a boy with bread. I had made
many a meal on bread, and inquiring where he got it, I
went immediately to the baker's he directed me to in Second Street; and asked for bisket, intending such as we had
in Boston, but they it seems were not made in Philadelphia; then I asked for a three-penny loaf, and was told
they had none such: so not considering or knowing the
difference of money and the greater cheapness nor the
names of his bread, I bad him give me three penny worth
of any sort. He gave me accordingly three great puffy

rolls. I was surprized at the quantity, but took it, and having no room in my pockets, walked off, with a roll under each arm, and eating the other. Thus I went up Market Street as far as Fourth Street, passing by the door of Mr. Read, my future wife's father, when she standing at the door saw me, and thought I made as I certainly did a most awkward ridiculous appearance. Then I turned and went down Chestnut Street and part of Walnut Street, eating my roll all the way, and coming round found my self again at Market Street Wharff, near the boat I came in, to which I went for a draught of the river water, and being filled with one of my rolls, gave the other two to a woman and her child that came down the river in the boat with us and were waiting to go farther. Thus refreshed I walked again up the street, which by this time had many clean dressed people in it who were all walking the same way; I joined them, and thereby was led into the great meeting house of the Quakers near the market. I sat down among them, and after looking round a while and hearing nothing said, being very drowzy thro' labour and want of rest the preceding night, I fell fast asleep, and continued so till the meeting broke up, when one was kind enough to rouse me. This was therefore the first house I was in or slept in, in Philadelphia.

Walking again down towards the river, and looking in the faces of people, I met a young Quaker man whose countenance I liked, and accosting him requested he would tell me where a stranger could get lodging. . . . He brought me to the Crooked Billet in Water-Street. Here I got a dinner. And while I was eating it, several sly questions were asked me, as it seemed to be suspected from my youth and appearance, that I might be some runaway. After dinner my sleepiness returned: and being shown to a bed, I lay down without undressing, and slept till six in the evening; was called to supper; went to bed again very early and slept soundly till the next morning. Then I made my self as tidy as I could, and went to Andrew Bradford the printer's. I found in the shop the old man his father, whom I had seen at New York, and who travelling on horse back had got to Philadelphia before me. He introduced me to his son, who received me civilly, gave me a breakfast, but told me he did not at present want a hand, being lately supplied with one. But there was another printer in town lately set up, one Keimer, who perhaps might employ me; if not, I should be welcome to lodge at his house, and he would give me a little work to do now and then till fuller business should offer.

The old gentleman said he would go with me to the new printer: and when we found him, neighbour, says Bradford, I have brought to see you a young man of your business, perhaps you may want such a one. He asked me a few questions, put a composing stick in my hand to see how I worked, and then said he would employ me soon, tho' he had just then nothing for me to do. . . . A few days after, Keimer sent for me. . . . And now he had got another pair of cases, and a pamphlet to reprint, on which he set me to work.

These two printers I found poorly qualified for their business. Bradford had not been bred to it, and was very illiterate; and Keimer tho' something of a scholar, was a mere compositor, knowing nothing of presswork. . . . He did not like my lodging at Bradford's while I worked with him. He had a house indeed, but without furniture, so he could not lodge me: but he got me a lodging at Mr. Read's before-mentioned, who was the owner of his house. And my chest and clothes being come by this time, I made

rather a more respectable appearance in the eyes of Miss
Read than I had done when she first happened to see me
eating my roll in the street.

I began now to have some acquaintance among the
young people of the town that were lovers of reading, with
whom I spent my evenings very pleasantly, and gaining
money by my industry and frugality, I lived very agreably,
forgetting Boston as much as I could, and not desiring
that any there should know where I resided, except my
friend Collins who was in my secret, and kept it when I
wrote to him. At length an incident happened that sent
me back again much sooner than I had intended.

I had a brother-in-law, Robert Holmes, master of a
sloop, that traded between Boston and Delaware. He
being at New Castle 40 miles below Philadelphia, heard
there of me, and wrote me a letter, mentioning the concern of my friends in Boston at my abrupt departure, as-
suring me of their goodwill to me, and that every thing
would be accommodated to my mind if I would return,
to which he exhorted me very earnestly. . . . Sir William
Keith, Governor of the Province, was then at New Castle,
and Capt. Holmes happening to be in company with
him . . . , spoke to him of me. . . . The Governor . . . said
I appeared a young man of promising parts, and therefore
should be encouraged: the printers at Philadelphia were
wretched ones, and if I would set up there, he made no
doubt I should succeed; for his part, he would procure me
the publick business, and do me every other service in his
power. . . .

[Franklin then went to Boston to find out whether his
father might help to set him up as a printer in Boston.
His father refused, giving as his reason Benjamin's ex-

treme youth. Franklin returned to Philadelphia and reported his failure to Sir William.]

And since he will not set you up, says he, I will do it my
self. Give me an inventory of the things necessary to be
had from England, and I will send for them. You shall
repay me when you are able; I am resolved to have a good
printer here, and I am sure you must succeed. This was
spoken with such an appearance of cordiality, that I had
not the least doubt of his meaning what he said. I had
hitherto kept the proposition of my setting up a secret in
Philadelphia, and I still kept it. Had it been known that
I depended on the Governor, probably some friend that
knew him better would have advised me not to rely on
him, as I afterwards heard it as his known character to
be liberal of promises which he never meant to keep. Yet
unsolicited as he was by me, how could I think his generous offers insincere? I believed him one of the best men
in the world.

I presented him an inventory of a little printing house,
amounting by my computation to about 100 £ Sterling.
He liked it, but asked me if my being on the spot in England to chuse the types and see that every thing was good
of the kind, might not be of some advantage. Then, says
he, when there, you may make acquaintances and establish correspondencies in the bookselling and stationary
way. I agreed that this might be advantageous. Then
says he, get yourself ready to go with Annis; which was
the annual ship, and the only one at that time usually
passing between London and Philadelphia. . . .

I had made some courtship during this time to Miss
Read. I had a great respect and affection for her, and had
some reason to believe she had the same for me: but as

I was about to take a long voyage, and we were both very young, only a little above 18, it was thought most prudent by her mother to prevent our going too far at present, as a marriage if it was to take place would be more convenient after my return, when I should be as I expected set up in my business. Perhaps too she thought my expectations not so wellfounded as I imagined them to be. . . .

The Governor, seeming to like my company, had me frequently to his house; and his setting me up was always mentioned as a fixed thing. I was to take with me letters recommendatory to a number of his friends, besides the letter of credit to furnish me with the necessary money for purchasing the press and types, paper, etc. For these letters I was appointed to call at different times, when they were to be ready, but a future time was still named. Thus we went on till the ship whose departure too had been several times postponed was on the point of sailing. Then when I called to take my leave and receive the letters, his secretary, Dr. Bard, came out to me and said the Governor was extreamly busy, in writing, but would be down at Newcastle before the ship, and there the letters would be delivered to me.

. . . Having taken leave of my friends, and interchanged some promises with Miss Read, I left Philadelphia in the ship, which anchored at Newcastle. The Governor was there. But when I went to his lodging, the secretary came to me from him with the civillest message in the world, that he could not then see me, being engaged in business of the utmost importance; but should send the letters to me on board, wished me heartily a good voyage and a speedy return, etc. I returned on board, a little puzzled, but still not doubting.

Mr. Andrew Hamilton, a famous lawyer of Philadelphia,

had taken passage in the same ship for himself and son: and with Mr. Denham, a Quaker merchant, and Messrs. Onion and Russel, masters of an iron work in Maryland, had engaged the great cabin; so that Ralph and I were forced to take up with a birth in the steerage: and none on board knowing us, were considered as ordinary persons. But Mr. Hamilton and his son (it was James, since Governor) returned from New Castle to Philadelphia, the father being recalled by a great fee to plead for a seized ship. And just before we sailed Col. French coming on board, and showing me great respect, I was more taken notice of, and with my friend Ralph invited by the other gentlemen to come into the cabin, there being now room. Accordingly we removed thither.

Understanding that Col. French had brought on board the Governor's dispatches, I asked the Captain for those letters that were to be under my care. He said all were put into the bag together; and he could not then come at them; but before we landed in England, I should have an opportunity of picking them out. So I was satisfied for the present, and we proceeded on our voyage. We had a sociable company in the cabin, and lived uncommonly well, having the addition of all Mr. Hamilton's stores, who had laid in plentifully. In this passage Mr. Denham contracted a friendship for me that continued during his life. The voyage was otherwise not a pleasant one, as we had a great deal of bad weather.

When we came into the Channel, the Captain kept his word with me, and gave me an opportunity of examining the bag for the Governor's letters. I found none upon which my name was put, as under my care; I picked out 6 or 7 that by the hand writing I thought might be the promised letters, especially as one of them was directed to

Basket the King's printer, and another to some stationer.
We arrived in London the 24th of December, 1724. I
waited upon the stationer who came first in my way, de-
livering the letter as from Gov. Keith. I don't know such
a person, says he: but opening the letter, O, this is from
Riddlesden; I have lately found him to be a compleat ras-
cal, and I will have nothing to do with him, nor receive
any letters from him. So putting the letter into my hand,
he turned on his heel and left me to serve some customer.
I was surprized to find these were not the Governor's letters. And after recollecting and comparing circumstances,
I began to doubt his sincerity. I found my friend Denham,
and opened the whole affair to him. He let me into Keith's
character, told me there was not the least probability that
he had written any letters for me, that no one who knew
him had the smallest dependance on him, and he laught
at the notion of the Governor's giving me a letter of credit,
having as he said no credit to give. On my expressing
some concern about what I should do: he advised me to
endeavour getting some employment in the way of my
business. Among the printers here, says he, you will improve yourself; and when you return to America, you will
set up to greater advantage. . . .

But what shall we think of a governor's playing such
pitiful tricks, and imposing so grossly on a poor ignorant
boy! It was a habit he had acquired. He wished to please
every body; and, having little to give, he gave expectations. He was otherwise an ingenious sensible man, a
pretty good writer, and a good governor for the people,
tho' not for his constituents the proprietaries, whose instructions he sometimes disregarded. Several of our best
laws were of his planning, and passed during his administration. . . .

I immediately got into work at Palmer's, then a famous printing house in Bartholomew Close; and here I continued near a year. I was pretty diligent; but spent with Ralph a good deal of my earnings in going to plays and other places of amusement. We had together consumed all my pistoles, and now just rubbed on from hand to mouth. He seemed quite to forget his wife and child, and I by degrees my engagements with Miss Read, to whom I never wrote more than one letter, and that was to let her know I was not likely soon to return. This was another of the great errata of my life, which I should wish to correct if I were to live it over again. In fact, by our expences, I was constantly kept unable to pay my passage.

At Palmer's I was employed in composing for the second edition of Woollaston's *Religion of Nature.* Some of his reasonings not appearing to me well-founded, I wrote a little metaphysical piece, in which I made remarks on them. It was entitled, *A Dissertation on Liberty and Necessity, Pleasure and pain.* I inscribed it to my friend Ralph. I printed a small number. It occasioned my being more considered by Mr. Palmer, as a young man of some ingenuity, tho' he seriously expostulated with me upon the principles of my pamphlet which to him appeared abominable. My printing this pamphlet was another erratum.

While I lodged in Little Britain I made an acquaintance with one Wilcox a bookseller, whose shop was at the next door. He had an immense collection of second-hand books. Circulating libraries were not then in use; but we agreed that on certain reasonable terms which I have now forgotten, I might take, read and return any of his books. This I esteemed a great advantage, and I made as much use of it as I could. . . .

. . . I left Palmer's to work at Watts's near Lincoln's Inn
Fields, a still greater printing house. Here I continued all
the rest of my stay in London.

At my first admission into this printing house, I took to
working at press, imagining I felt a want of the bodily
exercise I had been used to in America, where presswork
is mixed with composing. I drank only water; the other
workmen, near 50 in number, were great guzzlers of beer.
On occasion I carried up and down stairs a large form of
types in each hand, when others carried but one in both
hands. They wondered to see from this and several instances that the water-American as they called me was
stronger than themselves who drank *strong* beer. We had
an alehouse boy who attended always in the house to supply the workmen. My companion at the press drank
every day a pint before breakfast, a pint at breakfast with
his bread and cheese; a pint between breakfast and dinner; a pint at dinner; a pint in the afternoon about six
o'clock, and another when he had done his day's-work. I
thought it a detestable custom. But it was necessary, he
supposed, to drink *strong* beer that he might be *strong* to
labour. I endeavoured to convince him that the bodily
strength afforded by beer could only be in proportion to
the grain or flour of the barley dissolved in the water of
which it was made; that there was more flour in a penny-
worth of bread, and therefore if he would eat that with a
pint of water, it would give him more strength than a
quart of beer. He drank on however, and had 4 or 5
shillings to pay out of his wages every Saturday night for
that muddling liquor; an expence I was free from. And
thus these poor devils keep themselves always under. . . .

. . . My good friend Mr. Denham, with whom I often
spent an hour, when I had leisure, . . . told me he was

about to return to Philadelphia, and should carry over a great quantity of goods in order to open a store there: he proposed to take me over as his clerk, to keep his books (in which he would instruct me) copy his letters, and attend the store. He added, that as soon as I should be acquainted with mercantile business he would promote me by sending me with a cargo of flour and bread, etc., to the West Indies, and procure me commissions from others; which would be profitable, and if I managed well, would establish me handsomely. The thing pleased me, for I was grown tired of London, remembered with pleasure the happy months I had spent in Pennsylvania, and wished again to see it. Therefore I immediately agreed on the terms of fifty pounds a year, Pennsylvania money; less indeed than my present gettings as a compositor, but affording a better prospect.

I now took leave of printing, as I thought for ever, and was daily employed in my new business; going about with Mr. Denham among the tradesmen, to purchase various articles, and seeing them packed up, doing errands, calling upon workmen to dispatch, etc., and when all was on board, I had a few days leisure. . . .

Thus I spent about 18 months in London. Most part of the time, I worked hard at my business and spent but little upon my self except in seeing plays and in books. My friend Ralph had kept me poor. He owed me about 27 pounds; which I was now never likely to receive; a great sum out of my small earnings. I loved him notwithstanding, for he had many amiable qualities. . . . I had by no means improved my fortune. But I had picked up some very ingenious acquaintance whose conversation was of great advantage to me, and I had read considerably.

We sailed from Gravesend on the 23d of July 1726. For

the incidents of the voyage, I refer you to my Journal, where you will find them all minutely related. Perhaps the most important part of that Journal is the *Plan* to be found in it which I formed at sea, for regulating my future conduct in life. It is the more remarkable, as being formed when I was so young, and yet being pretty faithfully adhered to quite thro' to old age. We landed in Philadelphia the 11th of October, where I found sundry alterations. Keith was no longer Governor, being superceded by Major Gordon: I met him walking the streets as a common citizen. He seemed a little ashamed at seeing me, but passed without saying any thing. I should have been as much ashamed at seeing Miss Read, had not her fr[ien]ds, despairing with reason of my return, after the receipt of my letter, persuaded her to marry another, one Rogers, a potter, which was done in my absence. With him however she was never happy, and soon parted from him, refusing to cohabit with him, or bear his name, it being now said that he had another wife. He was a worthless fellow tho' an excellent workman, which was the temptation to her friends. He got into debt, and ran away in 1727 or 28. Went to the West Indies, and died there. Keimer had got a better house, a shop well supplied with stationary, plenty of new types, a number of hands tho' none good, and seemed to have a great deal of business.

Mr. Denham took a store in Water Street, where we opened our goods. I attended the business diligently, studied accounts, and grew in a little time expert at selling. We lodged and boarded together, he counselled me as a father, having a sincere regard for me: I respected and loved him: and we might have gone on together very happily: but in the beginning of Feb. 1726/7 when I had just passed my 21st year, we both were taken ill. My dis-

temper was a pleurisy, which very nearly carried me off:
I suffered a good deal, gave up the point in my own mind,
and was rather disappointed when I found my self re-
covering; regretting in some degree that I must now some
time or other have all that disagreable work to do over
again. I forget what his distemper was. It held him a
long time, and at length carried him off. He left me a
small legacy in a nuncupative will, as a token of his kindness for me, and he left me once more to the wide world.
For the store was taken into the care of his executors, and
my employment under him ended: my brother-in-law
Holmes, being now at Philadelphia, advised my return to
my business. And Keimer tempted me with an offer of
large wages by the year to come and take the management
of his printing-house, that he might better attend his
stationer's shop. I had heard a bad character of him in
London, from his wife and her friends, and was not fond
of having any more to do with him. I tried for farther
employment as a merchant's clerk; but not readily meeting with any, I closed again with Keimer.

I found in *his* house these hands; Hugh Meredith a
Welsh-Pennsylvanian, 30 years of age, bred to country
work: honest, sensible, had a great deal of solid observation, was something of a reader, but given to drink: Ste-
phen Potts, a young country man of full age, bred to the
same: of uncommon natural parts, and great wit and humour, but a little idle. These he had agreed with at extream
low wages, p[er] week, to be raised a shilling every 3
months, as they would deserve by improving in their business, and the expectation of these high wages to come on
hereafter was what he had drawn them in with. Meredith
was to work at press, Potts at bookbinding, which he by
agreement, was to teach them, tho' he knew neither one

nor t'other. John —— a wild Irishman brought up to no business, whose service for 4 years Keimer had purchased from the captain of a ship. He too was to be made a pressman. George Webb, an Oxford scholar, whose time for 4 years he had likewise bought, intending him for a compositor: of whom more presently. And David Harry, a country boy, whom he had taken apprentice. I soon perceived that the intention of engaging me at wages so much higher than he had been used to give, was to have these raw cheap hands formed thro' me, and as soon as I had instructed them, then, they being all articled to him, he should be able to do without me. I went on however, very chearfully; put his printing house in order, which had been in great confusion, and brought his hands by degrees to mind their business and to do it better. . . .

Our printing-house often wanted sorts, and there was no letter founder in America. I had seen types cast at James's in London, but without much attention to the manner: however I now contrived a mould, made use of the letters we had, as puncheons, struck the matrices in lead, and thus supplied in a pretty tolerable way all deficiencies. I also engraved several things on occasion. I made the ink, I was warehouse-man and every thing, in short quite a factotum.

But however serviceable I might be, I found that my services became every day of less importance, as the other hands improved in the business. And when Keimer paid my second quarter's wages, he let me know that he felt them too heavy, and thought I should make an abatement. He grew by degrees less civil, put on more of the master, frequently found fault, was captious and seemed ready for an out-breaking. I went on nevertheless with a good deal of patience, thinking that his incumbered circumstances were partly the cause. At length a trifle snapt our connexion. For a great noise happening near the court-house, I put my head out of the window to see what was the matter. Keimer being in the street looked up and saw me, called out to me in a loud voice and angry tone to mind my business, adding some reproachful words, that nettled me the more for their publicity, all the neighbours who were looking out on the same occasion being wit-nesses how I was treated. He came up immediately into the printing-house, continued the quarrel, high words passed on both sides, he gave me the quarter's warning we had stipulated, expressing a wish that he had not been obliged to so long a warning: I told him his wish was unnecessary for I would leave him that instant; and so taking my hat walked out of doors; desiring Meredith whom I saw below to take care of some things I left, and bring them to my lodging.

Meredith came accordingly in the evening, when we talked my affair over. He had conceived a great regard for me, and was very unwilling that I should leave the house while he remained in it. He dissuaded me from re-turning to my native country which I began to think of. He reminded me that Keimer was in debt for all he pos-sessed, that his creditors began to be uneasy, that he kept his shop miserably, sold often without profit for ready money, and often trusted without keeping accounts. That he must therefore fail; which would make a vacancy I might profit of. I objected my want of money. He then let me know that his father had a high opinion of me, and from some discourse that had passed between them, he was sure would advance money to set us up, if I would enter into partnership with him. My time, says he, will be out with Keimer in the spring. By that time we may

have our press and types in from London. I am sensible
I am no workman. If you like it, your skill in the business
shall be set against the stock I furnish; and we will share
the profits equally. The proposal was agreable, and I consented. His father was in town, and approved of it, the
more as he saw I had great influence with his son, had
prevailed on him to abstain long from dramdrinking, and
he hoped might break him of that wretched habit entirely,
when we came to be so closely connected. I gave an inventory to the father, who carried it to a merchant; the
things were sent for; the secret was to be kept till they
should arrive, and in the mean time I was to get work
if I could at the other printing house. But I found no
vacancy there, and so remained idle a few days, when
Keimer, on a prospect of being employed to print some
paper-money, in New Jersey, which would require cuts
and various types that I only could supply, and apprehending Bradford might engage me and get the jobb from
him, sent me a very civil message, that old friends should
not part for a few words, the effect of sudden passion,
and wishing me to return. Meredith persuaded me to
comply, as it would give more opportunity for his improvement under my daily instructions. So I returned,
and we went on more smoothly than for some time before. The New Jersey jobb was obtained. I contrived a
copper-plate press for it, the first that had been seen in
the country. I cut several ornaments and checks for the
bills. We went together to Burlington, where I executed
the whole to satisfaction, and he received so large a sum
for the work as to be enabled thereby to keep his head
much longer above water.

At Burlington I made an acquaintance with many principal people of the province. Several of them had been

appointed by the Assembly a committee to attend the press, and take care that no more bills were printed than the law directed. They were therefore by turns constantly with us, and generally he who attended brought with him a friend or two for company. My mind having been much more improved by reading than Keimer's, I suppose it was for that reason my conversation seemed to be more valued. They had me to their houses, introduced me to their friends and showed me much civility, while he, tho' the master, was a little neglected. In truth he was an odd fish, ignorant of common life, fond of rudely opposing received opinions, slovenly to extream dirtiness, enthusiastic in some points of religion, and a little knavish withal. We continued there near 3 months, and by that time I could reckon among my acquired friends, Judge Allen, Samuel Bustill, the secretary of the Province, Isaac Pearson, Joseph Cooper and several of the Smiths, members of Assembly, and Isaac Decow the Surveyor General. The latter was a shrewd sagacious old man, who told me that he began for himself when young by wheeling clay for the brickmakers, learnt to write after he was of age, carried the chain for surveyors, who taught him surveying, and he had now by his industry acquired a good estate; and says he, I foresee that you will soon work this man out of his business and make a fortune in it at Philadelphia. He had not then the least intimation of my intention to set up there or any where. These friends were afterwards of great use to me, as I occasionally was to some of them. They all continued their regard for me as long as they lived.

Before I enter upon my public appearance in business it may be well to let you know the then state of my mind, with regard to my principles and morals, that you may

see how far those influenced the future events of my life.
My parents had early given me religious impressions, and
brought me through my childhood piously in the dissent-
ing way. But I was scarce 15 when, after doubting by
turns of several points as I found them disputed in the
different books I read, I began to doubt of revelation it
self. Some books against deism fell into my hands; they
were said to be the substance of sermons preached at
Boyle's Lectures. It happened that they wrought an effect
on me quite contrary to what was intended by them: for
the arguments of the deists which were quoted to be re-
futed, appeared to me much stronger than the refutations.
In short I soon became a thorough deist. My arguments
perverted some others, particularly Collins and Ralph: but
each of them having afterwards wronged me greatly without the least compunction and recollecting Keith's conduct toward me, (who was another freethinker) and my
own towards Vernon and Miss Read, which at times gave
me great trouble, I began to suspect that this doctrine, tho'
it might be true, was not very useful. My London pamphlet, which . . . concluded that nothing could possibly
be wrong in the world, and that vice and virtue were
empty distinctions, no such things existing, appeared now
not so clever a performance as I once thought it; and I
doubted whether some error had not insinuated itself un-
perceived, into my argument, so as to infect all that followed, as is common in metaphysical reasonings. I grew
convinced that *truth, sincerity* and *integrity* in dealings
between man and man, were of the utmost importance to
the felicity of life, and I formed written resolutions (which
still remain in my Journal Book) to practice them ever
while I lived. Revelation had indeed no weight with me
as such; but I entertained an opinion, that tho' certain

actions might not be bad *because* they were forbidden by it, or good *because* it commanded them; yet probably those actions might be forbidden *because* they were bad for us, or commanded *because* they were beneficial to us, in their own natures, all the circumstances of things considered. And this persuasion, with the kind hand of Providence, or some guardian angel, or accidental favourable circumstances and situations, or all together, preserved me (thro' this dangerous time of youth and the hazardous situations I was sometimes in among strangers, remote from the eye and advice of my father) without any *wilful* gross immorality or injustice that might have been expected from my want of religion. I say *wilful*, because the instances I have mentioned had something of *necessity* in them, from my youth, inexperience, and the knavery of others. I had therefore a tolerable character to begin the world with, I valued it properly, and determined to preserve it.

We had not been long returned to Philadelphia, before the new types arrived from London. We settled with Keimer, and left him by his consent before he heard of it. We found a house to hire near the market, and took it. To lessen the rent, (which was then but 24 £ a year tho' I have since known it let for 70) we took in Tho. Godfrey, a glazier, and his family, who were to pay a considerable part of it to us, and we to board with them. We had scarce opened our letters and put our press in order, before George House, an acquaintance of mine, brought a country-man to us; whom he had met in the street enquiring for a printer. All our cash was now expended in the variety of particulars we had been obliged to procure and this countryman's five shillings being our first fruits, and coming so seasonably, gave me more pleasure than any

crown I have since earned; and from the gratitude I felt
toward House, has made me often more ready than perhaps I should otherwise have been to assist young begin-
ners. . . .

Brientnal particularly procured us from the Quakers,
the printing 40 sheets of their history, the rest being to
be done by Keimer: and upon this we worked exceeding
hard, for the price was low. It was a folio, pro patria size,
in pica with long primer notes. I composed of it a sheet a
day, and Meredith worked it off at press. It was often 11
at night and sometimes later before I had finished my dis-
tribution for the next day's work: for the little jobbs sent
in by our other friends now and then put us back. But so
determined I was to continue doing a sheet a day of the
folio, that one night when having imposed my forms, I
thought my day's work over, one of them by accident was
broken and two pages reduced to pie. I immediately distributed and composed it over again before I went to bed.
And this industry visible to our neighbours began to give
us character and credit; particularly I was told that mention being made of the new printing office at the merchants every-night-club, the general opinion was that it
must fail, there being already two printers in the place,
Keimer and Bradford; but Doctor Baird (whom you and
I saw many years after at his native place, St. Andrews in
Scotland) gave a contrary opinion; for the industry of that
Franklin, says he, is superior to any thing I ever saw of the
kind: I see him still at work when I go home from club;
and he is at work again before his neighbours are out of
bed. This struck the rest, and we soon after had offers
from one of them to supply us with stationary. But as yet
we did not chuse to engage in shop business.

I mention this industry the more particularly and the

more freely, tho' it seems to be talking in my own praise, that those of my posterity who shall read it, may know the use of that virtue, when they see its effects in my favour throughout this relation.

George Webb, who had found a female friend that lent him wherewith to purchase his time of Keimer, now came to offer himself as a journeyman to us. We could not then imploy him, but I foolishly let him know, as a secret, that I soon intended to begin a newspaper, and might then have work for him. My hopes of success as I told him were founded on this, that the then only newspaper, printed by Bradford, was a paltry thing, wretchedly managed, and no way entertaining; and yet was profitable to him. I therefore thought a good paper could scarcely fail of good encouragement. I requested Webb not to mention it, but he told it to Keimer, who immediately, to be beforehand with me, published proposals for printing one himself, on which Webb was to be employed. I resented this, and to counteract them, as I could not yet begin our paper, I wrote several pieces of entertainment for Bradford's paper, under the title of the Busy Body, which Brientnal continued some months. By this means the attention of the publick was fixed on that paper, and Keimer's proposals, which we burlesqued and ridiculed, were disregarded. He began his paper however, and after carrying it on three quarters of a year, with at most only 90 subscribers, he offered it to me for a trifle, and I having been ready some time to go on with it, took it in hand directly, and it proved in a few years extreamly profitable to me.

I perceive that I am apt to speak in the singular number, though our partnership still continued. The reason may be that in fact the whole management of the business lay upon me. Meredith was no compositor, a poor pressman, and seldom sober. My friends lamented my connection with him, but I was to make the best of it.

Our first papers made a quite different appearance from any before in the Province, a better type and better printed: but some spirited remarks of my writing on the dispute then going on between Governor Burnet and the Massachusetts Assembly, struck the principal people, occasioned the paper and the manager of it to be much talked of, and in a few weeks brought them all to be our subscribers. Their example was followed by many, and our number went on growing continually. This was one of the first good effects of my having learnt a little to scribble. Another was, that the leading men, seeing a news paper now in the hands of one who could also handle a pen, thought it convenient to oblige and encourage me. Bradford still printed the votes and laws and other publick business. He had printed an address of the House to the governor in a coarse blundering manner; we reprinted it elegantly and correctly, and sent one to every member. They were sensible of the difference, it strengthened the hands of our friends in the House, and they voted us their printers for the year ensuing. . . .

. . . Mr. Meredith's father, who was to have paid for our printing house according to the expectations given me, was able to advance only one hundred pounds, currency, which had been paid, and a hundred more was due to the merchant; who grew impatient and sued us all. We gave bail, but saw that if the money could not be raised in time, the suit must come to a judgment and execution, and our hopeful prospects must with us be ruined, as the press and letters must be sold for payment, perhaps at half price. In this distress two true friends whose kindness I have never forgotten nor ever shall forget while I can remember any thing, came to me separately unknown to each other, and without any application from me, offering each of them to advance me all the money that should be necessary to enable me to take the whole business upon my self if that should be practicable, but they did not like my continuing the partnership with Meredith, who as they said was often seen drunk in the streets, and playing at low games in alehouses, much to our discredit. These two friends were William Coleman and Robert Grace. I told them I could not propose a separation while any prospect remained of the Merediths fulfilling their part of our agreement. Because I thought myself under great obligations to them for what they had done and would do if they could. But if they finally failed in their performance, and our partnership must be dissolved, I should then think myself at liberty to accept the assistance of my friends. Thus the matter rested for some time. When I said to my partner, perhaps your father is dissatisfied at the part you have undertaken in this affair of ours, and is unwilling to advance for you and me what he would for you alone: if that is the case, tell me, and I will resign the whole to you and go about my business. No, says he, my father has really been disappointed and is really unable; and I am unwilling to distress him farther. I see this is a business I am not fit for. I was bred a farmer, and it was a folly in me to come to town and put my self at 30 years of age an apprentice to learn a new trade. Many of our Welsh people are going to settle in North Carolina where land is cheap: I am inclined to go with them, and follow my old employment. You may find friends to assist you. If you will take the debts of the company upon you, return to my father the hundred pound he has advanced, pay my little personal debts, and give me thirty pounds and a new saddle, I will relinquish the partnership and leave the whole in your hands. I agreed to this proposal. It was drawn up in writing, signed and sealed immediately. I gave him what he demanded and he went soon after to Carolina; from whence he sent me next year two long letters, containing the best account that had been given of that country, the climate, soil, husbandry, etc., for in those matters he was very judicious. I printed them in the papers, and they gave grate satisfaction to the publick.

As soon as he was gone, I recurred to my two friends; and because I would not give an unkind preference to either, I took half what each had offered, and I wanted, of one, and half of the other; paid off the company debts, and went on with the business in my own name, advertising that the partnership was dissolved. I think this was in or about the year 1729.

About this time there was a cry among the people for more paper-money, only 15,000 £ being extant in the province and that soon to be sunk. The wealthy inhabitants opposed any addition, being against all paper currency, from an apprehension that it would depreciate as it had done in New England to the prejudice of all creditors. We had discussed this point in our Junto, where I was on the side of an addition, being persuaded that the first small sum struck in 1723 had done much good, by increasing the trade, employment, and number of inhabitants in the province, since I now saw all the old houses inhabited, and many new ones building, where as I remembered well, that when I first walked about the streets of Philadelphia, eating my roll, I saw most of the houses in Walnut Street between Second and Front Streets with bills on their doors, to be let; and many likewise in Chesnut Street, and other streets; which made me then think the inhabitants of the city were one after another deserting it. Our debates possessed me so fully of the subject, that I wrote and printed an anonymous pamphlet on it, entituled, *The Nature and Necessity of a Paper Currency*. It was well received by the common people in general; but the rich men disliked it; for it increased and strengthened the clamour for more money; and they happening to have no writers among them that were able to answer it, their opposition slackened, and the point was carried by a majority in the House. My friends there, who conceived I had been of some service, thought fit to reward me, by employing me in printing the money, a very profitable jobb, and a great help to me. This was another advantage gained by my being able to write. The utility of this currency became by time and experience so evident, as never afterwards to be much disputed, so that it grew soon to 55,000 £, and in 1739 to 80,000 £, since which it arose during war to upwards of 350,000 £, trade, building and inhabitants all the while increasing. Tho' I now think there are limits beyond which the quantity may be hurtful.

I soon after obtained, thro' my friend Hamilton, the printing of the New Castle paper money, another profitable jobb, as I then thought it; small things appearing great to those in small circumstances. And these to me were really great advantages, as they were great encouragements. He procured me also the printing of the laws and votes of that government, which continued in my hands as long as I followed the business.

I now opened a little stationer's shop. I had in it blanks of all sorts, the correctest that ever appeared among us, being assisted in that by my friend Brientnal; I had also paper, parchment, chapmen's books, etc. One Whitemash, a compositor I had known in London, an excellent work-

man, now came to me and worked with me constantly and
diligently, and I took an apprentice, the son of Aquila
Rose. I began now gradually to pay off the debt I was
under for the printing-house. In order to secure my credit
and character as a tradesman, I took care not only to be
in *reality* industrious and frugal, but to avoid all *appearances* of the contrary. I drest plainly; I was seen at no
places of idle diversion; I never went out a-fishing or
shooting; a book, indeed, sometimes debauched me from
my work; but that was seldom, snug, and gave no scandal:
and to show that I was not above my business, I sometimes brought home the paper I purchased at the stores,
thro' the streets on a wheelbarrow. Thus being esteemed
an industrious thriving young man, and paying duly for
what I bought, the merchants who imported stationary
solicited my custom, others proposed supplying me with
books, and I went on swimmingly. In the mean time
Keimer's credit and business declining daily, he was at last
forced to sell his printing-house to satisfy his creditors.
He went to Barbadoes, and there lived some years, in
very poor circumstances. . . .

. . . There remained now no competitor with me at
Philadelphia, but the old one, Bradford, who was rich and
easy, did a little printing now and then by straggling
hands, but was not very anxious about the business. However, as he kept the post office, it was imagined he had
better opportunities of obtaining news, his paper was
thought a better distributer of advertisements than mine,
and therefore had many more, which was a profitable
thing to him and a disadvantage to me. For tho' I did indeed receive and send papers by post, yet the publick
opinion was otherwise; for what I did send was by bribing
the riders who took them privately: Bradford being un-

kind enough to forbid it: which occasioned some resentment on my part; and I thought so meanly of him for it, that when I afterwards came into his situation, I took care never to imitate it.

I had hitherto continued to board with Godfrey, who lived in part of my house with his wife and children, and had one side of the shop for his glazier's business, tho' he worked little, being always absorbed in his mathematics. Mrs. Godfrey projected a match for me with a relation's daughter, took opportunities of bringing us often together, till a serious courtship on my part ensued, the girl being in herself very deserving. The old folks encouraged me by continual invitations to supper, and by leaving us together, till at length it was time to explain. Mrs. Godfrey managed our little treaty. I let her know that I expected as much money with their daughter as would pay off my remaining debt for the printinghouse, which I believe was not then above a hundred pounds. She brought me word they had no such sum to spare. I said they might mortgage their house in the loan office. The answer to this after some days was, that they did not approve the match; that on enquiry of Bradford they had been informed the printing business was not a profitable one, the types would soon be worn out and more wanted, that S. Keimer and D. Harry had failed one after the other, and I should probably soon follow them; and therefore I was forbidden the house, and the daughter shut up. Whether this was a real change of sentiment, or only artifice, on a suppo[sit]ion of our being too far engaged in affection to retract, and therefore that we should steal a marriage, which would leave them at liberty to give or withold what they pleased, I know not: but I suspected the latter, resented it, and went no more. Mrs. Godfrey brought me afterwards some

more favourable accounts of their disposition, and would
have drawn me on again: but I declared absolutely my
resolution to have nothing more to do with that family.
This was resented by the Godfreys, we differed, and they
removed, leaving me the whole house, and I resolved to
take no more inmates. But this affair having turned my
thoughts to marriage, I looked round me, and made over-
tures of acquaintance in other places; but soon found that
the business of a printer being generally thought a poor
one, I was not to expect money with a wife unless with
such a one as I should not otherwise think agreable. In
the mean time, that hard-to-be-governed passion of youth
had hurried me frequently into intrigues with low women
that fell in my way, which were attended with some expence and great inconvenience, besides a continual risque
to my health by a distemper which of all things I dreaded,
tho' by great good luck I escaped it.

A friendly correspondence as neighbours and old acquaintances had continued between me and Mrs. Read's
family, who all had a regard for me from the time of my
first lodging in their house. I was often invited there and
consulted in their affairs, wherein I sometimes was of
service. I pitied poor Miss Read's unfortunate situation,
who was generally dejected, seldom chearful, and avoided
company. I considered my giddiness and inconstancy when
in London as in a great degree the cause of her unhappiness; tho' the mother was good enough to think the fault
more her own than mine, as she had prevented our marry-
ing before I went thither, and persuaded the other match
in my absence. Our mutual affection was revived, but
there were now great objections to our union. That match
was indeed looked upon as invalid, a preceding wife being said to be living in England; but this could not easily

be proved, because of the distance, and tho' there was a report of his death, it was not certain. Then, tho' it should be true, he had left many debts which his successor might be called on to pay. We ventured, however, over all these difficulties, and I took her to wife Sept. 1, 1730. None of the inconveniences happened that we had apprehended, she proved a good and faithful helpmate, assisted me much by attending the shop, we throve together, and have ever mutually endeavoured to make each other happy. Thus I corrected that great *erratum* as well as I could. . . .

III · Self-Improvement and Mutual Aid

BENJAMIN FRANKLIN's religious creed held that the best service to God is to be good to man. He leaned to the views of the "Dissenters" of his day, notably Joseph Priestley and Richard Price, who preached a doctrine somewhat like present Unitarianism. A moralist, he taught that man's soul is immortal and that man's conduct in this world will determine his condition in the next; so he made a creed of virtue, based on integrity and good deeds—man must help himself and others.

In the American tradition Franklin stands as a man who preached thrift, frugality, industry and enterprise as the "way to wealth." He grew to maturity in an American tradition that was older than he was, according to which such virtues as thrift and industry were not enough to bring a man success; he had also to practice charity and help his neighbor. Wealth was a token of esteem of the Divine Providence that governs men's affairs, and thus the accumulation of riches was not sought for its own sake alone. Furthermore, wealth and position, being marks of the divine favor, conferred an obligation; a successful man was a "steward," holding the world's goods in trust for the less fortunate. This "Protestant ethic" was a common denominator of Calvinistic Boston where Franklin spent his boyhood and of Quaker Philadelphia where he grew to young manhood.

112

One of Franklin's Puritan mentors was Cotton Mather; Franklin recalled in 1784 how as a boy he had found a copy of Mather's *Essays to Do Good.* This book, he said, "gave me such a turn of thinking, as to have an influence on my conduct through life; for I have always set a greater value on the character of a *doer of good* than on any other kind of reputation; and if I have been . . . a useful citizen, the public owes the advantage of it to that book." Cotton Mather explained to his congregation that a Christian "is a man in a boat, rowing for heaven"; to reach the "shoar of eternal blessedness," he must pull on both oars: praying is one, the other is attending to "some settled business, wherein a Christian should for the most part spend most of his time . . . that so he may glorify God by doing *Good* for *others,* and getting of *Good* for himself." A man who lays up an estate must remember that a portion of it must be used for the "happiness of mankind." Mather's *Essays,* which influenced Benjamin Franklin, described the "good" to be done by various members of society: sea captains, men of wealth, clergymen, etc. Since riches come from God, and are a mark of the divine favor, they are a kind of reward to charitable men for their virtue (especially charity and hard work in a "calling").

"Honor the Lord with thy substance," Mather wrote, "so shall thy barns be filled with plenty"; and Poor Richard echoed this sentiment in the warning, "Proportion your charity to the strength of your estate, or God will proportion your estate to the weakness of your charity." As the Lord's Steward, the man of property is charged with a sacred trust; he glorifies God not only in prayer but in his contribution, as Mather put it, "unto the welfare of mankind, and such a relief of their miseries as may give the children of men better opportunity to glorify Him."

Cotton Mather would have agreed with Poor Richard, "Serving God is doing good to man, but praying is thought an easier service, and therefore more generally chosen."

Quakers, too, accumulated wealth—in the words of a leading merchant of Philadelphia—for "the honour of God and Good of Mankind." Long before Franklin invented the character of Poor Richard, in fact half a century before Franklin's *Way to Wealth,* William Penn had written of the twin virtues, diligence and frugality: diligence "is the way to wealth" and frugality is a "way to be rich. . . ." It is proverbial, "*A penny saved is a penny got.*" Thus, when Franklin wrote that he adopted a morality common to all religions, he very likely had in mind that his own principles were part of both Quaker and Calvinistic beliefs. A life founded in virtue and charity was worth living because it was a good life, but it would also bring a material reward.

Success in business thus represented for Franklin, as it did for Bostonians and Philadelphians, more than the mere accumulation of material goods and power. Wealth was a public badge of just rewards for a good life; it enabled a man of virtue to do good to others. Year after year, Poor Richard inveighed against miserliness and the accumulation of riches for their own sake. "If worldly goods cannot save me from death," Poor Richard said, "they ought not to hinder me of eternal life." Money should be productive of good works because it was not yours to keep forever, but only yours to use. "You can't take it with you," we always say, in the spirit of Poor Richard's "If your riches are yours, why don't you take them with you to t'other world?" Men "keeping their money foolishly" are as much to be laughed at as those who spend it "idly." "He who multiplies riches, multiplies cares"; "He does not possess wealth, it possesses him"; "Wealth is not his that has it but his that enjoys it."

I. The Principle of Serving Others

At the age of sixteen, Franklin had resolved "to do for the future all that lies in my way for the service of my countryman." His heritage of service was also expressed in Poor Richard's saying, "The noblest question in the world is *What good may I do in it?*" At the age of forty-six he retired from business to devote the rest of his life to the study of science and to the service of his community and his country. In America the family names that are symbols of the greatest fortunes are apt to be the names associated with public trusts and benevolence: Rockefeller, Carnegie, Guggenheim and Ford. Franklin's way has become a common feature of the practice of American men of fortune, who are likely to dedicate a good portion of their wealth to public improvements and charitable works with the same ardor and intensity they spent in acquiring it.

A *Letter on Good Works from Benjamin Franklin to Joseph Huey*

Writing to his father at the age of thirty-two, Franklin noted that his mother had complained "that one of her sons is an Arian, another an Arminian. What an Arminian or an Arian is," Franklin replied, "I cannot say that I very well know. The truth is, I make such distinctions very little my study. I think vital religion has always suffered when orthodoxy is more regarded than virtue; and the Scriptures assure me that at the last day we shall not be

examined what we *thought* but what we *did;* and our
recommendation will not be that we said *Lord! Lord!* but
that we did good to our fellow-creatures. See Matt. XXV."
Franklin returned to this subject in a letter he wrote to
Ezra Stiles on March 9, 1790: "Here is my creed. I believe
in one God, creator of the universe. That He governs it by
His Providence. That He ought to be worshipped. That
the most acceptable service we render to Him is doing
good to His other children. That the soul of man is immortal, and will be treated with justice in another life
respecting its conduct in this." He enclosed to Stiles "the
copy of an old letter," which he had written to "a zealous
religionist" (supposed to have been Joseph Huey) who
had been helped by Franklin and who was afraid that
Franklin might "grow proud upon it, [&] sent me his serious though rather impertinent caution." Franklin's letter
to Huey contains the clearest exposition he ever wrote of
his doctrine of good works.

Philadelphia, June 6, 1753

Sir,

. . . As to the kindness you mention, I wish it could
have been of more service to you. But if it had, the only
thanks I should desire is, that you would always be equally
ready to serve any other person that may need your assistance, and so let good offices go round, for mankind
are all of a family.

For my own part, when I am employed in serving
others, I do not look upon myself as conferring favours,
but as paying debts. In my travels, and since my settlement, I have received much kindness from men to whom
I shall never have any opportunity of making the least di-

rect return. And numberless mercies from God, who is
infinitely above being benefited by our services. Those
kindnesses from men, I can therefore only return on their
fellow men; and I can only shew my gratitude for these
mercies from God by a readiness to help His other children
and my brethren. For I do not think that thanks and compliments, tho' repeated weekly, can discharge our real obligations to each other, and much less those to our Creator.
You will see in this my notion of good works, that I am
far from expecting to merit Heaven by them. By Heaven
we understand a state of happiness, infinite in degree and
eternal in duration. I can do nothing to deserve such rewards. He that for giving a draught of water to a thirsty
person should expect to be paid with a good plantation,
would be modest in his demands compared with those who
think they deserve Heaven for the little good they do on
earth. Even the mixed imperfect pleasures we enjoy in
this world are rather from God's goodness than our merit;
how much more such happiness of Heaven. For my own
part I have not the vanity to think I deserve it, the folly
to expect it, nor the ambition to desire it; but content myself in submitting to the will and disposal of that God who
made me, who has hitherto preserved and blessed me, and
in whose Fatherly Goodness I may well confide, that he
will never make me miserable, and that even the afflictions
I may at any time suffer shall tend to my benefit.

The faith you mention has doubtless its use in the world.
I do not desire to see it diminished, nor would I endeavour
to lessen it in any man. But I wish it were more productive of good works, than I have generally seen it: I mean
real good works, works of kindness, charity, mercy, and
publick spirit; not holiday-keeping, sermon-reading or

hearing; performing church ceremonies, or making long prayers, filled with flatteries and compliments, despised even by wise men, and much less capable of pleasing the Deity. The worship of God is a duty; the hearing and reading of sermons may be useful; but, if men rest in hearing and praying, as too many do, it is as if a tree should value itself on being watered and putting forth leaves, tho' it never produced any fruit.

Your great Master thought much less of these outward appearances and professions than many of His modern disciples. He preferred the *Doers* of the Word, to the meer *Hearers;* the son that seemingly refused to obey his father, and yet performed his commands, to him that professed his readiness, but neglected the work; the heretical but charitable Samaritan, to the uncharitable tho' orthodox priest and sanctified Levite; & those who gave food to the hungry, drink to the thirsty, raiment to the naked, entertainment to the stranger, and relief to the sick, tho' they never heard of His name, He declares shall in the last day be accepted, when those who cry Lord! Lord! who value themselves on their faith, tho' great enough to perform miracles, but have neglected good works, shall be rejected. He professed that He came not to call the righteous but sinners to repentance; which implied His modest opinion, that there were some in His time so good, that they need not hear even Him for improvement; but now-a-days we have scarce a little parson, that does not think it the duty of every man within his reach to sit under his petty ministrations; and that whoever omits them offends God. I wish to such more humility, and to you health and happiness, being your friend and servant,

B. Franklin

II. Moral Improvement

Franklin was neither an orthodox Calvinist nor a Quaker, but he had absorbed enough of their common morality to be a "doer of good," and to devote himself to charity and public works. While, perhaps as a result of his own experience, he held that religion is the common source of morality, he also believed that teaching morals and virtue required a technique to be applied by those people leading "bad lives" who "would gladly lead good ones, but know not *how* to make the change." Franklin was aware that many such people "have frequently *resolved* and *endeavoured*" to improve themselves "but in vain, because their endeavours have not been properly conducted." To him it seemed that expecting "people to be good, to be just, to be temperate, etc., without *shewing* them *how* they should *become* so, seems like the ineffectual charity mentioned by the Apostle, which consisted in saying to the hungry, the cold, and the naked, 'Be ye fed, be ye warmed, be ye clothed,' without shewing them how they should get food, fire, or clothing." Acquiring virtue was an art and required tools as all arts do. Franklin therefore applied himself to the needs of an artisan of virtue, showing him the actual steps to take. The moral gadgets Franklin invented included a "moral algebra," in which a man might keep a ledger of his good and bad deeds, and the device he used so successfully for his own improvement and which is described in the following pages from the *Autobiography*. Franklin's advice to the artisan of virtue is nondenominational, and is secular to some extent. He never stated explicitly whether his method was in-

tended to supplement orthodox religious teaching or practice or to be a substitute; it probably wouldn't have
mattered very much to him. His aim, after all, was to
teach men how to improve their moral character and acquire virtue, and his own experience had shown him that
his method worked and that virtue was rewarded in this
world.

The following selection, taken from the second part of
Franklin's *Autobiography*, written in Passy in 1784, is
based on Franklin's original manuscript, published by the
University of California Press in 1949.

I had been religiously educated as a Presbyterian; and
tho' some of the dogmas of that persuasion, such as the
eternal decrees of God, election, reprobation, etc., appeared to me unintelligible, others doubtful, & I early ab-
sented myself from the public assemblies of the sect,
Sunday being my studying-day, I never was without some
religious principles; I never doubted, for instance, the ex-
istance of the Deity, that He made the world, & governed
it by His Providence; that the most acceptable service of
God was the doing good to Man; that our souls are immortal; and that all crime will be punished & virtue rewarded either here or hereafter; these I esteemed the
essentials of every religion, and being to be found in all
the religions we had in our country I respected them all,
tho' with different degrees of respect as I found them
more or less mixed with other articles which without any
tendency to inspire, promote or confirm morality, served
principally to divide us & make us unfriendly to one another. This respect to all, with an opinion that the worst
had some good effects, induced me to avoid all discourse
that might tend to lessen the good opinion another might

have of his own religion; and as our province increased
in people and new places of worship were continually
wanted & generally erected by voluntary contribution, my
mite for such purpose, whatever might be the sect, was
never refused.

Tho' I seldom attended any public worship, I had still
an opinion of its propriety, and of its utility when rightly
conducted, and I regularly paid my annual subscription
for the support of the only Presbyterian minister or meeting we had in Philadelphia. He used to visit me sometimes as a friend, and admonish me to attend his adminis-
trations, and I was now and then prevailed on to do so,
once for five Sundays successively. Had he been, *in my
opinion,* a good preacher, perhaps I might have continued,
notwithstanding the occasion I had for the Sunday's leisure in my course of study. But his discourses were chiefly
either polemic arguments, or explications of the peculiar
doctrines of our sect, and were all to me very dry, uninter-
esting and unedifying, since not a single moral principle
was inculcated or enforced, their aim seeming to be rather
to make us Presbyterians than good citizens. At length he
took for his text that verse of the 4th chapter of Philippians, *Finally, brethren, whatsoever things are true, honest, just, pure, lovely, or of good report, if there be any
virtue, or any praise, think on those things;* & I imagined,
in a sermon on such a text, we could not miss of having
some morality. But he confined himself to five points only
as meant by the Apostle, *viz.* 1. Keeping holy the Sabbath
day. 2. Being diligent in reading the Holy Scriptures.
3. Attending duly the publick worship. 4. Partaking of the
sacrament. 5. Paying a due respect to God's ministers.
These might be all good things, but as they were not the
kind of good things that I expected from that text, I de-

spaired of ever meeting with them from any other, was
disgusted, and attended his preaching no more. I had
some years before composed a little liturgy or form of
prayer for my own private use, *viz.*, in 1728, entitled, *Articles of Belief & Acts of Religion.* I returned to the use of
this, and went no more to the public assemblies. My conduct might be blameable, but I leave it without attempting farther to excuse it, my present purpose being to relate
facts and not to make apologies for them.

It was about this time that I conceived the bold and
arduous project of arriving at moral perfection. I wished
to live without committing any fault at any time; I would
conquer all that either natural inclination, custom, or company might lead me into. As I knew, or thought I knew,
what was right and wrong, I did not see why I might not
always do the one and avoid the other. But I soon found
I had undertaken a task of more difficulty than I had imagined. While my *attention was taken up* in guarding
against one fault, I was often surprized by another. Habit
took the advantage of inattention. Inclination was sometimes too strong for reason. I concluded at length, that
the mere speculative conviction that it was our interest to
be compleatly virtuous, was not sufficient to prevent our
slipping, and that the contrary habits must be broken and
good ones acquired and established, before we can have
any dependance on a steady uniform rectitude of conduct. For this purpose I therefore contrived the following
method.

In the various enumerations of the moral virtues I had
met with in my reading, I found the catalogue more or
less numerous, as different writers included more or fewer
ideas under the same name. Temperance, for example,
was by some confined to eating & drinking, while by others

it was extended to mean the moderating every other pleasure, appetite, inclination or passion, bodily or mental, even to our avarice & ambition. I proposed to myself, for the sake of clearness, to use rather more names with fewer ideas annexed to each, than a few names with more ideas; and I included under thirteen names of virtues all that at that time occurred to me as necessary or desirable, and annexed to each a short precept, which fully expressed the extent I gave to its meaning.

These names of virtues with their precepts were

1. Temperance.

Eat not to dulness.
Drink not to elevation.

2. Silence.

Speak not but what may benefit others or yourself.
Avoid trifling conversation.

3. Order.

Let all your things have their places.
Let each part of your business have its time.

4. Resolution.

Resolve to perform what you ought.
Perform without fail what you resolve.

5. Frugality.

Make no expence but to do good to others or yourself:
i.e. waste nothing.

6. Industry.

Lose no time.
Be always employed in something useful.
Cut off all unnecessary actions.

7. Sincerity.

Use no hurtful deceit.
Think innocently and justly; and, if you speak, speak
accordingly.

8. Justice.

Wrong none, by doing injuries or omitting the benefits
that are your duty.

9. Moderation.

Avoid extreams. Forbear resenting injuries so much as
you think they deserve.

10. Cleanliness.

Tolerate no uncleanness in body, cloaths or habitation.

11. Tranquility.

Be not disturbed at trifles, or at accidents common or
unavoidable.

12. Chastity.

Rarely use venery but for health or offspring; never to
dulness, weakness, or the injury of your own or
another's peace or reputation.

13. Humility.

Imitate Jesus and Socrates.

My intention being to acquire the *habitude* of all these virtues, I judged it would be well not to distract my attention by attempting the whole at once, but to fix it on one of them at a time, and when I should be master of that, then to proceed to another, and so on till I should have gone thro' the thirteen. And as the previous acquisition of some might facilitate the acquisition of certain others, I arranged them with that view as they stand above. *Temperance* first, as it tends to procure that coolness & clearness of head, which is so necessary where constant vigilance was to be kept up, and guard maintained, against the unremitting attraction of ancient habits and the force of perpetual temptations. This being acquired & established, *silence* would be more easy and, my desire being to gain knowledge at the same time that I improved in virtue, and considering that in conversation it was obtained rather by the use of the ears than of the tongue, & therefore wishing to break a habit I was getting into of prattling, punning & joking, which only made me acceptable to trifling company, I gave *silence* the second place. This, and the next, *order*, I expected would allow me more time for attending to my project and my studies; RESOLUTION, once become habitual, would keep me firm in my endeavours to obtain all the subsequent virtues; *frugality* & *industry*, by freeing me from my remaining debt, & producing affluence & independance, would make more easy the practice of *sincerity* and *justice*, etc. etc. Conceiving then that, agreable to the advice of Pythagoras in his Golden Verses, daily examination would be necessary, I contrived the following method for conducting that examination.

I made a little book in which I allotted a page for each of the virtues. I ruled each page with red ink, so as to

FORM OF THE PAGES

TEMPERANCE							
Eat not to Dulness. *Drink not to Elevation.*							
	SUN.	MON.	TUES.	WED.	THURS.	FRI.	SAT.
T [Temperance]							
S [Silence]	● ●	●		●		●	
O [Order]	●	●	●		●	●	●
R [Resolution]			●			●	
F [Frugality]		●			●		
I [Industry]			●				
S [Sincerity]							
J [Justice]							
M [Moderation]							
Cl. [Cleanliness]							
T [Tranquility]							
Ch. [Chastity]							
H [Humility]							

have seven columns, one for each day of the week, marking each column with a letter for the day. I crossed these columns with thirteen red lines, marking the beginning of each line with the first letter of one of the virtues, on which line & in its proper column I might mark by a little black spot every fault I found upon examination to have been committed respecting that virtue upon that day.

I determined to give a week's strict attention to each of the virtues successively. Thus in the first week my great guard was to avoid every the least offence against *temperance,* leaving the other virtues to their ordinary chance, only marking every evening the faults of the day. Thus if in the first week I could keep my first line marked T clear of spots, I supposed the habit of that virtue so much strengthened and its opposite weakened, that I might venture extending my attention to include the next, and for the following week keep both lines clear of spots. Proceeding thus to the last, I could go thro' a course compleat in thirteen weeks, and four courses in a year. And like him who having a garden to weed, does not attempt to eradicate all the bad herbs at once, which would exceed his reach and his strength, but works on one of the beds at a time, & having accomplished the first proceeds to a second; so I should have, (I hoped) the encouraging pleasure of seeing on my pages the progress I made in virtue, by clearing successively my lines of their spots, till in the end by a number of courses, I should be happy in viewing a clean book after a thirteen weeks daily examination.

This my little book had for its motto these lines from Addison's Cato;

Here will I hold: If there is a Pow'r above us, (And that there is, all Nature cries aloud Thro' all her Works) he

must delight in Virtue, And that which he delights in must
be happy.

Another from Cicero

*O Vitæ Philosophia Dux! O Virtutum indagatrix, ex-
pultrixque vitiorum! Unus dies bene, & ex preceptis tuis
actus, peccanti immortalitati est anteponendus.*

Another from the Proverbs of Solomon speaking of wisdom or virtue;

Length of days is in her right hand, and in her left hand
riches and honours; her ways are ways of pleasantness, and
all her paths are peace.

III, 16, 17.

And conceiving God to be the fountain of wisdom, I
thought it right and necessary to solicit His assistance for
obtaining it; to this end I formed the following little
prayer, which was prefixed to my tables of examination;
for daily use.

O Powerful Goodness! bountiful Father! merciful Guide!
Increase in me that wisdom which discovers my truest interests; strengthen my resolutions to perform what that
wisdom dictates. Accept my kind offices to Thy other
children, as the only return in my power for Thy continual
favours to me.

I used also sometimes a little prayer which I took from
Thomson's poems, viz.,

Father of Light and Life, thou Good supreme,
O teach me what is good, teach me thy self!

> Save me from Folly, Vanity and Vice,
> From every low Pursuit, and fill my Soul
> With Knowledge, conscious Peace, & Virtue pure,
> Sacred, substantial, neverfading Bliss!

The precept of *order* requiring that *every part of my business should have its allotted time,* one page in my little book contained the following scheme of employment for the twenty-four hours of a natural day:

The morning question: What good shall I do this day?	5 6 7 8	Rise, wash, and address *powerful goodness;* contrive day's business and take the resolution of the day; prosecute the present study: and breakfast.
	9 10 11	Work.
	12 1	Read, or overlook my accounts, and dine.
	2 3 4 5	Work.
	6 7 8	Put things in their places, supper, musick or diversion, or conversation.
	9	Examination of the day.
Evening question: What good have I done to day?	10 11 12 1 2 3 4	Sleep.

I entered upon the execution of this plan for self-examination, and continued it with occasional intermissions for some time. I was surprized to find my self so much fuller of faults than I had imagined, but I had the satisfaction of seeing them diminish. To avoid the trouble of renewing now & then my little book, which, by scraping out the marks on the paper of old faults to make room for new ones in a new course, became full of holes, I transferred my tables and precepts to the ivory leaves of a memorandum book, on which the lines were drawn with red ink that made a durable stain, and on those lines I marked my faults with a black lead pencil, which marks I could easily wipe out with a wet sponge. After a while I went thro' one course only in a year, and afterward only one in several years, till at length I omitted them entirely, being employed in voyages & business abroad, with a multiplicity of affairs that interfered; but I always carried my little book with me.

My scheme of ORDER gave me the most trouble; and I found that, tho' it might be practicable where a man's business was such as to leave him the disposition of his time, that of a journey-man printer, for instance, it was not possible to be exactly observed by a master, who must mix with the world, and often receive people of business at their own hours. *Order,* too, with regard to places for things, papers, etc., I found extreamly difficult to acquire. I had not been early accustomed to *method,* &, having an exceeding good memory, I was not so sensible of the inconvenience attending want of method. This article, therefore, cost me so much painful attention, & my faults in it vexed me so much, & I made so little progress in amendment, & had such frequent relapses, that I was almost ready to give up the attempt, and content my self with a faulty character in that respect. Like the man who, in buying an ax of a smith, my neighbour, desired to have the whole of its surface as bright as the edge; the smith consented to grind it bright for him if he would turn the wheel. He turned, while the smith pressed the broad face of the ax hard and heavily on the stone, which made the turning of it very fatiguing. The man came every now & then from the wheel to see how the work went on & at length would take his ax as it was, without farther grinding. No, says the smith, turn on, turn on; we shall have it bright by and by; as yet, 'tis only speckled. Yes, says the man, but—*I think I like a speckled ax best.* And I believe this may have been the case with many, who, having, for want of some such means as I employed, found the difficulty of obtaining good, & breaking bad habits, in other points of vice and virtue, have given up the struggle, and concluded that *a speckled ax was best.* For something, that pretended to be reason, was every now and then suggesting to me that such extream nicety as I exacted of my self might be a kind of foppery in morals, which, if it were known, would make me ridiculous; that a perfect character might be attended with the inconvenience of being envied and hated; and that a benevolent man should allow a few faults in himself, to keep his friends in countenance. In truth, I found myself incorrigible with respect to *order;* and now I am grown old, and my memory bad, I feel very sensibly the want of it. But, on the whole, tho' I never arrived at the perfection I had been so ambitious of obtaining, but fell far short of it, yet I was, by the endeavour, a better and a happier man than I otherwise should have been if I had not attempted it; as those who aim at perfect writing by imitating the engraved copies, tho' they never reach the wished for excellence of those copies, their hand is mended by the endeavour, and is tolerable while it continues fair & legible.

It may be well my posterity should be informed that to this little artifice, with the blessing of God, their ancestor owed the constant felicity of his life, down to his 79th year in which this is written. What reverses may attend the remainder is in the hand of Providence; but, if they arrive, the reflection on past happiness enjoyed ought to help his bearing them with more resignation. To *temperance* he ascribes his long-continued health, & what is still left to him of a good constitution; to *industry* & *frugality*, the early easiness of his circumstances & acquisition of his fortune, with all that knowledge that enabled him to be an useful citizen, and obtained for him some degree of reputation among the learned; to *sincerity* & *justice*, the confidence of his country, and the honourable employs it conferred upon him. And to the joint influence of the whole mass of the virtues, even in the imperfect state he was able to acquire them, all that evenness of temper & that chearfulness in conversation which makes his company still sought for, & agreeable even to his younger acquaintance. I hope, therefore, that some of my descendants may follow the example & reap the benefit.

It will be remarked that tho' my scheme was not wholly without religion, there was in it no mark of any of the distinguishing tenets of any particular sect. I had purposely avoided them; for, being fully persuaded of the utility and excellency of my method, and that it might be serviceable to people in all religions, and intending some time or other to publish it, I would not have any thing in it that should prejudice any one, of any sect, against it. I purposed writing a little comment on each virtue, in which I would have shown the advantages of possessing it, & the mischiefs attending its opposite vice; and I should have called my book THE ART OF VIRTUE,* because it would have shown the *means & manner* of obtaining virtue, which would have distinguished it from the mere exhortation to be good, that does not instruct & indicate the means, but is like the apostle's man of verbal charity, who only without showing to the naked & the hungry *how* or where they might get cloaths or victuals, exhorted them to be fed and clothed.—James ii. 15, 16.

. . . My list of virtues contained at first but twelve. But a Quaker friend having kindly informed me that I was generally thought proud; that my pride showed itself frequently in conversation; that I was not content with being in the right when discussing any point, but was overbearing, & rather insolent, of which he convinced me by mentioning several instances;—I determined endeavouring to cure myself, if I could, of this vice or folly among the rest, and I added *humility* to my list, giving an extensive meaning to the word.

I cannot boast of much success in acquiring the *reality* of this virtue, but I had a good deal with regard to the *appearance* of it. I made it a rule to forbear all direct contradiction to the sentiments of others, and all positive assertion of my own. I even forbid myself, agreeable to the old laws of our Junto, the use of every word or expression in the language that imported a fixed opinion; such as *certainly, undoubtedly,* etc., and I adopted, instead of them, *I conceive, I apprehend,* or *I imagine* a thing to be so or so, or it so appears to me at present. When another asserted something that I thought an error, I denied my self the pleasure of contradicting him abruptly, and of show-

---

* Nothing so likely to make a man's fortune as virtue. [Franklin's note.]

ing immediately some absurdity in his proposition; and in
answering I began by observing that in certain cases or
circumstances his opinion would be right, but, in the present case there *appeared* or *seemed* to me some difference,
etc. I soon found the advantage of this change in my manners. The conversations I engaged in went on more pleasantly. The modest way in which I proposed my opinions
procured them a readier reception and less contradiction;
I had less mortification when I was found to be in the
wrong, and I more easily prevailed with others to give up
their mistakes & join with me when I happened to be in
the right.

And this mode, which I at first put on, with some violence to natural inclination, became at length so easy, &
so habitual to me, that perhaps for these fifty years past
no one has ever heard a dogmatical expression escape me.
And to this habit (after my character of integrity) I think
it principally owing that I had early so much weight with
my fellow citizens when I proposed new institutions, or
alterations in the old, and so much influence in public
councils when I became a member. For I was but a bad
speaker, never eloquent, subject to much hesitation in my
choice of words, hardly correct in language, and yet I generally carried my points.

In reality, there is, perhaps, no one of our natural passions so hard to subdue as *pride.* Disguise it, struggle
with it, beat it down, stifle it, mortify it as much as one
pleases, it is still alive, and will every now and then peep
out and show itself. You will see it, perhaps, often in this
history. For, even if I could conceive that I had compleatly overcome it, I should probably be proud of my
humility.

Thus far written at Passy, 1784.

III. The Maxims of "Poor Richard"

Franklin's almanac, *Poor Richard,* was a best seller from the start; three printings were required to satisfy the demand for the first issue. "Poor Dick" was the exponent of American folk wisdom and illustrates Franklin's talent for knowing the average man and being able to speak to him. His precepts were practical, telling men how to get on in this world, how to be successful. They were the distillation of practical experience from many lands and many places, and although Franklin created *ad hoc* only a few of them, most were transformed by his pen into a style characteristically his and characteristically American; over the years, the sayings of Poor Richard have become as well known to Americans as the Bible.

Often Poor Richard is known through the preface prepared by Franklin for the issue of 1758, reprinted separately as *The Way to Wealth* or *Father Abraham's Speech,* in which were collected maxims on thrift and frugality. This American classic has tended to obscure the Poor Richard of Benjamin Franklin who wrote precepts about love, good fellowship and the joys of living. Late in life, Franklin said that he had filled the empty spaces of his almanac with "proverbial sentences, chiefly such as inculcated industry and frugality, as the means of procuring wealth and thereby securing virtue." But in the almanac for 1739, Poor Richard himself explained: "Be not thou disturbed, O grave and sober reader, if among the many serious sentences in my book thou findest me trifling now and then, and talking idly. In all the dishes I have hitherto cooked for thee, there is solid meat enough for thy money. There are scraps from the table of wisdom that

will, if well digested, yield strong nourishment to thy
mind. But squeamish stomachs cannot eat without pickles;
which, 'tis true, are good for nothing else, but they provoke an appetite."

No one can read the maxims of Poor Richard without
becoming aware of that earthy or worldly flavor which
in almost every line bespeaks the actual occurrences in
men's lives, perhaps Franklin's own life or those of his
friends and associates and often the collective lives of nations embodied in the folk wisdom of the proverbs he
adapted to the life of America. Poor Richard spoke with
the stubborn voice of experience.

"Never spare the parson's wine nor the baker's pudding." (1733)

"Hunger never saw bad bread." (1733)

"He's a fool that makes his doctor his heir." (1733)

"The heart of the fool is in his mouth, but the mouth of
the wise man is in his heart." (1733)

"He that drinks fast pays slow." (1733)

"A house without a woman and firelight is like a body
without soul or sprite." (1733)

"As charms are nonsense, nonsense is a charm." (1734)

"Where there's marriage without love there will be love
without marriage." (1734)

"A lie stands on one leg, truth on two." (1735)

"Sloth and silence are a fool's virtues." (1735)

"Opportunity is the great bawd." (1735)

"A little house well filled, a little field well tilled, and
a little wife well willed, are great riches." (1735)

"A ship under sail and a big-bellied woman are the
handsomest two things that can be seen common." (1735)

"There's more old drunkards than old doctors." (1736)

"He that has neither fools nor beggars among his kindred is the son of thunder-gust." (1736)

"Bargaining has neither friends nor relations." (1736)

"None preaches better than the ant, and she says nothing." (1736)

"The absent are never without fault, nor the present without excuse." (1736)

"Poverty, poetry, and new titles of honour make men ridiculous." (1736)

"Let thy maidservant be faithful, strong, and homely." (1736)

"Fish and visitors stink in three days." (1736)

"The rotten apple spoils his companions." (1736)

"A countryman between two lawyers is like a fish between two cats." (1737)

"There are no ugly loves nor handsome prisons." (1737)

"The worst wheel of the cart makes the most noise." (1737)

"Write with the learned, pronounce with the vulgar." (1738)

"The ancients tell us what is best; but we must learn from the moderns what is fittest." (1738)

"He that falls in love with himself will have no rivals." (1739)

"Thou hadst better eat salt with the philosophers of Greece than sugar with the courtiers of Italy." (1740)

"Up, sluggard, and waste not life; in the grave will be sleeping enough." (1741)

"The eye of a master will do more work than his hand." (1744)

"Help, hands; for I have no lands." (1745)

"The most exquisite folly is made of wisdom spun too fine." (1746)

"A plowman on his legs is higher than a gentleman on his knees." (1746)

"Liberality is not giving much, but giving wisely." (1748)

"Little strokes fell great oaks." (1750)

"Genius without education is like silver in the mine." (1750)

"The cat in gloves catches no mice." (1754)

THE WAY TO WEALTH

Preface to Poor Richard Improved: 1758.

Courteous Reader

I have heard that nothing gives an author so great pleasure, as to find his works respectfully quoted by other learned authors. This pleasure I have seldom enjoyed; for tho' I have been, if I may say it without vanity, an *eminent author* of almanacks annually now a full quarter of a century, my brother authors in the same way, for what reason I know not, have ever been very sparing in their applauses, and no other author has taken the least notice of me, so that did not my writings produce me some solid *pudding*, the great deficiency of *praise* would have quite discouraged me.

I concluded at length, that the people were the best judges of my merit; for they buy my works; and besides, in my rambles, where I am not personally known, I have frequently heard one or other of my adages repeated, with, *as Poor Richard says*, at the end on 't; this gave me some satisfaction, as it showed not only that my instructions were regarded, but discovered likewise some respect for my authority; and I own, that to encourage the practice of remembering and repeating those wise sentences, I have sometimes *quoted myself* with great gravity.

Judge, then, how much I must have been gratified by an incident I am going to relate to you. I stopt my horse lately where a great number of people were collected at a vendue of merchant goods. The hour of sale not being come, they were conversing on the badness of the times and one of the company called to a plain clean old man, with white locks, "Pray, Father Abraham, what think you of the times? Won't these heavy taxes quite ruin the country? How shall we be ever able to pay them? What would you advise us to?" Father Abraham stood up, and replyed, "If you'd have my advice, I'll give it you in short, for *A word to the wise is enough*, and *many words won't fill a bushel*, as Poor Richard says." They joined in desiring him to speak his mind, and gathering round him, he proceeded as follows;

"Friends," says he, and neighbours, "the taxes are indeed very heavy, and if those laid on by the Government were the only ones we had to pay, we might more easily discharge them; but we have many others, and much more grievous to some of us. We are taxed twice as much by our *idleness*, three times as much by our *pride*, and four times as much by our *folly*; and from these taxes the commissioners cannot ease or deliver us by allowing an abatement. However let us hearken to good advice, and something may be done for us; *God helps them that help themselves*, as Poor Richard says, in his Almanack of 1733.

It would be thought a hard Government that should tax its people one-tenth part of their *time*, to be employed in its service. But *idleness* taxes many of us much more, if we reckon all that is spent in absolute *sloth*, or doing of nothing, with that which is spent in idle employments or

amusements, that amount to nothing. *Sloth,* by bringing
on diseases, absolutely shortens life. *Sloth, like rust, con-
sumes faster than labour wears; while the used key is
always bright,* as Poor Richard says. *But dost thou love
life, then do not squander time, for that's the stuff life is
made of,* as Poor Richard says. How much more than is
necessary do we spend in sleep, forgetting that *The sleeping fox catches no poultry,* and that *There will be sleeping
enough in the grave,* as Poor Richard says.

*If time be of all things the most precious, wasting time
must be,* as Poor Richard says, *the greatest prodigality;*
since, as he elsewhere tells us, *Lost time is never found
again; and what we call time enough, always proves little
enough:* Let us then up and be doing, and doing to the
purpose; so by diligence shall we do more with less per-
plexity. *Sloth makes all things difficult, but industry all
easy,* as Poor Richard says; and *He that riseth late must
trot all day, and shall scarce overtake his business at night;*
while *Laziness travels so slowly, that poverty soon over-
takes him,* as we read in Poor Richard, who adds, *Drive
thy business, let not that drive thee;* and, *Early to bed,
early to rise, makes a man healthy, wealthy, and wise. . . .*

Methinks I hear some of you say, *Must a man afford
himself no leisure?* I will tell thee, my friend, what Poor
Richard says, *Employ thy time well, if thou meanest to
gain leisure; and, since thou art not sure of a minute, throw
not away an hour.* Leisure is time for doing something
useful; this leisure the diligent man will obtain, but the
lazy man never; so that, as Poor Richard says, *A life of
leisure and a life of laziness are two things.* Do you imagine that sloth will afford you more comfort than labour?
No, for as Poor Richard says, *Trouble springs from idleness, and grievous toil from needless ease. Many without*

labour, would live by their wits only, but they break for want of stock. Whereas industry gives comfort, and plenty, and respect: *fly pleasures, and they'll follow you. The diligent spinner has a large shift; and now I have a sheep and a cow, everybody bids me good morrow;* all which is well said by Poor Richard.

But with our industry, we must likewise be *steady, settled,* and *careful,* and oversee our own affairs *with our own eyes,* and not trust too much to others; for, as Poor Richard says

> I never saw an oft-removed tree,
> Nor yet an oft-removed family,
> That throve so well as those that settled be.

And again, *Three removes is as bad as a fire;* and again, *Keep thy shop, and thy shop will keep thee;* and again, *If you would have your business done, go; if not, send.* And again,

> He that by the plough would thrive,
> Himself must either hold or drive.

And again, *The eye of a master will do more work than both his hands;* and again, *Want of care does us more damage than want of knowledge;* and again, *Not to oversee workmen, is to leave them your purse open.* Trusting too much to others' care is the ruin of many; for, as the Almanack says, *In the affairs of this world, men are saved, not by faith, but by the want of it;* but a man's own care is profitable; for, saith Poor Dick, *Learning is to the studious,* and *Riches to the careful,* as well as *Power to the bold,* and *Heaven to the virtuous.* And farther, *If you would have a faithful servant, and one that you like, serve yourself.*

And again, he adviseth to circumspection and care, even
in the smallest matters, because sometimes *A little neglect
may breed great mischief;* adding, *for want of a nail the
shoe was lost; for want of a shoe the horse was lost; and
for want of a horse the rider was lost, being overtaken and
slain by the enemy; all for want of care about a horse-shoe
nail.*

So much for industry, my friends, and attention to one's
own business; but to these we must add *frugality,* if we
would make our *industry* more certainly successful. A
man may, if he knows not how to save as he gets, *keep his
nose all his life to the grindstone,* and die not worth a
groat at last. *A fat kitchen makes a lean will,* as Poor Richard says; and

> Many estates are spent in the getting,
> Since women for tea forsook spinning and knitting,
> And men for punch forsook hewing and splitting.

If you would be wealthy, says he, in another almanack,
*think of saving as well as of getting: The Indies have not
made Spain rich, because her outgoes are greater than
her incomes.*

Away then with your expensive follies, and you will
not then have so much cause to complain of hard times,
heavy taxes, and chargeable families; for, as Poor Dick
says,

> Women and wine, game and deceit,
> Make the wealth small and the wants great.

And farther, *What maintains one vice, would bring up two
children.* You may think perhaps, that a *little* tea, or a
little punch now and then, diet a *little* more costly, clothes

a *little* finer, and a *little* entertainment now and then, can be no *great* matter; but remember what Poor Richard says, *Many a little makes a mickle;* and farther, *Beware of little expences; a small leak will sink a great ship;* and again, *Who dainties love, shall beggars prove;* and moreover, *Fools make feasts, and wise men eat them.* . . .

And now to conclude, *Experience keeps a dear school, but fools will learn in no other, and scarce in that;* for it is true, *we may give advice, but we cannot give conduct,* as Poor Richard says: However, remember this, *They that won't be counselled, can't be helped,* as Poor Richard says: and farther, that, *if you will not hear reason, she'll surely rap your knuckles.*"

Thus the old gentleman ended his harangue. The people heard it, and approved the doctrine, and immediately practised the contrary, just as if it had been a common sermon; for the vendue opened, and they began to buy extravagantly, notwithstanding his cautions and their own fear of taxes. I found the good man had thoroughly studied my almanacks, and digested all I had dropt on these topicks during the course of five and twenty years. The frequent mention he made of me must have tired any one else, but my vanity was wonderfully delighted with it, though I was conscious that not a tenth part of the wisdom was my own, which he ascribed to me, but rather the *gleanings* I had made of the sense of all ages and nations. However, I resolved to be the better for the echo of it; and though I had at first determined to buy stuff for a new coat, I went away resolved to wear my old one a little longer. Reader, if thou wilt do the same, thy profit will be as great as mine. I am, as ever, thine to serve thee,

Richard Saunders.

July 7, 1757.

IV. Mutual Aid in the Junto

Benjamin Franklin knew that a group of men acting together in a common cause may accomplish far more than
the same men working independently of one another. He
founded a club for mutual improvement, called the Junto,
which met once a week to discuss practical problems, philosophy and science; members of the club educated one
another by reports on their reading, but they also helped
one another in business. Through the Junto Franklin and
his partner Meredith obtained their first major printing
jobs and were able to survive; later, two Junto members
loaned Franklin the money to buy out Meredith. But
Franklin used the Junto (and its affiliated societies) to
further good works that benefited the members and all
Philadelphians and Pennsylvanians. It was the spearhead
in the Defense Association; its activities produced the idea
of the library; and such projects as organizing a fire company, improving the "city watch," and founding an academy which grew into the University of Pennsylvania,
originated in discussions at Junto meetings and became
reality through Junto support. Helping one another, the
Junto members achieved material success; they became
men of influence in local affairs because they were associated with Franklin in the useful projects he had proposed to them and which they had supported. Thus the
Junto served Franklin's self-interest in acquiring affluence
and position, but it also was of value to the other members
and to the community as a whole.

The Junto was Franklin's organization on the "leather-
apron" level. He was just as eager for an organization
of the colonies for their general welfare; he proposed

the Albany Plan of Union in 1754 and presented the Articles of Confederation to the Second Continental Congress in 1776. On May 9, 1754, he published in the *Gazette* what is considered to be the first American cartoon. It represents a snake broken into pieces labeled "N.E.," "N.Y.," "N.J.," "P.," "M.," "V.," "N.C." and "S.C.," and it is thought to be of his design and perhaps engraved after his own drawing. Referring to the old "vulgar error'" that a "joint snake" can be broken into bits and still live if the parts are brought together again, this cartoon—widely reprinted during the outbreak of the Revolution—bore the challenging legend: JOIN, *or* DIE. Here is the perfect symbol of the citizen as well as the state; no man and no state may long survive alone—the good life and the secure world may be achieved only by joint effort. The very name Junto that Franklin gave to his club was derived from the Latin word *juncta,* united or joined, as in the popular phrase *juncta juvant* ("united they assist"); usually said of things which are trifling of themselves but which acquire strength when put together. Although the name had been often used for men who had joined together for political action, the sense in which Franklin used it probably came from a publication of William Penn's in 1708, suggesting the formation of "a small junto . . . for publick ends." In the Junto we see the principle expressed in *E pluribus unum,* one out of many, strength through union, symbolized in the strength of a bundle of sticks tied together (where each one alone may be weak) as pictured on the old dime. No American needs to be reminded that a feature of our national life is our banding together in associations for mutual aid and public benefit, but that Franklin's Junto was the ancestor of them all may not be so well known.

Two major sources of the Junto idea are known. One is Defoe's *Essay upon Projects,* which Franklin read as a boy and which posterity has passed by in favor of *Robinson Crusoe.* The projects that were sponsored by Defoe were political, civic, commercial and philanthropic: national banks, good roads, lunatic asylums, professional or trade schools for young men and colleges for girls, military academies, and friendly associations for the mutual help of members, especially in the event of distress to any one of them. The other source, as Franklin wrote in a letter dated May 12, 1784, was Cotton Mather's *Essays to Do Good:* it consists of twenty-two essays which laud benevolence in general and give specific instructions for doing good to each group in society, *viz.,* magistrates, clergymen, doctors, lawyers, teachers, ship captains, mechanics, gentlemen, ladies, husbands, wives. Mather organized "neighborhood benefit societies," one of which he hoped to have in each church; he belonged to twenty such societies himself. His son Samuel relates that Mather drew up a series of "Points of Consideration," which were to be read at every meeting; following the reading of each "point" there was to be a pause so that any member who chose might offer some proposal or comment. This procedure may be compared to the Junto rules which required a number of questions to be asked at meetings, with members given a chance to reply. Unlike Mather, Franklin was concerned with the business affairs of the members and with a defense of fundamental freedoms and independence of the mind; he was not content to improve man's piety and virtue, but sought to develop a knowledge of practical politics, science and good literature.

Some of the twenty-four questions Franklin devised for

Junto meetings derive simply from Cotton Mather's "Points of Consideration." Mather asked, "Is there any matter to be humbly moved unto the legislative power, to be enacted into a law for public benefit?"—which is similar to one of Franklin's. But where Mather asked, "Is there any particular person whose disorderly behaviour may be so scandalous and so notorious that we may do well to send unto the said person our charitable admonitions?"—Franklin inquired about any fellow citizen "who has committed an error proper for us to be warned against or avoid," but first he wanted to know about fellow citizens who had "lately done a worthy action, deserving praise or imitation." Mather was interested in uncovering "any instance of oppression or fraudulence in the dealings of any sort of people," but Franklin sought out "any encroachment on the just liberties of the people," a subject that did not particularly interest the New England theocrat. Franklin had no concern for Mather's "methods [to] be devised" that "household piety" might flourish.

That Cotton Mather was inept compared to Benjamin Franklin is in the very saying supererogatory. Mather belonged to twenty clubs; if they met only once a month he could scarcely attend all their meetings and, even if he did, his effect would be so divided as to be minimal. But Franklin's club met once a week and became a tightly knit effective group. To make the group's influence more telling Franklin conceived the idea that each member should form a "subordinate club, with the same rules respecting queries, etc., and without informing them of the connection with the Junto." Thus the Junto could produce "the improvement of . . . many more citizens by the use of our institutions," and other advantages would

be "our better acquaintance with the general sentiments
of the inhabitants on any occasion, as the Junto member
might propose what queries we should desire, and was
to report to the Junto what passed in his separate club;
the promotion of our particular interests in business by
more extensive recommendation, and the increase of our
influence in public affairs, and our power of doing good
by spreading thro' the several clubs the sentiments of
the Junto." Five or six such clubs were formed, with
names like the Vine, the Union and the Band. They were
useful, Franklin wrote, "and afforded us a good deal of
amusement, information, and instruction, besides answering in some considerable degree, our views of influencing
the public opinion on particular occasions."

Each member of the Junto was expected to produce
"one or more queries on any point of morals, politics or
natural philosophy, to be discussed by the company."
The debates were conducted without heat of passion, and
"all expressions of positiveness in opinions, or direct contradiction," were expressly prohibited under penalty of
a fine, since the aim was to achieve a "sincere spirit of
inquiry after truth, without fondness for dispute, or desire of victory." At the meetings the Junto members
studied the standards of good writing, the concepts of
philosophy, the fundamental principles of politics and
economics, and the nature of wisdom, happiness, dew,
tides and the phenomena of vapors. The discussions were
not confined to natural and moral philosophy, or literature,
but embraced the empirical approach to wealth: success
was to be sought in examination of the actual experience
of Philadelphians who had succeeded or failed. The
members brought to one another's attention examples of
citizens who had failed in business and the *cause* of fail-

ure, businessmen who had been "thriving well" and by what *means*, the facts of *how* any "present rich man, here or elsewhere," obtained his wealth. This was the "case" method, now widely used in business schools.

Junto members came to one another's aid whenever the reputation of any one of them was attacked, they helped "deserving strangers" lately arrived in town, encouraged good young men starting out in business, and crusaded against intemperance, imprudence, passion or "any other vice or folly." Every member swore to respect truth for its own sake, to love all mankind regardless of religion, and to uphold the freedom of any man to hold whatever "speculative opinions" he might wish and follow his own conscience in "his external way of worship."

The character of the Junto may be seen in the "Rules" drawn up by Franklin, sample discussions written out by him, and questions debated at the meetings. The combination of self-interest, mutual improvement, civic responsibility and curiosity about the external world made the Junto a mirror of the mind of Benjamin Franklin: at once philosopher, scientist, businessman and citizen. The Junto fed his mind, increased his business and brought him political power; and he in return educated the Junto— the first example of adult education in America—in science, literature and philosophy and in the principles of liberty, the rights and duties of free men and the ways of increasing profits. To conceive of a club with these aims anywhere else but in America is just as difficult as to imagine the Junto leading a successful life for thirty years without the direction of Benjamin Franklin.*

* The following materials relating to the Junto are reprinted from *The Writings of Benjamin Franklin,* edited by Jared Sparks, vol. 2 (Philadelphia, revised edition, Childs & Peterson [1840]), pp. 9-13, 551-557.

Rules for a Club Established for Mutual Improvement
(drawn up in 1728)

Previous Question, to be Answered at Every Meeting

Have you read over these queries this morning, in order to consider what you might have to offer the Junto touching any one of them? *viz.*

1. Have you met with any thing in the author you last read, remarkable, or suitable to be communicated to the Junto? particularly in history, morality, poetry, physic, travels, mechanic arts, or other parts of knowledge.

2. What new story have you lately heard agreeable for telling in conversation?

3. Hath any citizen in your knowledge failed in his business lately, and what have you heard of the cause?

4. Have you lately heard of any citizen's thriving well, and by what means?

5. Have you lately heard how any present rich man, here or elsewhere, got his estate?

6. Do you know of a fellow citizen, who has lately done a worthy action, deserving praise and imitation; or who has lately committed an error, proper for us to be warned against and avoid?

7. What unhappy effects of intemperance have you lately observed or heard; of imprudence, of passion, or of any other vice or folly?

8. What happy effects of temperance, of prudence, of moderation, or of any other virtue?

9. Have you or any of your acquaintance been lately sick or wounded? If so, what remedies were used, and what were their effects?

10. Whom do you know that are shortly going [on]

voyages or journeys, if one should have occasion to send by them?

11. Do you think of any thing at present, in which the Junto may be serviceable to mankind, to their country, to their friends, or to themselves?

12. Hath any deserving stranger arrived in town since last meeting, that you have heard of? And what have you heard or observed of his character or merits? And whether, think you, it lies in the power of the Junto to oblige him, or encourage him as he deserves?

13. Do you know of any deserving young beginner lately set up, whom it lies in the power of the Junto any way to encourage?

14. Have you lately observed any defect in the laws of your country, of which it would be proper to move the legislature for an amendment? Or do you know of any beneficial law that is wanting?

15. Have you lately observed any encroachment on the just liberties of the people?

16. Hath any body attacked your reputation lately? And what can the Junto do towards securing it?

17. Is there any man whose friendship you want, and which the Junto, or any of them, can procure for you?

18. Have you lately heard any member's character attacked, and how have you defended it?

19. Hath any man injured you, from whom it is in the power of the Junto to procure redress?

20. In what manner can the Junto, or any of them, assist you in any of your honourable designs?

21. Have you any weighty affair on hand, in which you think the advice of the Junto may be of service?

22. What benefits have you lately received from any man not present?

23. Is there any difficulty in matters of opinion, of justice, and injustice, which you would gladly have discussed at this time?

24. Do you see any thing amiss in the present customs or proceedings of the Junto, which might be amended?

———

Any person to be qualified [as a member of the Junto is] to stand up, and lay his hand upon his breast, and be asked these questions, viz.

Question 1. Have you any particular disrespect to any present members? *Answer.* I have not.

Question 2. Do you sincerely declare, that you love mankind in general, of what profession or religion soever? *Answer.* I do.

Question 3. Do you think any person ought to be harmed in his body, name, or goods, for mere speculative opinions, or his external way of worship? *Answer.* No.

Question 4. Do you love truth for truth's sake, and will you endeavour impartially to find and receive it yourself, and communicate it to others? *Answer.* Yes.

Some Queries for the Consideration of the Junto

Question. Can a man arrive at perfection in this life, as some believe; or is it impossible, as others believe?

Answer. Perhaps they differ in the meaning of the word *perfection.* I suppose the perfection of any thing to be only the greatest the nature of the thing is capable of. Different things have different degrees of perfection, and the same thing at different times. Thus, a horse is more perfect than an oyster, yet the oyster may be a perfect oyster, as well as the horse a perfect horse. And an egg is not so perfect as a chicken, nor a chicken as a hen; for the hen has more strength than the chicken, and the chicken more life than the egg; yet it may be a perfect egg, chicken, and hen.

If they mean a man cannot in this life be so perfect as an angel, it may be true; for an angel, by being incorporeal, is allowed some perfections we are at present incapable of, and less liable to some imperfections than we are liable to. If they mean a man is not capable of being as perfect here as he is capable of being in heaven, that may be true likewise. But that a man is not capable of being so perfect here, as he is capable of being here, is not sense; it is as if I should say, a chicken, in the state of a chicken, is not capable of being so perfect as a chicken is capable of being in that state.

In the above sense, there may be a perfect oyster, a perfect horse, a perfect ship; why not a perfect man? That is, as perfect as his present nature and circumstances admit.

Question. Wherein consists the happiness of a rational creature?

Answer. In having a sound mind and a healthy body, a sufficiency of the necessaries and conveniences of life, together with the favor of God and the love of mankind.

Question. Is there any difference between knowledge and prudence? If there is any, which of the two is most eligible?

Question. Is it justifiable to put private men to death for the sake of public safety or tranquillity, who have committed no crime? As, in the case of the plague, to

stop infection; or, as in the case of the Welshmen here
executed?

Question. If the sovereign power attempts to deprive
a subject of his right (or, which is the same thing, of
what he thinks his right), is it justifiable in him to resist,
if he is able?

Question. What general conduct of life is most suitable for men in such circumstances as most of the members of the Junto are? Or, of the many schemes of living
which are in our power to pursue, which will be most
probably conducive to our happiness?

Question. Which is best, to make a friend of a wise
and good man that is poor, or of a rich man that is neither
wise nor good? Which of the two is the greatest loss to
a country if they both die? Which of the two is happiest
in life?

Question. Does it not, in a general way, require great
study and intense application for a poor man to become
rich and powerful, if he would do it without the for-
feiture of his honesty?

Question. Does it not require as much pains, study,
and application, to become truly wise and strictly virtuous, as to become rich? Can a man of common capacity
pursue both views with success, at the same time? If
not, which of the two is it best for him to make his whole
application to?

Question. Whence comes the dew, that stands on the
outside of a tankard that has cold water in it in the summer time?

Question. Does the importation of servants increase
or advance the wealth of our country? Would not an
office of insurance for servants be of service, and what
methods are proper for the erecting of such an office?

Some Questions Debated at Junto Meetings

Is sound an entity or body?

How may the phenomena of vapors be explained?

Is self-interest the rudder that steers mankind, the universal monarch to whom all are tributaries?

Which is the best form of government, and what was that form which first prevailed among mankind?

Can any one particular form of government suit all mankind?

What is the reason that the tides rise higher in the Bay of Fundy, than the Bay of Delaware?

Is the emission of paper money safe?

What is the reason that men of the greatest knowledge are not the most happy?

Why are tumultuous, uneasy sensations, united with our desires?

How may smoky chimneys be best cured?

Why does the flame of a candle tend upwards in a spire?

Which is least criminal, a *bad* action joined with a *good* intention, or a *good* action with a *bad* intention?

Is it inconsistent with the principles of liberty in a free government, to punish a man as a libeller, when he speaks the truth?

V. PUBLIC TRUSTS

Benjamin Franklin was not willing to allow his good works to cease at his death and, in his last will and testament, he made provision for two public trusts which continue active in Boston and Philadelphia to this day. In his last will and testament, Franklin bequeathed to his son-in-law, Richard Bache, "the bond I have against him, of two thousand and one hundred and seventy-two pounds, . . . requesting that, in consideration thereof, he would immediately after my decease manumit and set free his negro man Bob." He gave his daughter Sarah the portrait of the King of France, "set with four hundred and eight diamonds, . . . requesting, however, that she would not form any of those diamonds into ornaments . . . and thereby introduce or countenance the expensive, vain, and useless fashion of wearing jewels in this country." He bequeathed two thousand pounds "of the salary that may remain due to me as President of the State" of Pennsylvania to be used "for making the River Schuylkill navigable." The debts owing to him he bequeathed "to the contributors to the Pennsylvania Hospital, hoping that those debtors, and the descendants of such as are deceased, who now, as I find, make some difficulty of satisfying such antiquated demands as just debts, may, however, be induced to pay or give them as charity to that excellent institution." In the codicil to his will, printed in full below, Franklin established the first large-scale charitable foundations in America.

Codicil to the Last Will & Testament of B. Franklin

I, Benjamin Franklin, in the foregoing or annexed last will and testament named, having further considered the same, do think proper to make and publish the following codicil or addition thereto.

It having long been a fixed political opinion of mine, that in a democratical state there ought to be no offices of profit, for the reasons I had given in an article of my drawing in our constitution, it was my intention when I accepted the office of President, to devote the appointed salary to some public uses. Accordingly, I had already, before I made my will in July last, given large sums of it to colleges, schools, building of churches, etc.; and in that will I bequeathed two thousand pounds more to the State for the purpose of making the Schuylkill navigable. But understanding since that such a sum will do but little towards accomplishing such a work, and that the project is not likely to be undertaken for many years to come, and having entertained another idea, that I hope may be more extensively useful, I do hereby revoke and annul that bequest, and direct that the certificates I have for what remains due to me of that salary be sold, towards raising the sum of two thousand pounds sterling, to be disposed of as I am now about to order.

It has been an opinion, that he who receives an estate from his ancestors is under some kind of obligation to transmit the same to their posterity. This obligation does not lie on me, who never inherited a shilling from any ancestor or relation. I shall, however, if it is not diminished by some accident before my death, leave a considerable estate among my descendants and relations. The above observation is made merely as some apology to my family for making bequests that do not appear to have any immediate relation to their advantage.

I was born in Boston, New England, and owe my first instructions in literature to the free grammar-schools established there. I have, therefore, already considered

these schools in my will.* But I am also under obligations
to the State of Massachusetts for having, unasked, appointed me formerly their agent in England, with a handsome salary, which continued some years; and although
I accidentally lost in their service, by transmitting Governor Hutchinson's letters, much more than the amount
of what they gave me, I do not think that ought in the
least to diminish my gratitude.

I have considered that, among artisans, good apprentices are most likely to make good citizens, and, having
myself been bred to a manual art, printing, in my native
town, and afterwards assisted to set up my business in
Philadelphia by kind loans of money from two friends
there, which was the foundation of my fortune, and of
all the utility in life that may be ascribed to me, I wish
to be useful even after my death, if possible, in forming
and advancing other young men, that may be serviceable
to their country in both these towns. To this end, I devote two thousand pounds sterling, of which I give one
thousand thereof to the inhabitants of the town of Boston, in Massachusetts, and the other thousand to the
inhabitants of the city of Philadelphia, in trust, to and
for the uses, intents, and purposes hereinafter mentioned
and declared.

The said sum of one thousand pounds sterling, if accepted by the inhabitants of the town of Boston, shall
be managed under the direction of the selectmen, united

---

* In the last will and testament, Franklin bequeathed one hundred
pounds sterling "to the managers or directors of the free schools in my
native town of Boston, to be by them . . . put out to interest, and so continued at interest for ever, which interest annually shall be laid out in
silver medals, and given as honourary rewards annually by the directors
of the said free schools belonging to the said town, in such a manner as
to the discretion of the selectmen of the said town shall seem meet."

with the ministers of the oldest Episcopalian, Congrega-
tional, and Presbyterian churches in that town, who are
to let out the sum upon interest, at five per cent. per annum, to such young married artificers, under the age of
twenty-five years, as have served an apprenticeship in
the said town, and faithfully fulfilled the duties required
in their indentures, so as to obtain a good moral character from at least two respectable citizens, who are willing
to become their sureties, in a bond with the applicants,
for the repayment of the moneys so lent, with interest,
according to the terms hereinafter prescribed; all which
bonds are to be taken for Spanish milled dollars, or the
value thereof in current gold coin; and the managers
shall keep a bound book or books, wherein shall be entered the names of those who shall apply for and receive
the benefits of this institution, and of their sureties, together with the sums lent, the dates, and other necessary
and proper records respecting the business and concerns
of this institution. And as these loans are intended to
assist young married artificers in setting up their business,
they are to be proportioned by the discretion of the
managers, so as not to exceed sixty pounds sterling to
one person, nor to be less than fifteen pounds; and if the
number of appliers so entitled should be so large as that
the sum will not suffice to afford to each as much as might
otherwise not be improper, the proportion to each shall
be diminished so as to afford to every one some assistance.
These aids may, therefore, be small at first, but, as the
capital increases by the accumulated interest, they will
be more ample. And in order to serve as many as possible
in their turn, as well as to make the repayment of the
principal borrowed more easy, each borrower shall be
obliged to pay, with the yearly interest, one tenth part

of the principal, which sums of principal and interest, so paid in, shall be again let out to fresh borrowers.

And, as it is presumed that there will always be found in Boston virtuous and benevolent citizens, willing to bestow a part of their time in doing good to the rising generation, by superintending and managing this institution gratis, it is hoped that no part of the money will at any time be dead, or be diverted to other purposes, but be continually augmenting by the interest; in which case there may, in time, be more than the occasions in Boston shall require, and then some may be spared to the neighbouring or other towns in the said State of Massachusetts, who may desire to have it; such towns engaging to pay punctually the interest and the portions of the principal, annually, to the inhabitants of the town of Boston.

If this plan is executed, and succeeds as projected without interruption for one hundred years, the sum will then be one hundred and thirty-one thousand pounds; of which I would have the managers of the donation to the town of Boston then lay out, at their discretion, one hundred thousand pounds in public works, which may be judged of most general utility to the inhabitants, such as fortifications, bridges, aqueducts, public buildings, baths, pavements, or whatever may make living in the town more convenient to its people, and render it more agreeable to strangers resorting thither for health or a temporary residence. The remaining thirty-one thousand pounds I would have continued to be let out on interest, in the manner above directed, for another hundred years, as I hope it will have been found that the institution has had a good effect on the conduct of youth, and been of service to many worthy characters and useful citizens.

At the end of this second term, if no unfortunate accident has prevented the operation, the sum will be four millions and sixty one thousand pounds sterling, of which I leave one million sixty one thousand pounds to the disposition of the inhabitants of the town of Boston, and three millions to the disposition of the government of the state, not presuming to carry my views farther.

All the directions herein given, respecting the disposition and management of the donation to the inhabitants of Boston, I would have observed respecting that to the inhabitants of Philadelphia, only, as Philadelphia is incorporated, I request the corporation of that city to undertake the management agreeably to the said directions; and I do hereby vest them with full and ample powers for that purpose. And, having considered that the covering a ground plot with buildings and pavements, which carry off most of the rain and prevent its soaking into the Earth and renewing and purifying the Springs, whence the water of wells must gradually grow worse, and in time be unfit for use, as I find has happened in all old cities, I recommend that at the end of the first hundred years, if not done before, the corporation of the city employ a part of the hundred thousand pounds in bringing, by pipes, the water of Wissahickon Creek into the town, so as to supply the inhabitants, which I apprehend may be done without great difficulty, the level of the creek being much above that of the city, and may be made higher by a dam. I also recommend making the Schuylkill completely navigable. At the end of the second hundred years, I would have the disposition of the four million and sixty one thousand pounds divided between the inhabitants of the city of Philadelphia and the government of Pennsylvania, in the same manner as herein directed with respect to that of the inhabitants of Boston and the government of Massachusetts.

It is my desire that this institution should take place and begin to operate within one year after my decease, for which purpose due notice should be publickly given previous to the expiration of that year, that those for whose benefit this establishment is intended may make their respective applications. And I hereby direct my executors, the survivors or survivor of them, within six months after my decease, to pay over the said sum of two thousand pounds sterling to such persons as shall be duly appointed by the Selectmen of Boston and the corporation of Philadelphia, to receive and take charge of their respective sums, of one thousand pounds each, for the purposes aforesaid.

Considering the accidents to which all human affairs and projects are subject in such a length of time, I have, perhaps, too much flattered myself with a vain fancy that these dispositions, if carried into execution, will be continued without interruption and have the effects proposed. I hope, however, that if the inhabitants of the two cities should not think fit to undertake the execution, they will, at least, accept the offer of these donations as a mark of my good will, a token of my gratitude, and a testimony of my earnest desire to be useful to them after my departure.

I wish, indeed, that they may both undertake to endeavour the execution of the project, because I think that, though unforeseen difficulties may arise, expedients will be found to remove them, and the scheme be found practicable. If one of them accepts the money, with the conditions, and the other refuses, my will then is, that both Sums be given to the inhabitants of the city accepting the whole, to be applied to the same purposes, and under the same regulations directed for the separate parts; and, if both refuse, the money of course remains in the mass of my Estate, and is to be disposed of therewith according to my will made the Seventeenth day of July, 1788.

I wish to be buried by the side of my wife, if it may be, and that a marble stone, to be made by Chambers, six feet long, four feet wide, plain, with only a small moulding round the upper edge, and this inscription:

Benjamin ⎫
And ⎬ Franklin
Deborah ⎭

178——

to be placed over us both. My fine crab-tree walking-stick, with a gold head curiously wrought in the form of the cap of liberty, I give to my friend, and the friend of mankind, General Washington. If it were a Sceptre, he has merited it, and would become it. . . .

And lastly, it is my desire that this, my present codicil, be annexed to, and considered as part of, my last will and testament to all intents and purposes.

In witness whereof, I have hereunto set my hand and Seal this twenty-third day of June, [SEAL.] Anno Domini one thousand Seven hundred and eighty nine.

B. Franklin.

Signed, sealed, published, and declared by the above named Benjamin Franklin to be a codicil to his last will and testament, in the presence of us.

Francis Bailey,
Thomas Lang,
Abraham Shoemaker.

IV · In the Service of the Community

In FRANKLIN's civic pride and his projects for
the improvement of Philadelphia, we see another aspect
of the philosophy of doing good. At the same time we may
recognize the zeal for reform that has long been a characteristic of American life. In his attention to the details
of daily living, Franklin shows himself as the observant
empiricist. As the successful engineer of ways to make the
city he loved cleaner, safer and more attractive he continually sponsored new institutions that were proof that
the applications of reason to experience were fruitful in
the real world.

"Human felicity," he wrote, "is produced not so much
by great pieces of good fortune that seldom happen, as
by little advantages that occur every day." Franklin typi-
fies that aspect of the American character that is attentive
to small details as well as over-all great plans. The practical idealism of America lies in our capacity to work for
our ideals step by step, to recognize that the perfect world
is never achieved but that we may approach it gradually
by a creative attentiveness to each aspect of life around
us.

I. CIVIC IMPROVEMENTS

Franklin watched his city and his country grow and—
being a man of action rather than an armchair philosopher

—he put his energy into reforms that made his community a better place to live in. These reforms and the institutions he helped to found are described in the following selections from the *Autobiography,* taken from the manuscript version published by the University of California Press in 1949.

At the time I established my self in Pensylvania, there was not a good bookseller's shop in any of the colonies to the southward of Boston. In New York & Philadelphia the printers were indeed stationers, they sold only paper, etc., almanacks, ballads, and a few common school books. Those who loved reading were obliged to send for their books from England. The members of the Junto had each a few. We had left the alehouse where we first met, and hired a room to hold our club in. I proposed that we should all of us bring our books to that room, where they would not only be ready to consult in our conferences, but become a common benefit, each of us being at liberty to borrow such as he wished to read at home. This was accordingly done, and for some time contented us. Finding the advantage of this little collection, I proposed to render the benefit from books more common by commencing a public subscription library. I drew a sketch of the plan and rules that would be necessary, and got a skilful conveyancer, Mr. Charles Brockden, to put the whole in form of articles of agreement to be subscribed; by which each subscriber engaged to pay a certain sum down for the first purchase of books and an annual contribution for encreasing them. So few were the readers at that time in Philadelphia, and the majority of us so poor, that I was not able with great industry to find more than fifty persons, mostly young tradesmen, willing to pay down for this purpose forty shillings each, & ten shillings per annum. On this little fund we began. The books were imported. The library was open one day in the week for lending them to the subscribers, on their promisory notes to pay double the value if not duly returned. The institution soon manifested its utility, was imitated by other towns and in other provinces, the libraries were augmented by donations, reading became fashionable, and our people having no publick amusements to divert their attention from study became better acquainted with books, and in a few years were observed by strangers to be better instructed & more intelligent than people of the same rank generally are in other countries. . . .

The objections & reluctances I met with in soliciting the subscriptions made me soon feel the impropriety of presenting one's self as the proposer of any useful project that might be supposed to raise one's reputation in the smallest degree above that of one's neighbours, when one has need of their assistance to accomplish that project. I therefore put my self as much as I could out of sight, and stated it as a scheme of a *number of friends,* who had requested me to go about and propose it to such as they thought lovers of reading. In this way my affair went on more smoothly, and I ever after practised it on such occasions; and from my frequent successes, can heartily recommend it. The present little sacrifice of your vanity will afterwards be amply repaid. If it remains a while uncertain to whom the merit belongs, some one more vain than yourself will be encouraged to claim it, and then even envy will be disposed to do you justice, by plucking those assumed feathers, & restoring them to their right owner.

This library afforded me the means of improvement by constant study, for which I set apart an hour or two each day; and thus repaired in some degree the loss of the learned education my father once intended for me. Reading was the only amusement I allowed my self. I spent no time in taverns, games or frolicks of any kind. And my industry in my business continued as indefatigable as it was necessary. I was in debt for my printing-house, I had a young family coming on to be educated, and I had to contend with for business two printers who were established in the place before me. My circumstances however grew daily easier: my original habits of frugality continuing. And my father having among his instructions to me when a boy, frequently repeated a proverb of Solomon, *"Seest thou a man diligent in his calling, he shall stand before kings, he shall not stand before mean men,"* I from thence considered industry as a means of obtaining wealth and distinction, which encouraged me, tho' I did not think that I should ever literally stand before Kings, which however since happened—for I have stood before five, & even had the honour of sitting down with one, the King of Denmark, to dinner. . . .

In 1737, Col. Spotswood, late Governor of Virginia, & then Post-Master General, being dissatisfied with the conduct of his deputy at Philadelphia, respecting some negligence in rendering, & inexactitude of his accounts, took from him the commission & offered it to me. I accepted it readily, and found it of great advantage; for tho' the salary was small, it facilitated the correspondence that improved my newspaper, encreased the number demanded, as well as the advertisements to be inserted, so that it came to afford me a very considerable income. . . .

I began now to turn my thoughts a little to public affairs, beginning however with small matters. The city watch was one of the first things that I conceived to want

regulation. It was managed by the constables of the respective wards in turn. The constable warned a number
of housekeepers to attend him for the night. Those who
chose never to attend paid him six shillings a year to be
excused, which was supposed to be for hiring substitutes;
but was in reality much more than was necessary for
that purpose, and made the constableship a place of profit.
And the constable for a little drink often got such raga-
muffins about him as a watch that reputable housekeepers
did not chuse to mix with. Walking the rounds too was
often neglected, and most of the night spent in tippling. I
thereupon wrote a paper to be read in Junto, representing
these irregularities, but insisting more particularly on the
inequality of this six shilling tax of the constables, respecting the circumstances of those who paid it, since a poor
widow housekeeper, all whose property to be guarded
by the watch did not perhaps exceed the value of fifty
pounds, paid as much as the wealthiest merchant who had
thousands of pounds worth of goods in his stores. On the
whole I proposed as a more effectual watch, the hiring of
proper men to serve constantly in that business; and as a
more equitable way of supporting the charge, the levying
a tax that should be proportioned to property. This idea
being approved by the Junto, was communicated to the
other clubs, but as arising in each of them. And tho' the
plan was not immediately carried into execution, yet by
preparing the minds of people for the change, it paved
the way for the law obtained a few years after, when the
members of our clubs were grown into more influence.

About this time I wrote a paper (first to be read in
Junto but it was afterwards published) on the different
accidents and carelessness by which houses were set on
fire, with cautions against them, and means proposed of

avoiding them. This was much spoken of as a useful piece, and gave rise to a project, which soon followed it, of forming a company for the more ready extinguishing of fires, and mutual assistance in removing & securing of goods when in danger. Associates in this scheme were presently found amounting to thirty. Our articles of agreement obliged every member to keep always in good order and fit for use, a certain number of leather buckets, with strong bags & baskets (for packing & transporting of goods) which were to be brought to every fire; and we agreed to meet once a month & spend a social evening together, in discoursing and communicating such ideas as occurred to us upon the subject of fires as might be useful in our conduct on such occasions. The utility of this institution soon appeared, and many more desiring to be admitted than we thought convenient for one company, they were advised to form another, which was accordingly done. And this went on, one new company being formed after another, till they became so numerous as to include most of the inhabitants who were men of property; and now at the time of my writing this, tho' upwards of fifty years since its establishment, that which I first formed, called the Union Fire Company, still subsists and flourishes, tho' the first members are all deceased but myself & one who is older by a year than I am. The small fines that have been paid by members for absence at the monthly meetings, have been applied to the purchase of fire-engines, ladders, firehooks, and other useful implements, for each company, so that I question whether there is a city in the world better provided with means of putting a stop to beginning conflagrations; and in fact since those institutions, the city has never lost by fire more than one or two houses at a time, and the flames have often been

extinguished before the house in which they began has
been half consumed.

In 1739 arrived among us from England the Rev. Mr.
Whitefield, who had made himself remarkable there as an
itinerant preacher. He was at first permitted to preach
in some of our churches; but the clergy taking a dislike to
him, soon refused him their pulpits and he was obliged to
preach in the fields. . . . And it being found inconvenient
to assemble in the open air, subject to its inclemencies,
the building of a house to meet in was no sooner proposed
and persons appointed to receive contributions, but sufficient sums were soon received to procure the ground
and erect the building which was 100 feet long & 70 broad,
about the size of Westminster-hall; and the work was
carried on with such spirit as to be finished in a much
shorter time than could have been expected. Both house
and ground were vested in trustees, expressly for the use
of any preacher of any religious persuasion who might desire to say something to the people of Philadelphia, the
design in building not being to accommodate any particular sect, but the inhabitants in general, so that even if the
Mufti of Constantinople were to send a missionary to
preach Mahometanism to us, he would find a pulpit at his
service. . . .

. . . I had on the whole abundant reason to be satisfied
with my being established in Pennsylvania. There were
however two things that I regretted: there being no provision for defence, nor for a compleat education of youth;
no militia nor any college. I therefore in 1743, drew up a
proposal for establishing an academy; & at that time thinking the Reverend Mr. Peters, who was out of employ, a fit
person to superintend such an institution, I communicated
the project to him. But he having more profitable views

in the service of the proprietors, which succeeded, declined the undertaking. And not knowing another at that time suitable for such a trust, I let the scheme lie a while dormant. I succeeded better the next year, 1744, in proposing and establishing a philosophical society. The paper I wrote for that purpose will be found among my writings when collected. . . .

. . . I turned my thoughts again to the affair of establishing an academy. The first step I took was to associate in the design a number of active friends of whom the Junto furnished a good part: the next was to write and publish a pamphlet intitled, *Proposals relating to the Education of Youth in Pennsylvania.* This I distributed among the principal inhabitants gratis; and as soon as I could suppose their minds a little prepared by the perusal of it, I set on foot a subscription for opening and supporting an academy; it was to be paid in quotas yearly for five years; by so dividing it I judged the subscription might be larger, and I believe it was so, amounting to no less (if I remember right) than five thousand pounds. In the introduction to these proposals, I stated their publication not as an act of mine, but of some *publick-spirited gentlemen;* avoiding as much as I could, according to my usual rule, the presenting myself to the publick as the author of any scheme for their benefit.

The subscribers, to carry the project into immediate execution, chose out of their number twenty-four trustees, and appointed Mr. Francis, then attorney general, and myself, to draw up constitutions for the government of the academy, which being done and signed, a house was hired, masters engaged and the schools opened I think in the same year 1749. The scholars encreasing fast, the house was soon found too small, and we were looking out for a piece of ground, properly situated, with intention to build, when Providence threw into our way a large house ready built, which with a few alterations might well serve our purpose; this was the building, before mentioned, erected by the hearers of Mr. Whitefield, and was obtained for us in the following manner.

It is to be noted that the contributions to this building being made by people of different sects, care was taken in the nomination of trustees, in whom the building & ground was to be vested, that a predominancy should not be given to any sect, lest in time that predominancy might be a means of appropriating the whole to the use of such sect, contrary to the original intention; it was therefore that one of each sect was appointed, *viz.* one Church-of-England-man, one Presbyterian, one Baptist, one Moravian, etc. those in case of vacancy by death were to fill it by election from among the contributors. The Moravian happened not to please his colleagues, and on his death, they resolved to have no other of that sect. The difficulty then was, how to avoid having two of some other sect, by means of the new choice. Several persons were named and for that reason not agreed to. At length one mentioned me, with the observation that I was merely an honest man, & of no sect at all; which prevailed with them to chuse me. The enthusiasm which existed when the house was built, had long since abated, and its trustees had not been able to procure fresh contributions for paying the ground rent, and discharging some other debts the building had occasioned, which embarrassed them greatly. Being now a member of both sets of trustees, that for the building & that for the academy, I had good opportunity of negociating with both, & brought them finally to an agreement, by which the trustees for the building were to

cede it to those of the academy, the latter undertaking
to discharge the debt, to keep forever open in the building a large hall for occasional preachers according to the
original intention, and maintain a free school for the instruction of poor children. Writings were accordingly
drawn, and on paying the debts the trustees of the academy were put in possession of the premises, and by dividing the great and lofty hall into stories, and different rooms
above & below for the several schools, and purchasing
some additional ground, the whole was soon made fit for
our purpose, and the scholars removed into the building.
The care and trouble of agreeing with the workmen, purchasing materials, and superintending the work fell upon
me, and I went through it the more chearfully, as it did not
then interfere with my private business, having the year
before taken a very able, industrious & honest partner, Mr.
David Hall, with whose character I was well acquainted,
as he had worked for me four years. He took off my hands
all care of the printing-office, paying me punctually my
share of the profits. This partnership continued eighteen
years, successfully for us both.

The trustees of the academy after a while were incorporated by a charter from the Governor; their funds were
increased by contributions in Britain, and grants of land
from the proprietaries, to which the Assembly has since
made considerable addition, and thus was established the
present University of Philadelphia. I have been continued
one of its trustees from the beginning, now near forty
years, and have had the very great pleasure of seeing a
number of the youth who have received their education
in it, distinguished by their improved abilities, serviceable
in public stations, and ornaments to their country.

When I disengaged myself as above mentioned from

private business, I flattered myself that by the sufficient tho' moderate fortune I had acquired, I had secured leisure during the rest of my life, for philosophical studies and amusements; I purchased all Dr. Spence[r]'s apparatus, who had come from England to lecture here; and I proceeded in my electrical experiments with great alacrity; but the publick now considering me as a man of leisure, laid hold of me for their purposes; every part of our civil government and almost at the same time, imposing some duty upon me. The Governor put me into the commission of the peace; the Corporation of the City chose me of the common council, and soon after an alderman; and the citizens at large chose me a burgess to represent them in Assembly. This latter station was the more agreable to me, as I was at length tired with sitting there to hear debates in which as clerk I could take no part, and which were often so unentertaining, that I was induced to amuse myself with making magic squares or circles, or any thing to avoid weariness. And I conceived my becoming a member would enlarge my power of doing good. I would not however insinuate that my ambition was not flattered by all these promotions. It certainly was. For considering my low beginning they were great things to me. And they were still more pleasing, as being so many spontaneous testimonies of the publick's good opinion, and by me entirely unsolicited.

. . . Our city, tho' laid out with a beautiful regularity, the streets large, strait, and crossing each other at right angles, had the disgrace of suffering those streets to remain long unpaved, and in wet weather the wheels of heavy carriages ploughed them into a quagmire, so that it was difficult to cross them. And in dry weather the dust was offensive. I had lived near what was called the Jersey

Market, and saw with pain the inhabitants wading in mud while purchasing their provisions. A strip of ground down the middle of that market was at length paved with brick, so that being once in the market they had firm footing, but were often over shoes in dirt to get there. By talking and writing on the subject, I was at length instrumental in getting the street paved with stone between the market and the bricked foot pavement that was on each side next the houses. This for some time gave an easy access to the market, dry-shod. But the rest of the street not being paved, whenever a carriage came out of the mud upon this pavement, it shook off and left its dirt on it, and was soon covered with mire, which was not removed, the city as yet having no scavengers. After some enquiry I found a poor industrious man, who was willing to undertake keeping the pavement clean, by sweeping it twice a week & carrying off the dirt from before all the neighbours' doors, for the sum of sixpence per month, to be paid by each house. I then wrote and printed a paper, setting forth the advantages to the neighbourhood that might be obtained by this small expence; the greater ease in keeping our houses clean, so much dirt not being brought in by people's feet; the benefit to the shops by more custom, as buyers could more easily get at them, and by not having in windy weather the dust blown in upon their goods, etc. etc. I sent one of these papers to each house, and in a day or two went round to see who would subscribe an agreement to pay these sixpences. It was unanimously signed, and for a time well executed. All the inhabitants of the city were delighted with the cleanliness of the pavement that surrounded the market, it being a convenience to all; and this raised a general desire to have all the streets paved; & made the people more willing to submit to a tax for

that purpose. After some time I drew a bill for paving the
city, and brought it into the Assembly. It was just before
I went to England in 1757 and did not pass till I was gone,
and then with an alteration in the mode of assessment,
which I thought not for the better, but with an additional
provision for lighting as well as paving the streets, which
was a great improvement. It was by a private person, the
late Mr. John Clifton, his giving a sample of the utility of
lamps by placing one at his door, that the people were first
impressed with the idea of enlightning all the city. The
honour of this public benefit has also been ascribed to me,
but it belongs truly to that gentleman. I did but follow
his example; and have only some merit to claim respecting
the form of our lamps as differing from the globe lamps
we at first were supplied with from London. . . .

. . . Some may think these trifling matters not worth
minding or relating. But when they consider, that tho'
dust blown into the eyes of a single person, or into a single
shop on a windy day, is but of small importance, yet the
great number of the instances in a populous city, and its
frequent repetitions, give it weight & consequence; perhaps they will not censure very severely those who bestow
some . . . attention to affairs of this seemingly low nature.
Human felicity is produced not so much by great pieces
of good fortune that seldom happen, as by little advantages
that occur every day. Thus if you teach a poor young man
to shave himself and keep his razor in order, you may contribute more to the happiness of his life than in giving
him a 1000 Guineas. The money may be soon spent, the
regret only remaining of having foolishly consumed it.
But in the other case he escapes the frequent vexation of
waiting for barbers, & of their some times, dirty fingers,
offensive breaths and dull razors. He shaves when most

convenient to him, and enjoys daily the pleasure of its being done with a good instrument. With these sentiments I have hazarded the few preceding pages, hoping they may afford hints which some time or other may be useful to a city I love, having lived many years in it very happily; and perhaps to some of our towns in America. . . .

II. The Pennsylvania Hospital

Franklin was not the founder of the Pennsylvania Hospital—the idea was Thomas Bond's—but without Franklin this hospital would never have been established. To this project he brought his unique gifts of printer and pamphleteer, his shrewd judgment of men's characters and his ingenuity in politics. First Franklin "prepared" the minds of Pennsylvanians by articles in the *Pennsylvania Gazette,* but even so the subscriptions were not sufficient, and he saw that assistance from the Assembly would be needed. "The country members," he related, "did not at first relish the project. They objected that it could only be serviceable to the city, and therefore the citizens should alone be at the expence of it; and they doubted whether the citizens themselves generally approved of it." Franklin then formed his plan, which was to draw up the "bill for incorporating the contributors" so as "to make the important clause a conditional one, *viz.* 'And be it enacted . . . that when the said contributors shall have . . . *raised by their contributions a capital stock of £2000 value* . . . and *shall make the same appear to the satisfaction of the Speaker of the Assembly* for the time being; that *then* . . . the said Speaker . . . is hereby required to sign an order on the Provincial Treasurer for the payment of two thousand pounds. . . .' " This account comes from the *Autobiography.*

Franklin described the success of the "condition" in carrying "the bill through; . . . the members who had opposed
the grant . . . now conceived they might have the credit
of being charitable without the expence [&] agreed to
its passage; and then in soliciting subscriptions among
the people, we urged the conditional promise of the law
as an additional motive to give, since every man's donation would be doubled. Thus the clause worked both
ways." Adequate donations were accumulated to the sur-
prise of some members of the Assembly, which had then
to make its gift, and a building was erected for the first
permanent hospital in America. Franklin wrote in later
life that he did "not remember any of my political ma-
noeuvres, the success of which gave me at the time more
pleasure" or that "in after-thinking of it, I more easily excused myself for having made some use of cunning."

His interest in the Pennsylvania Hospital continued
after the initial funds were raised. He published a book
about the institution, its history and purpose, in which he
presented a stirring plea for each reader to contribute. It
contains the finest statement of his belief that the best
way of doing good is to have an organized group working
toward a common goal. Here is an empirical demonstration—based on facts and figures—that the whole community benefits by a joint effort. His argument that hospitals
provide a means of restoring sick individuals to a useful
place in society has a modern tone, as has the statement
that hospitals may serve the community by acquainting
physicians with a greater variety of diseases than they
might otherwise encounter and by offering a training
ground for young and inexperienced physicians.

Franklin, a stanch republican, was pleased to observe
that the Pennsylvania Hospital "gave to the beggar in

America a degree of comfort and chance for recovery equal to that of a European prince in his palace." And not only did such a hospital afford better and cleaner surroundings, more conducive to recovery, than a private home, but the cost of hospital care was only one tenth of similar care in "private lodgings." Presenting the record of the new Pennsylvania Hospital to the inhabitants of the province, Franklin made his book handsome; the message was to be conveyed in a form worthy of the contents. This book is to my mind the most beautiful example of Franklin's skill in printing and it outrivals by far the better-known *Cato Major* in which he took so much pride.

The following selection is taken from the original edition of *Some Account of the Pennsylvania Hospital* which, for some unaccountable reason, has never been incorporated into collections of Franklin's writings.*

> *Some Account of the Pennsylvania Hospital; From its first Rise, to the Beginning of the Fifth Month, called May, 1754. Philadelphia: Printed by B. Franklin, and D. Hall, Mdccliv.*

About the end of the year 1750, some persons, who had frequent opportunities of observing the distress of such distempered poor as from time to time came to Philadelphia, for the advice and assistance of the physicians and surgeons of that city; how difficult it was for them to procure suitable lodgings, and other conveniences proper for their respective cases, and how expensive the providing good and careful nurses, and other attendants, for want whereof, many must suffer greatly, and some probably

---

* The extracts printed below are taken from the copy of this rare Franklin imprint in the Boston Athenaeum.

perish, that might otherwise have been restored to health and comfort, and become useful to themselves, their families, and the publick, for many years after; and considering, moreover, that even the poor inhabitants of this city, tho' they had homes, yet were therein but badly accommodated in sickness, and could not be so well and so easily taken care of in their separate habitations, as they might be in one convenient house, under one inspection, and in the hands of skilful practitioners; and several of the inhabitants of the province, who unhappily became disordered in their senses, wandered about, to the terror of their neighbours, there being no place (except the House of Correction) in which they might be confined, and subjected to proper management for their recovery, and that house was by no means fitted for such purposes; did charitably consult together, and confer with their friends and acquaintances, on the best means of relieving the distressed, under those circumstances; and an infirmary, or hospital, in the manner of several lately established in Great Britain, being proposed, was so generally approved, that there was reason to expect a considerable subscription from the inhabitants of this city, towards the support of such an hospital; but the expence of erecting a building sufficiently large and commodious for the purpose, it was thought would be too heavy, unless the subscription could be made general through the Province, and some assistance could be obtained from the Assembly; the following petition was therefore drawn, and presented to the House on the 23d of January, 1750-51.

To the Honourable House of Representatives of the Province of Pennsylvania,

> The Petition of sundry inhabitants of the said Province. Humbly sheweth,

"That with the numbers of people the number of
"lunaticks, or persons distempered in mind, and deprived
"of their rational faculties, hath greatly encreased in this
"Province.

"That some of them going at large are a terror to their
"neighbours, who are daily apprehensive of the violences
"they may commit; and others are continually wasting
"their substance, to the great injury of themselves and
"families, ill disposed persons wickedly taking advantage
"of their unhappy condition, and drawing them into un-
"reasonable bargains, etc.

"That few or none of them are so sensible of their con-
"dition as to submit voluntarily to the treatment their re-
"spective cases require, and therefore continue in the same
"deplorable state during their lives; whereas it has been
"found, by the experience of many years, that above two
"thirds of the mad people received into Bethlehem Hos-
"pital, and there treated properly, have been perfectly
"cured. . . ."

On the second reading of the petition, January 29, the
House gave leave to the petitioners to bring in a bill, which
was read the first time on the first of February. For some
time it was doubtful whether the bill would not miscarry,
many of the members not readily conceiving the necessity or usefulness of the design; and apprehending, moreover, that the expence of paying physicians and surgeons
would eat up the whole of any fund that could be reasonably expected to be raised; but three of the profession, *viz.*,
Doctors Lloyd Zachary, Thomas Bond, and Phineas Bond,
generously offering to attend the hospital gratis for three
years, and the other objections being by degrees got over,
the bill, on the seventh of the same month, passed the
House, *nemine contradicente*, and in May following it re-

ceived the Governor's assent, and was enacted into a
law. . . .

As soon as the law was published, the promoters of the
design set on foot a subscription which in a short time
amounted to considerable more than the sum required by
the act. And on the first of the month called July, 1751,
a majority of the contributors met at the State-House in
Philadelphia, and pursuant to the act chose by ballot
twelve managers, and a treasurer. . . .

The managers met soon after the choice, and viewed
several spots of ground in and near the city which were
thought suitable to erect buildings on for this purpose;
and agreeing in judgment, that one particular lot belonging to the Proprietaries would suit as well or better than
any other, they drew up the following respectful address,
and sent it (with the following letter) to Thomas Hyam,
and Sylvanus Bevan, to be presented by them to the Proprietaries. And that it may be seen at one view, what has
been hitherto done in that affair, it is thought proper to
add the answers the managers received from their agents,
and other papers relative thereto. . . .

The following papers were published in the *Pennsylvania Gazette*, of August the eighth, and fifteenth, 1751,
viz.

> *Post obitum benefacta manent, æternaque Virtus*
> *Non metuit, Stygiis nec rapiatur Aquis.*
> I was sick, and ye visited me. Matth. xxv.

"Among all the innumerable species of animals which
"inhabit the air, earth and water, so exceedingly different
"in their production, their properties, and the manner of
"their existence, and so varied in form, that even of the
"same kind it can scarce be said there are two individuals
"in all respects alike; it is remarkable there are none within

"our observation distinguished from the rest by this par-
"ticular, that they are by nature incapable of diseases. . . .
"But tho' every animal that hath life is liable to death,
"man, of all other creatures, has the greatest number of
"diseases to his share; whether they are the effects of our
"intemperance and vice, or are given us that we may have
"a greater opportunity of exercising towards each other
"that virtue which most of all recommends us to the Deity,
"I mean Charity. . . .

"But the good particular men may do separately in re-
"lieving the sick, is small compared with what they may
"do collectively, or by a joint endeavour and interest.
"Hence the erecting of hospitals or infirmaries by sub-
"scription for the reception, entertainment, and cure of
"the sick poor, has been found by experience exceedingly
"beneficial, as they turn out annually great numbers of
"patients perfectly cured, who might otherwise have been
"lost to their families, and to society. Hence infirmaries
"spread more and more in Europe, new ones being con-
"tinually erected in large cities and populous towns, where
"generally the most skilful physicians and surgeons in-
"habit. And the subscribers have had the satisfaction in
"a few years of seeing the good they proposed to do be-
"come much more extensive than was at first expected; for
"the multitude and variety of cases continually treated in
"those infirmaries, not only render the physicians and sur-
"geons who attend them still more expert and skilful for
"the benefit of others, but afford such speedy and effectual
"instruction to the young students of both professions,
"who come from different and remote parts of the country
"for improvement, that they return with a more ample
"stock of knowledge in their art, and become blessings to
"the neighbourhoods in which they fix their residence.

"It is therefore a great pleasure to all the benevolent
"and charitable, who have been acquainted with these
"things in other countries, to observe that an institution of
"the same kind has met with such encouragement in Penn-
"sylvania, and is in such forwardness that there is reason
"to expect it may be carried into execution the ensuing
"year. May the Father of Mercies grant it His blessing, and
"thousands of our unhappy fellow creatures, yet unborn,
"will have cause to bless Him, for putting it into the hearts
"of the generous contributors, and enabling them thus to
"provide for their relief."

Homines ad Deos, nulla re propius accedunt, quam
Salutem Hominibus dando. Cicer. Orat.

"This motto, taken from a pagan author, expresses the
"general sense of mankind, even in the earliest ages, con-
"cerning that great duty and extensive charity, the admin-
"istring comfort and relief to the sick. If men, without any
"other assistance than the dictates of natural reason, had
"so high an opinion of it, what may be expected from
"Christians, to whom it has been so warmly recommended
"by the best example of human conduct. To visit the sick,
"to feed the hungry, to clothe the naked, and comfort the
afflicted, are the inseparable duties of a Christian life. . . .

"The difference between nursing and curing the sick in
"an hospital, and separately in private lodgings, with re-
"gard to the expence is at least as ten to one. For instance,
"suppose a person under the necessity of having a limb
"amputated, he must have the constant attendance of a
"nurse, a room, fire, etc., which cannot for the first three
"or four weeks be procured at less expence than fifteen
"shillings a week, and never after at less than ten. If he
"continues two months, his nursing will be five pounds,
"his surgeon's fee and other accidental charges commonly

"amounts to three pounds, in the whole near ten pounds;
"whereas in an hospital, one nurse, one fire, etc., will be
"sufficient for ten patients, the extra expences will be in-
"considerable, and the surgeons fees taken off, which will
"bring the above calculation within the limits of truth.

"But the difference with regard to the unhappy sufferer
"is still greater. In an hospital his case will be treated
"according to the best rules of art, by men of experience
"and known abilities in their profession. His lodgings will
"be commodious, clean and neat, in an healthy and open
"situation; his diet will be well chosen and properly ad-
"ministred. He will have many other necessary conven-
"iences for his relief, such as hot and cold baths, sweating-
"rooms, chirurgic machines, bandage, etc., which can
"rarely be procured in the best private lodgings, much less
"in those miserable loathsome holes which are the com-
"mon receptacles of the diseased poor that are brought to
"this city. In short, a beggar in a well regulated hospital
"stands an equal chance with a prince in his palace for a
"comfortable subsistence and an expeditious and effectual
"cure of his diseases. . . ."

On the sixteenth of August it being made appear to
the satisfaction of the Assembly that the contributions
amounted to upwards of two thousand pounds, an order
was obtained for the two thousand pounds that had been
conditionally granted by the act, one thousand pounds to
be paid immediately, the other in twelve months. The
money, when received, was lett out at interest on good
security, that it might be improving till it should be
wanted for the building, which the managers were obliged
to postpone till a piece of ground could be obtained that
would afford sufficient room in an airy, healthy situation,
and yet so nigh the built streets of the city as that the

managers, physicians and surgeons, might readily and conveniently visit the house on every occasion. [And] that
some good might be doing in the meantime, the managers concluded to hire a house, and take in some patients
for a beginning; but some doubts arising concerning the
power and duty of the managers, a general meeting of the
contributors was called to settle the same, and the following law was passed for those and other purposes. . . .

About the beginning of this year twelve tin boxes were
provided, on which were written these words in gold letters, CHARITY FOR THE HOSPITAL. One box for each manager, to be put up in his house, ready to receive casual
benefactions, in imitation of a good custom practiced in
some foreign countries, where these kind of boxes are frequent in shops, stores, and other places of business, and
into which the buyer and seller (when different prices are
proposed) often agree to throw the difference, instead of
splitting it, in which the successful in trade sometimes
piously deposite a part of their extraordinary gains, and
magistrates throw their petty fees; a custom worthy of imitation! But these boxes among us have produced but little
for the hospital as yet, not through want of charity in our
people, but from their being unacquainted with the nature and design of them.

From the foregoing accounts it appears, that from the
tenth of February, 1752, to the twenty-seventh of April,
1754, which is but about two years and two months, sixty
persons afflicted with various distempers have been cured,
besides many others that have received considerable relief, both in and out-patients; and if so much good has
been done by so small a number of contributors, how much
more then may reasonably be expected from the liberal
aid and assistance of the well-disposed who hitherto have

not joined in the undertaking? Experience has more and
more convinced all concerned, of the great usefulness of
this charity. . . . The careful attendance afforded to the
sick poor; the neatness, cleanness, and regularity of diet
with which they are kept in the hospital, are found to
contribute to their recovery much sooner than their own
manner of living at home, and render the physick they
take more effectual. Here they have the best advice and
the best medicines, which are helps to recovery, that many
in better circumstances in different parts of the Province
do not enjoy. In short, there is scarce any one kind of
doing good, which is not hereby in some manner promoted; for not only the sick are visited and relieved, but
the stranger is taken in, the ignorant instructed, and the
bad reclaimed;* present wants are supplied, and the future prevented, and (by easing poor families of the burthen of supporting and curing their sick) it is also the
means of feeding the hungry, and cloathing the naked.

It is therefore hoped, that by additional benefactions
from pious and benevolent persons (an account of which
will be published yearly according to law) this charity
may be farther extended, so as to embrace with open arms
all the sick poor that need the relief it affords, and that the
managers will not in time to come be under a necessity,
from the narrowness of the funds, of refusing admittance
to any proper object. . . .

It ought in justice to be here observed that the practitioners have not only given their advice and attendance
gratis, but have made their visits with even greater as-

---

* The kind visits and conversation of some serious persons, and the
pious books that have been left in the hospital, recommended to the
perusal of the patients, together with the exact regularity kept in the
house, have been attended with a blessing in these respects. [Franklin's
note.]

siduity and constancy than is sometimes used to their richer patients; and that the managers have attended their monthly boards, and the committees the visitations of two days in every week, with greater readiness and punctuality than has been usually known in any other publick business, where interest was not immediately concerned; owing, no doubt, to that satisfaction which naturally arises in humane minds from a consciousness of doing good, and from the frequent pleasing sight of misery relieved, distress removed, grievous diseases healed, health restored, and those who were admitted languishing, groaning, and almost despairing of recovery, discharged sound and hearty, with chearful and thankful countenances, gratefully acknowledging the care that has been taken of them, praising God and blessing their benefactors, who by their bountiful contributions founded so excellent an institution.

N. B. *All persons who shall be disposed to contribute to the support of this hospital by will, are advised to do it in the following manner.*

Item, *I give and bequeath to the contributors to the* Pennsylvania *Hospital, the sum of*
to be paid to their treasurer for the time being, and applied towards carrying on the charitable design of the said hospital.

V · Inventions and
Applications of Science

FRANKLIN believed in the exercise of reason to make life healthier, more comfortable and more secure. Science, he conceived, bears continual fruit in the production of useful devices based on discoveries which are the outcome of even such research as might not at first have seemed likely to have such an end product. This is the sense in which he took such pride in the lightning rod, a practical issue of his general exploration of electrical phenomena. But Franklin knew that inventions and useful discoveries are only abstractions in the minds of their creators until people accept them and apply them in their lives. Thus a major part of his program of doing good for the sake of man and the community was to advocate the introduction of new and worth-while practices, whether his own inventions or those of others.

I. INOCULATION

A typical example of Franklin as practical educator is provided by his services in furthering the practice of inoculation. In vaccination, discovered by Edward Jenner, a case of the mild disease cowpox is given to the patient who then acquires an immunity to smallpox, but in inocu-

189

lation the patient obtains immunity by being given a mild case of smallpox—sometimes a dangerous procedure, since "mild" cases are not always easy to identify. When the new and untried method of inoculation was first introduced into Boston, the Mathers had been in favor of it; so the Franklins opposed it. But by 1736, when Franklin's son Francis died of smallpox "taken in the common way," he had changed his views. In his *Autobiography*, he wrote that he had "long regretted bitterly, and still regret that I had not given it to him by inoculation. This I mention for the sake of parents who omit that operation, on the supposition that they should never forgive themselves if a child died under it; my example showing that the regret may be the same either way, and that, therefore, the safer should be chosen."

Some suspicion had been rumored around Philadelphia that young "Franky" had not died from the smallpox caught in the normal way, but rather from inoculation. Recognizing that a newspaper must correct error and teach important lessons to its readers, Franklin published the following advertisement in his *Pennsylvania Gazette*.

Understanding 'tis a current report that my son Francis, who died lately of the small pox, had it by inoculation; and being desired to satisfy the publick in that particular; inasmuch as some people are, by that report (joined with others of the like kind, and perhaps equally groundless) deterred from having that operation performed on their children, I do hereby sincerely declare, that he was not inoculated, but received the distemper in the common way of infection. And I suppose the report could only arise from its being my known opinion that inoculation was a safe and beneficial practice; and from my having said among my acquaintance, that I intended to have my child inoculated, as soon as he should have recovered sufficient strength from a flux with which he had been long afflicted.

B. Franklin.

Franklin saw that many lives might be lost by smallpox if the new preventive were not adopted, and he used the press to help spread the practice of inoculation.

Articles and advertisements in the *Pennsylvania Gazette* would never reach all Americans. Franklin therefore joined forces with an eminent London physician, William Heberden, to educate his countrymen. Franklin told Dr. Heberden about the success already achieved in America by using inoculation and persuaded him to write a pamphlet giving simple rules that anyone might follow in inoculating himself and his family. Heberden was convinced of the utility of the project and even paid for the full cost of printing the pamphlet, which was entitled *Plain Instructions for Inoculation in the Small-Pox; By which any person may be enabled to perform the operation and conduct the patient through the distemper.* The title page contained a note: "Printed at the expence of the author, to be given away in America. M,DCC,LIX." Heberden began his *Instructions* as follows:

Inoculation, as I am well assured, would be much more general among the English on the Continent of America, and of course many lives would be saved, if all who are desirous of being inoculated could easily be furnished with the means of having it done.

This consideration has engaged me to draw up a few short and plain instructions by which any person may be enabled to perform the operation in a tolerable manner, and to conduct the patient through the distemper in those

places where it is not easy to procure the assistance of
physicians and surgeons. . . .

Heberden's pamphlet was published anonymously, but
Franklin knew that its influence would be greater if readers were aware of the name of the distinguished author.
Furthermore, if Heberden's practical suggestions were to
be followed, supporting evidence on the usefulness of inoculation was required. To meet these two needs, Franklin wrote a pamphlet of his own to be distributed with
Heberden's, in which he disclosed Heberden's name and
presented statistics to show that inoculation was a tested
public-health measure. Fifteen hundred were sent to
David Hall in Philadelphia to be given away in America
in the hopes that the facts in Franklin's four-page pamphlet would convince Americans to adopt the procedure
outlined by Heberden.

Franklin had always been concerned with the health of
the man of little or moderate means; the inoculation
pamphlets were intended to remove the objection of the
expense of the practice by "encouraging parents to inoculate their own children"; the Pennsylvania Hospital was
designed primarily to provide medical care for those who
could not otherwise afford it; and the book he published,
Every Man his own Doctor, was advertised as providing
"plain and easy means for persons to cure themselves of
all, or most of the distempers incident in this climate, and
with very little charge, the medicines being chiefly of the
growth and production of this country"—and he reduced
the low price (one shilling) to anyone who would buy
the book in quantity to "give away in charity."

Franklin's pamphlet on inoculation, although twice reprinted in modern medical journals, has never before been included in a volume of Franklin's writings, nor in any of the editions of his works. It is printed below in full.*

Some Account of the Success of Inoculation for the Small-pox in England and America. Together with plain instructions, by which any person may be enabled to perform the Operation, and conduct the patient through the distemper.

London: Printed by W. Strahan, M,DCC,LIX.

London, Feb. 16, 1759.

Having been desired by my greatly esteemed friend Dr. William Heberden, F.R.S., *one of the principal physicians of this city, to communicate what account I had of the success of* inoculation *in* Boston, New England, *I some time since wrote and sent to him the following paper,* viz.

About 1753 or 54, the small-pox made its appearance in Boston, New England. It had not spread in the town for many years before, so that there were a great number of the inhabitants to have it. At first, endeavours were used to prevent its spreading, by removing the sick, or guarding the houses in which they were; and with the same view inoculation was forbidden; but when it was found that these endeavours were fruitless, the distemper breaking out in different quarters of the town and increasing, inoculation was then permitted.

Upon this, all that inclined to inoculation for themselves or families hurried into it precipitately, fearing the infection might otherwise be taken in the common way; the

---

* The text below is taken from the copy in the Harvard College Library.

numbers inoculated in every neighbourhood spread the infection likewise more speedily among those who did not chuse inoculation; so that in a few months the distemper went thro' the town, and was extinct; and the trade of the town suffered only a short interruption, compared with what had been usual in former times, the country people during the seasons of that sickness fearing all intercourse with the town.

As the practice of inoculation always divided people into parties, some contending warmly for it, and others as strongly against it; the latter asserting that the advantages pretended were imaginary, and that the surgeons, from views of interest, concealed or diminished the true number of deaths occasioned by inoculation, and magnified the number of those who died of the small-pox in the common way: it was resolved by the magistrates of the town to cause a strict and impartial enquiry to be made by the constables of each ward, who were to give in their returns upon oath; and that the enquiry might be made more strictly and impartially, some of the partisans for and against the practice were joined as assistants to the officers, and accompanied them in their progress through the wards from house to house. Their several returns being received, and summed up together, the numbers turned out as follows,

Had the Small-pox in the common way,		Of these died		Received the distemper by Inoculation,		Of these died	
Whites	Blacks	Whites	Blacks	Whites	Blacks	Whites	Blacks
5059	485	452	62	1974	139	23	7

It appeared by this account that the deaths of persons inoculated were more in proportion at this time than had been formerly observed, being something more than one in a hundred. The favourers of inoculation however would not allow that this was owing to any error in the former accounts, but rather to the inoculating at this time many unfit subjects, partly through the impatience of people who would not wait the necessary preparation, lest they should take it in the common way; and partly from the importunity of parents prevailing with the surgeons against their judgment and advice to inoculate weak children labouring under other disorders; because the parents could not immediately remove them out of the way of the distemper, and thought they would at least stand a better chance by being inoculated, than in taking the infection, as they would probably do, in the common way. The surgeons and physicians were also suddenly oppressed with the great hurry of business, which so hasty and general an inoculation and spreading of the distemper in the common way must occasion, and probably could not so particularly attend to the circumstances of the patients offered for inoculation.

Inoculation was first practiced in Boston by Dr. Boylstone in 1720. It was not used before in any part of America, and not in Philadelphia till 1730. Some years since, an enquiry was made in Philadelphia of the several surgeons and physicians who had practised inoculation, what numbers had been by each inoculated, and what was the success. The result of this enquiry was that upwards of 800 (I forget the exact number) had been inoculated at different times, and that only four of them had died.— If this account was true, as I believe it was, the reason of greater success there than had been found in Boston, where the general loss by inoculation used to be estimated at about one in 100, may probably be from this circumstance: that in Boston they always keep the distemper out as long as they can, so that when it comes, it finds a greater number of adult subjects than in Philadelphia, where since 1730 it has gone through the town once in four or five years, so that the greatest number of subjects for inoculation must be under that age.

Notwithstanding the now uncontroverted success of inoculation, it does not seem to make that progress among the common people in America, which at first was expected. *Scruples of conscience* weigh with many concerning the *lawfulness* of the practice. And if one parent or near relation is against it, the other does not chuse to inoculate a child without free consent of all parties, lest in case of a disastrous event, perpetual blame should follow. These *scruples* a *sensible Clergy* may in time remove.—— The *expence* of having the operation performed by a surgeon weighs with others, for that has been pretty high in some parts of America; and where a common tradesman or artificer has a number in his family to have the distemper, it amounts to more money than he can well spare. Many of these, rather than own the *true motive* for declining inoculation, join with the scrupulous in the cry *against it*, and influence others. A small pamphlet wrote in plain language by some skilful physician and published, directing what preparations of the body should be used before the inoculation of children, what precautions to avoid giving the infection at the same time in the common way, and how the operation is to be performed, the incisions dressed, the patient treated, and on the appearance of what symptoms a physician is to be called, etc., might, by encouraging parents to inoculate their own children, be a means of removing that objection of the expence, render the practice much more general, and thereby save the lives of thousands.

The Doctor [William Heberden], after perusing and considering the above, humanely took the trouble (tho' his extensive practice affords him scarce any time to spare) of writing the following PLAIN INSTRUCTIONS* and generously, at his own private expence, printed a very large impression of them, which was put into my hands to be distributed *gratis* in America. Not aiming at the praise which however is justly due to such disinterested benevolence, he has omitted his name; but as I thought the advice of a nameless physician might possibly on that account be less regarded, I have without his knowledge here divulged it. And I have prefixed to his small but valuable work these pages, containing the facts that gave rise to it; because *facts* generally have, as indeed they ought to have, great weight in persuading to the practice they favour. To these I may also add an account I have been favoured with by Dr. Archer, physician to the small-pox hospital here, *viz.*

                                                    PERSONS

There have been inoculated in this Hospital since
  its first institution to this day, Dec. 31, 1758..... 1601
Of which number died   6

Patients who had the small-pox in the common way
  in this hospital, to the same day................ 3856
Of which number have died..................... 1002

---

* To make them the plainer and more generally intelligible, the Doctor purposely avoided, as much as possible, the medical terms and expressions used by physicians in their writings. [Franklin's note.]

By this account it appears that in the way of inoculation there has died but *one* patient in 267, whereas in the common way there has died more than *one* in *four*. The mortality indeed in the latter case appears to have been greater than usual (one in seven, when the distemper is not very favourable, being reckoned the common loss in towns by the small-pox, all ages and ranks taken together), but these patients were mostly adults and were received, it is said, into the hospital after great irregularities had been committed. By the Boston account it appears that, whites and blacks taken together, but about one in eleven died in the common way, and the distemper then was therefore reckoned uncommonly favourable. I have also obtained from the Foundling Hospital (where all the children admitted that have not had the small-pox are inoculated at the age of five years), an account to this time of the success of that practice there, which stands thus, *viz.*

Inoculated, boys 162, girls 176, in all.............. 338
Of these died in Inoculation, only................   2

And the death of one of those two was occasioned by a worm fever.

On the whole, if the chance were only as *two* to *one* in favour of the practice among children, would it not be sufficient to induce a tender parent to lay hold of the advantage? But when it is so much greater, as it appears to be by these accounts (in some even as *thirty* to *one*), surely parents will no longer refuse to accept and thankfully use a discovery God in His mercy has been pleased to bless mankind with; whereby some check may now be put to the ravages that cruel disease has been accustomed to make, and the human species be again suffered to increase as it did before the small-pox made its appearance. This increase has indeed been more obstructed by that distemper than is usually imagined. For the loss of one in ten thereby is not merely the loss of so many persons, but the accumulated loss of all the children and children's children the deceased might have had, multiplied by successive generations.

B. Franklin,
of Philadelphia.

II. THE LIGHTNING ROD

Franklin's invention of the lightning rod was based on the discoveries he had made in electricity. His research on lightning and electricity thus had the immediate usefulness of lessening the terrors of man and helping him to preserve his buildings and ships. In 1753, Franklin published in *Poor Richard's Almanack* some simple directions for erecting lightning rods, his first communication to the nonscientific public on this subject; it has not been reprinted in the editions of his writings. It may be compared to the more complete account of the whole subject written fifteen years later and published in the fourth edition (London, 1769) of Franklin's book on electricity.

How to Make a Lightning Rod

It has pleased God in his goodness to mankind, at length to discover to them the means of securing their habitations and other buildings from mischief by thunder and lightning. The method is this: Provide a small iron rod (it may be made of the rod-iron used by the nailers) but of such a length that one end being three or four feet in the moist ground, the other may be six or eight feet above the highest part of the building. To the upper end of the rod fasten a foot of brass wire, the size of a common knitting-needle, sharpened to a fine point; the rod may be secured to the house by a few small staples. If the house or barn be long, there may be a rod and point at each end, and a middling wire along the ridge from one to the other. A house thus furnished will not be damaged by lightning, it being attracted by the points, and passing thro' the metal into the ground without hurting any thing. Vessels also, having a sharp pointed rod fixed on the top of their masts, with a wire from the foot of the rod reaching down round one of the shrouds to the water, will not be hurt by lightning.

Of Lightning, and the Method (now used in America) of securing Buildings and Persons from its mischievous Effects

Paris, Sept., 1767.

Experiments made in electricity first gave philosophers a suspicion that the matter of lightning was the same with the electric matter. Experiments afterwards made on lightning obtained from the clouds by pointed rods, received into bottles, and subjected to every trial, have since proved this suspicion to be perfectly well founded; and that whatever properties we find in electricity, are also the properties of lightning.

This matter of lightning, or of electricity, is an extream

subtile fluid, penetrating other bodies, and subsisting in them, equally diffused.

When by any operation of art or nature, there happens to be a greater proportion of this fluid in one body than in another, the body which has most will communicate to that which has least, till the proportion becomes equal; provided the distance between them be not too great; or, if it is too great, till there be proper conductors to convey it from one to the other.

If the communication be through the air without any conductor, a bright light is seen between the bodies, and a sound is heard. In our small experiments we call this light and sound the electric spark and snap; but in the great operations of nature, the light is what we call *lightning*, and the sound (produced at the same time, tho' generally arriving later at our ears than the light does to our eyes) is, with its echoes, called *thunder*.

If the communication of this fluid is by a conductor, it may be without either light or sound, the subtle fluid passing in the substance of the conductor.

If the conductor be good and of sufficient bigness, the fluid passes through it without hurting it. If otherwise, it is damaged or destroyed.

All metals, and water, are good conductors. Other bodies may become conductors by having some quantity of water in them, as wood, and other materials used in building, but not having much water in them, they are not good conductors, and therefore are often damaged in the operation.

Glass, wax, silk, wool, hair, feathers, and even wood, perfectly dry are non-conductors: that is, they resist instead of facilitating the passage of this subtle fluid.

When this fluid has an opportunity of passing through two conductors, one good, and sufficient, as of metal, the other not so good, it passes in the best, and will follow it in any direction.

The distance at which a body charged with this fluid will discharge itself suddenly, striking through the air into another body that is not charged, or not so highly charged, is different according to the quantity of the fluid, the dimensions and form of the bodies themselves, and the state of the air between them. This distance, whatever it happens to be between any two bodies, is called their *striking distance,* as till they come within that distance of each other, no stroke will be made.

The clouds have often more of this fluid in proportion than the earth; in which case as soon as they come near enough (that is, within the striking distance) or meet with a conductor, the fluid quits them and strikes into the earth. A cloud fully charged with this fluid, if so high as to be beyond the striking distance from the earth, passes quietly without making noise or giving light; unless it meets with other clouds that have less.

Tall trees, and lofty buildings, as the towers and spires of churches, become sometimes conductors between the clouds and the earth; but not being good ones, that is, not conveying the fluid freely, they are often damaged.

Buildings that have their roofs covered with lead, or other metal, and spouts of metal continued from the roof into the ground to carry off the water, are never hurt by lightning, as, whenever it falls on such a building, it passes in the metals and not in the walls.

When other buildings happen to be within the striking distance from such clouds, the fluid passes in the walls whether of wood, brick or stone, quitting the walls only when it can find better conductors near them, as metal rods, bolts, and hinges of windows or doors, gilding on wainscot, or frames of pictures; the silvering on the backs of looking-glasses; the wires for bells; and the bodies of animals, as containing watry fluids. And in passing thro' the house it follows the direction of these conductors, taking as many in its way as can assist it in its passage, whether in a strait or crooked line, leaping from one to the other, if not far distant from each other, only rending the wall in the spaces where these partial good conductors are too distant from each other.

An iron rod being placed on the outside of a building, from the highest part continued down into the moist earth, in any direction, strait or crooked, following the form of the roof or other parts of the building, will receive the lightning at its upper end, attracting it so as to prevent its striking any other part; and, affording it a good conveyance into the earth, will prevent its damaging any part of the building.

A small quantity of metal is found able to conduct a great quantity of this fluid. A wire no bigger than a goose quill, has been known to conduct (with safety to the building as far as the wire was continued) a quantity of lightning that did prodigious damage both above and below it; and probably larger rods are not necessary, tho' it is common in America, to make them of half an inch, some of three quarters, or an inch diameter.

The rod may be fastened to the wall, chimney, etc., with staples of iron. The lightning will not leave the rod (a good conductor), to pass into the wall (a bad conductor), through those staples. It would rather, if any were in the wall, pass out of it into the rod to get more readily by that conductor into the earth.

If the building be very large and extensive, two or more rods may be placed at different parts, for greater security.

Small ragged parts of clouds suspended in the air between the great body of clouds and the earth (like leaf gold in electrical experiments), often serve as partial conductors for the lightning, which proceeds from one of them to another, and by their help comes within the striking distance to the earth or a building. It therefore strikes through those conductors a building that would otherwise be out of the striking distance.

Long sharp points communicating with the earth, and presented to such parts of clouds, drawing silently from them the fluid they are charged with, they are then attracted to the cloud, and may leave the distance so great as to be beyond the reach of striking.

It is therefore that we elevate the upper end of the rod six or eight feet above the highest part of the building, tapering it gradually to a fine sharp point, which is gilt to prevent its rusting.

Thus the pointed rod either prevents a stroke from the cloud, or, if a stroke is made, conducts it to the earth with safety to the building.

The lower end of the rod should enter the earth so deep as to come at the moist part, perhaps two or three feet; and, if bent when under the surface so as to go in a horizontal line six or eight feet from the wall, and then bent again downwards three or four feet, it will prevent damage to any of the stones of the foundation.

A person apprehensive of danger from lightning, happening during the time of thunder to be in a house not so secured, will do well to avoid sitting near the chimney, near a looking-glass, or any gilt pictures or wainscot; the safest place is in the middle of the room, (so it be not under a metal lustre suspended by a chain) sitting in one chair and laying the feet up in another. It is still safer to bring two or three mattrasses or beds into the middle of the room, and folding them up double, place the chair upon them; for they not being so good conductors as the walls, the lightning will not chuse an interrupted course through the air of the room and the bedding, when it can go thro' a continued better conductor, the wall. But, where it can be had, a hamock or swinging bed, suspended by silk cords equally distant from the walls on every side, and from the cieling and floor above and below, affords the safest situation a person can have in any room whatever; and what indeed may be deemed quite free from danger of any stroke by lightning.

III. Useful Gadgets

In 1787, Manasseh Cutler visited Franklin in his home in Philadelphia; Franklin invited him into the library, which was also his study, and showed him many useful contrivances and natural curiosities. Cutler later described how Franklin showed him "a rolling press, for taking the copies of letters or any other writing. A sheet of paper is completely copied in less than two minutes: the copy as fair as the original, and without defacing it in the smallest degree. It is an invention of his own, extremely useful in many situations of life. He also showed us his long, artificial arm and hand, for taking down and putting up books on high shelves, which are out of reach; and his great arm-chair, with rockers, and a large fan placed over it, with which he fans himself, keeps off the flies, etc., while he sits reading, with only a small motion of the foot; and many other curiosities and inventions, all his own, but of lesser note."

The production of ingenious and useful devices is well established as part of the American character. Franklin as gadgeteer may be seen in his descriptions of the "long arm" and the bifocal glasses he contrived.

The Invention of Bifocal Glasses

[Franklin's description of the bifocal glasses which he invented comes from a letter written to George Whatley, dated Passy, May 23, 1785.]

. . . By Mr. Dollond's saying that my double spectacles can only serve particular eyes, I doubt he has not been rightly informed of their construction. I imagine it will be found pretty generally true that the same convexity of glass through which a man sees clearest and best at the distance proper for reading, is not the best for greater distances. I therefore had formerly two pair of spectacles which I shifted occasionally, as in travelling I sometimes read and often wanted to regard the prospects. Finding this change troublesome, and not always sufficiently ready, I had the glasses cut, and half of each kind associated in the same circle, thus,

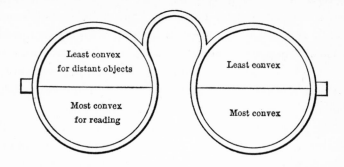

By this means, as I wear my spectacles constantly, I have only to move my eyes up or down, as I want to see distinctly far or near, the proper glasses being always ready. This I find more particularly convenient since my being in France, the glasses that serve me best at table to see what I eat, not being the best to see the faces of those on the other side of the table who speak to me; and when one's ears are not well accustomed to the sounds of a language, a sight of the movements in the features of him that speaks helps to explain; so that I understand French better by the help of my spectacles. . . .

Description of an Instrument for taking down Books from high Shelves

January, 1786.

Old men find it inconvenient to mount a ladder or steps for that purpose, their heads being sometimes subject to giddinesses, and their activity, with the steadiness of their joints, being abated by age; besides the trouble of removing the steps every time a book is wanted from a different part of their library.

For a remedy, I have lately made the following simple machine, which I call the *long arm*.

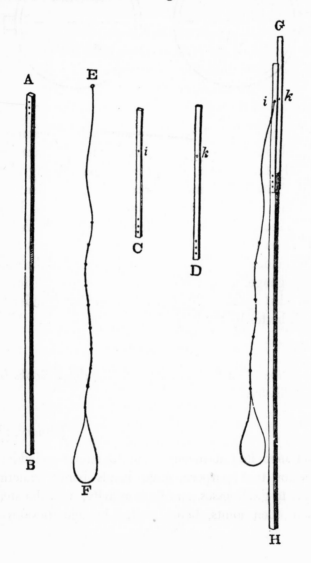

A B, the *arm*, is a stick of pine, an inch square and 8 feet long. *C, D*, the *thumb* and *finger*, are two pieces of ash lath, an inch and half wide, and a quarter of an inch thick. These are fixed by wood screws on opposite sides of the end *A* of the arm *A B;* the finger *D* being longer and standing out an inch and half farther than the thumb *C*. The outside of the ends of these laths are pared off sloping and thin, that they may more easily enter between books that stand together on a shelf. Two small holes are bored through them at *i, k. E F*, the sinew, is a cord of the size of a small goosequill, with a loop at one end. When applied to the machine it passes through the two laths, and is stopped by a knot in its other end behind the longest at *k*. The hole at *i* is nearer the end of the arm than that at *k*, about an inch. A number of knots are also on the cord, distant three or four inches from each other.

To use this instrument; put one hand into the loop, and draw the sinew straight down the side of the arm; then enter the end of the finger between the book you would take down and that which is next to it. The laths being flexible, you may easily, by a slight pressure sideways, open them wider if the book is thick, or close them if it is thin, by pulling the string, so as to enter the shorter lath or thumb between your book and that which is next to its other side, then push till the back of your book comes to touch the string. Then draw the string or sinew tight, which will cause the thumb and finger to pinch the book strongly, so that you may draw it out. As it leaves the other books, turn the instrument a *quarter* round, so that the book may lie flat and rest on its side upon the under lath or finger. The knots on the sinew will help you to keep it tight and close to the side of the arm as you take it down hand over hand, till the book comes to you; which would drop from between the thumb and finger if the sinew was let loose.

All new tools require some practice before we can become expert in the use of them. This requires very little.

Made in the proportions above given, it serves well for books in duodecimo or octavo. Quartos and folios are too heavy for it; but those are usually placed on the lower shelves within reach of hand.

The book taken down, may, when done with, be put up again into its place by the same machine.

IV. A FRANKLIN STOVE

Franklin devoted considerable attention to the improvement of stoves or fireplaces and design of chimneys. Many different types of iron fireplaces which are set into a room are called today "Franklin stoves," so that this expression has become a kind of generic term rather than a description of his particular invention. His own account of the stove he invented, which follows, was published so that anyone who wished might construct one. Being more concerned with improving the heating and ventilation of houses and the saving of fuel—in other words, helping his fellow men to better lives—Franklin did not take out a patent on his invention. In the account, Franklin reveals a kind of ingenuity and practicality that Americans have always admired, and the little pamphlet on the "Pennsylvania Fire-places" is thus in the main tradition of the improvement of man's living conditions which has become so characteristic of America.

An
ACCOUNT
of the New-Invented
PENNSYLVANIAN FIRE-PLACES;
wherein

Their construction and manner of operation is particu-
larly explained; their advantages above every other
method of warming rooms demonstrated; and all ob-
jections that have been raised against the use of them
answered and obviated. With directions for putting
them up, and for using them to the best advantage.
And a copper-plate in which the several parts of the
machine are exactly laid down, from a scale of equal
parts.

PHILADELPHIA:
Printed and Sold by B. Franklin. 1744

In these Northern Colonies the inhabitants keep fires
to sit by, generally seven months in the year; that is, from
the beginning of October to the end of April; and in
some winters near eight months, by taking in part of
September and May.

Wood, our common fewel, which within these 100
years might be had at every man's door, must now be
fetched near 100 miles to some towns, and makes a very
considerable article in the expence of families.

As therefore so much of the comfort and conveniency
of our lives, for so great a part of the year, depends on
the article of fire; since fuel is become so expensive, and
(as the country is more cleared and settled) will of course
grow scarcer and dearer; any new proposal for saving

the wood, and for lessening the charge and augmenting the benefit of fire, by some particular method of making and managing it, may at least be thought worth consideration.

The new fire-places are a late invention to that purpose, (experienced now three winters by a great number of families in Pennsylvania) of which this paper is intended to give a particular account.

That the reader may the better judge whether this method of managing fire has any advantage over those heretofore in use, it may be proper to consider both the old and new methods, separately and particularly, and afterwards make the comparison.

In order to do this 'tis necessary to understand well some few of the properties of air and fire, *viz.*

1. Air is rarified by heat, and condensed by cold, *i.e.* the same quantity of air takes up more space when warm than when cold. This may be shown by several very easy experiments. Take any clear glass bottle (a Florence flask stript of the straw is best), place it before the fire, and, as the air within is warmed and rarified, part of it will be driven out of the bottle; turn it up, place its mouth in a vessel of water, and remove it from the fire; then, as the air within cools and contracts, you will see the water rise in the neck of the bottle, supplying the place of just so much air as was driven out. Hold a large hot coal near the side of the bottle, and as the air within feels the heat, it will again distend and force out the water. Or, fill a bladder half-full of air, tie the neck tight, and lay it before a fire as near as may be without scorching the bladder; as the air within heats, you will perceive it to swell and fill the bladder, till it becomes tight, as if full

blown. Remove it to a cool place, and you will see it fall gradually, till it becomes as lank as at first.

2. Air rarified and distended by heat is specifically* lighter than it was before, and will rise in other air of greater density. As wood, oil, or any other matter specifically lighter than water, if placed at the bottom of a vessel of water, will rise till it comes to the top; so rarified air will rise in common air, till it either comes to air of equal weight, or is by cold reduced to its former density.

A fire then being made in any chimney, the air over the fire is rarified by the heat, becomes lighter and therefore immediately rises in the funnel, and goes out; the other air in the room (flowing towards the chimney) supplies its place, is rarified in its turn, and rises likewise; the place of the air thus carried out of the room is supplied by fresh air coming in thro' doors and windows, or, if they be shut, thro' every crevice with violence, as may be seen by holding a candle to a key-hole. If the room be so tight as that all the crevices together will not supply so much air as is continually carried off, then in a little time the current up the funnel must flag, and the smoke, being no longer driven up, must come into the room.

1. Fire (*i.e.* common fire) throws out light, heat, and smoke (or fume). The two first move in right lines, and with great swiftness; the latter is but just separated from the fuel, and then moves only as it is carried by the stream of rarified air. And without a continual accession and

---

* Body or matter of any sort is said to be *specifically* heavier or lighter than other matter, when it has more or less substance or weight in the same dimensions. [Franklin's note.]

recession of air, to carry off the smoaky fumes, they would remain crouded about the fire, and stifle it.

2. Heat may be separated from the smoke as well as from the light, by means of a plate of iron, which will suffer heat to pass through it without the others.

3. Fire sends out its rays of heat, as well as rays of light, equally every way. But the greatest sensible heat is over the fire, where there is, besides the rays of heat shot upwards, a continual rising stream of hot air, heated by the rays shot round on every side.

These things being understood, we proceed to consider the fire-places heretofore in use, *viz.*

1. The large open fire-places used in the days of our fathers, and still generally in the country, and in kitchens.

2. The newer-fashioned fire-places, with low breasts and narrow hearths.

3. Fire-places with hollow backs, hearths and jams of iron, . . . for warming the air as it comes into the room.

4. The Holland stoves, with iron doors opening into the room.

5. The German stoves, which have no opening in the room where they are used, but the fire is put in from some other room, or from without.

6. Iron pots, with open charcoal fires, placed in the middle of a room.

. . . To avoid the several inconveniences, and at the same time retain all the advantages of other fire-places, was contrived the PENNSYLVANIA FIRE-PLACE, now to be described. . . .

Its operation may be conceived by observing the plate entitled, *Profile of the Chimney and Fire-place.*

PROFILE OF THE PENNSYLVANIA CHIMNEY AND FIRE-PLACE

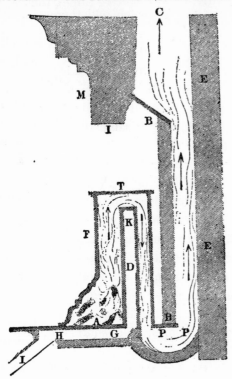

M The mantel-piece, or breast of the chimney.
C The funnel.
B The false back and closing.
E True back of the chimney.
T Top of the fire-place.
F The front of it.
A The place where the fire is made.
D The air-box.
K The hole in the side plate, thro' which the warmed air is discharged out of the air-box into the room.
H The hollow filled with fresh air, entring at the passage I, and ascending into the air-box thro' the air-hole in the bottom plate, near
G The partition in the hollow to keep the air and smoke apart.
P The passage under the false back and part of the hearth for the smoke.
[The arrows show] the course of the smoke.

The fire being made at A, the flame and smoke will
ascend and strike the top T, which will thereby receive
a considerable heat. The smoke, finding no passage upwards, turns over the top of the air-box, and descends
between it and the back plate to the holes in the bottom
plate, heating, as it passes, both plates of the air-box,
and the said back plate; the front plate, bottom and side
plates are also all heated at the same time. The smoke
proceeds in the passage that leads it under and behind
the false back, and so rises into the chimney. The air
of the room, warmed behind the back plate, and by the
sides, front, and top plates, becoming specifically lighter
than the other air in the room, is obliged to rise; but the
closure over the fire-place hindring it from going up the
chimney, it is forced out into the room, rises by the mantle-
piece to the cieling, and spreads all over the top of the
room, whence being crouded down gradually by the
stream of newly-warmed air that follows and rises above
it, the whole room becomes in a short time equally
warmed.

At the same time the air, warmed under the bottom
plate and in the air-box, rises and comes out of the holes
in the side plates, very swiftly if the door of the room
be shut, and joins its current with the stream before mentioned, rising from the side, back, and top plates.

The air that enters the room thro' the air-box is fresh,
tho' warm; and computing the swiftness of its motion
with the areas of the holes, 'tis found that near 10 barrels
of fresh air are hourly introduced by the air-box; and
by this means the air in the room is continually changed,
and kept at the same time sweet and warm.

'Tis to be observed, that the entring air will not be

warm at first lighting the fire, but heats gradually as the fire encreases.

A square opening for a trap-door should be left in the closing of the chimney, for the sweeper to go up. The door may be made of slate or tin, and commonly kept close shut, but so placed as that turning up against the back of the chimney when open, it closes the vacancy behind the false back, and shoots the soot, that falls in sweeping, out upon the hearth. This trap-door is a very convenient thing.

In rooms where much smoking of tobacco is used, 'tis also convenient to have a small hole, about five or six inches square, cut near the cieling through into the funnel. This hole must have a shutter, by which it may be closed or opened at pleasure. When open, there will be a strong draught of air through it into the chimney, which will presently carry off a cloud of smoke, and keep the room clear. If the room be too hot likewise, it will carry off as much of the warm air as you please, and then you may stop it intirely, or in part, as you think fit. By this means it is that the tobacco smoke does not descend among the heads of the company near the fire, as it must do before it can get into common chimneys.

. . . .

The Advantages of this Fire-place

Its advantages above the common fire-places are,

1. That your whole room is equally warmed; so that people need not croud so close round the fire, but may

sit near the window, and have the benefit of the light for
reading, writing, needlework, etc. They may sit with
comfort in any part of the room, which is a very considerable advantage in a large family, where there must often
be two fires kept, because all cannot conveniently come
at one.

2. If you sit near the fire, you have not that cold
draught of uncomfortable air nipping your back and
heels, as when before common fires, by which many
catch cold, being scorcht before, and, as it were, froze
behind.

3. If you sit against a crevice, there is not that sharp
draught of cold air playing on you, as in rooms where
there are fires in the common way; by which many catch
cold, whence proceed coughs, catarrhs, tooth-achs, fe-
vers, pleurisies, and many other diseases.

4. In case of sickness, they make most excellent nurs-
ing-rooms; as they constantly supply a sufficiency of fresh
air, so warmed at the same time as to be no way inconvenient or dangerous. A small one does well in a chamber;
and, the chimneys being fitted for it, it may be removed
from one room to another, as occasion requires, and fixed
in half an hour. The equal temper, too, and warmth, of
the air of the room, is thought to be particularly advantageous in some distempers. For 'twas observed in the
winters of 1730 and 1736, when the small-pox spread in
Pennsylvania, that very few of the children of the Ger-
mans died of that distemper in proportion to those of
the English; which was ascribed by some to the warmth
and equal temper of air in their stove-rooms; which made
the disease as favourable as it commonly is in the West
Indies. But this conjecture we submit to the judgment
of physicians.

5. In common chimneys, the strongest heat from the fire, which is upwards, goes directly up the chimney, and is lost; and there is such a strong draught into the chimney, that not only the upright heat, but also the back, sides, and downward heats are carried up the chimney by that draught of air; and the warmth given before the fire, by the rays that strike out towards the room, is continually driven back, crouded into the chimney, and carried up, by the same draught of air. But here the upright heat strikes and heats the top plate, which warms the air above it, and that comes into the room. The heat likewise, which the fire communicates to the sides, back, bottom and air-box, is all brought into the room; for you will find a constant current of warm air coming out of the chimney-corner into the room. Hold a candle just under the mantle-piece, or breast of your chimney, and you will see the flame bent outwards. By laying a piece of smoaking paper on the hearth, on either side, you may see how the current of air moves, and where it tends, for it will turn and carry the smoke with it.

6. Thus, as very little of the heat is lost, when this fire-place is used, *much less wood** will serve you, which is a considerable advantage where wood is dear.

7. When you burn candles near this fire-place, you will find that the flame burns quite upright, and does

---

* People who have used these fire-places, differ much in their accounts of the wood saved by them. Some say five-sixths, others three-fourths, and others much less. This is owing to the great difference there was in their former fires; some (according to the different circumstances of their rooms and chimneys) having been used to make very large, others middling, and others, of a more sparing temper, very small ones. While in these fire-places (their size and draught being nearly the same) the consumption is more equal. I suppose, taking a number of families together, that two-thirds, or half the wood, at least, is saved. My common room, I know, is made twice as warm as it used to be, with a quarter of the wood I formerly consumed there. [Franklin's note.]

not blare and run the tallow down, by drawing towards
the chimney, as against common fires.

8. This fire-place cures most smoaky chimneys, and
thereby preserves both the eyes and furniture.

9. It prevents the fouling of chimneys; much of the
lint and dust that contributes to foul a chimney, being
by the low arch obliged to pass thro' the flame, where 'tis
consumed. Then, less wood being burnt, there is less
smoke made. Again, the shutter, or trap-bellows, soon
blowing the wood into a flame, the same wood does not
yield so much smoke as if burnt in a common chimney.
For as soon as flame begins, smoke, in proportion, ceases.

10. And, if a chimney should be foul, 'tis much less
likely to take fire. If it should take fire, 'tis easily stifled
and extinguished.

11. A fire may be very speedily made in this fire-place,
by the help of the shutter, or trap-bellows, as aforesaid.

12. A fire may be soon extinguished by closing it with
the shutter before, and turning the register behind, which
will stifle it, and the brands will remain ready to rekindle.

13. The room being once warm, the warmth may be
retained in it all night.

14. And lastly, the fire is so secured at night, that not
one spark can fly out into the room to do damage.

With all these conveniencies, you do not lose the pleasing sight nor use of the fire, as in the Dutch stoves, but
may boil the tea-kettle, warm the flat-irons, heat heaters,
keep warm a dish of victuals by setting it on the top,
etc., etc.

Objections answered

There are some objections commonly made by people
that are unacquainted with these fire-places, which it
may not be amiss to endeavour to remove, as they arise

from prejudices which might otherwise obstruct in some degree the general use of this beneficial machine. We frequently hear it said, *They are of the nature of Dutch stoves; stoves have an unpleasant smell; stoves are unwholesome; and warm rooms make people tender, and apt to catch cold.* As to the first, that they are of the nature of Dutch stoves, . . . there is a most material difference, and . . . these have vastly the advantage, if it were only in the single article of the admission and circulation of fresh air. But it must be allowed there may have been some cause to complain of the offensive smell of iron stoves. This smell, however, never proceeded from the iron itself, which in its nature, whether hot or cold, is one of the sweetest of metals, but from the general uncleanly manner of using those stoves. If they are kept clean, they are as sweet as an ironing-box, which, tho' ever so hot, never offends the smell of the nicest lady; but it is common to let them be greased by setting candlesticks on them, or otherwise; to rub greasy hands on them, and, above all, to spit upon them to try how hot they are, which is an inconsiderate, filthy unmannerly custom; for the slimy matter of spittle drying on, burns and fumes when the stove is hot, as well as the grease, and smells most nauseously; which makes such close stoverooms, where there is no draught to carry off those filthy vapours, almost intolerable to those that are not from their infancy accustomed to them. At the same time, nothing is more easy than to keep them clean; for when by any accident they happen to be fouled, a lee made of ashes and water, with a brush, will scour them perfectly; as will also a little strong soft soap and water.

That hot iron of itself gives no offensive smell, those know very well who have (as the writer of this has) been present at a furnace when the workmen were pouring out the flowing metal to cast large plates, and not the least smell of it to be perceived. That hot iron does not, like lead, brass, and some other metals, give out unwholesome vapours, is plain from the general health and strength of those who constantly work in iron, as furnace-men, forge-men, and smiths. That it is in its nature a metal perfectly wholesome to the body of man, is known from the beneficial use of chalybeat or iron-mine waters; from the good done by taking steel filings in several disorders; and that even the smithy water, in which hot irons are quenched, is found advantageous to the human constitution. The ingenious and learned Dr. Desaguliers, to whose instructive writings the contriver of this machine acknowledges himself much indebted, relates an experiment he made, to try whether heated iron would yield unwholesome vapours. He took a cube of iron, and having given it a very great heat, he fixed it so to a receiver, exhausted by the air-pump, that all the air rushing in to fill the receiver, should first pass thro' a hole in the hot iron. He then put a small bird into the receiver, who breathed that air without any inconvenience, or suffering the least disorder. But the same experiment being made with a cube of hot brass, a bird put into that air died in a few minutes. Brass, indeed, stinks even when cold, and much more when hot; lead too, when hot, yields a very unwholesome steam; but iron is always sweet, and every way taken is wholesome and friendly to the human body,—except in weapons.

That warm rooms make people tender and apt to catch cold, is a mistake as great as it is (among the English) general. We have seen in the preceding pages how the common rooms are apt to give colds; but the writer of this paper may affirm, from his own experience, and that of his family and friends who have used warm rooms for these four winters past, that by the use of such rooms, people are rendered *less liable* to take cold, and, indeed, *actually hardened.* If sitting warm in a room made one subject to take cold on going out, lying warm in bed should, by a parity of reason, produce the same effect when we rise. Yet we find we can leap out of the warmest bed naked in the coldest morning, without any such danger; and in the same manner out of warm clothes into a cold bed. The reason is, that in these cases the pores all close at once, the cold is shut out, and the heat within augmented, as we soon after feel by the glowing of the flesh and skin. Thus, no one was ever known to catch cold by the use of the cold bath. And are not cold baths allowed to harden the bodies of those that use them? Are they not therefore frequently prescribed to the tenderest constitutions? Now, every time you go out of a warm room into the cold freezing air, you do as it were plunge into a cold bath, and the effect is in proportion the same; for (tho' perhaps you may feel somewhat chilly at first) you find in a little time your bodies hardened and strengthened, your blood is driven round with a brisker circulation, and a comfortable, steady, uniform inward warmth succeeds that equal outward warmth you first received in the room. Farther to confirm this assertion, we instance the Swedes, the Danes, the Russians; these nations are said to live in rooms, compared to ours, as hot as ovens; yet where are the hardy soldiers, tho' bred in their boasted cool houses, that can, like these people, bear the fatigues of a winter campaign in so severe a climate, march whole days to the neck in snow, and at night entrench in ice, as they do?

The mentioning of those northern nations puts me in

mind of a considerable *publick advantage* that may arise
from the general use of these fire-places. It is observable,
that tho' those countries have been well inhabited for
many ages, wood is still their fuel, and yet at no very
great price; which could not have been if they had not
universally used stoves, but consumed it as we do in
great quantities, by open fires. By the help of this saving
invention our wood may grow as fast as we consume it,
and our posterity may warm themselves at a moderate
rate, without being obliged to fetch their fuel over the
Atlantick; as, if pit-coal should not be here discovered
(which is an uncertainty) they must necessarily do.

We leave it to the political arithmetician to compute
how much money will be saved to a country, by its spending two thirds less of fuel; how much labour saved in
cutting and carriage of it; how much more land may be
cleared for cultivation; how great the profit by the additional quantity of work done, in those trades particularly
that do not exercise the body so much, but that the work-
folks are obliged to run frequently to the fire to warm
themselves. And to physicians to say, how much healthier thick-built towns and cities will be, now half suffo-
cated with sulphury smoke, when so much less of that
smoke shall be made, and the air breathed by the inhabitants be consequently so much purer. These things it
will suffice just to have mentioned. . . .

. . . People are at first apt to make their rooms too
warm, not imagining how little a fire will be sufficient.
When the plates are no hotter than that one may just
bear the hand on them, the room will generally be as warm
as you desire it.

VI · The Style of Being American

Being an American meant for Franklin a passionate love of country and a devotion to a democratic point of view in which the rights and liberties of his fellow men were guaranteed and protected. As her foremost citizen in the eyes of the world, he was the champion of her cause in Britain for more than a decade before the Revolution and her representative in France during the years of conflict. America was fortunate in having a man of his stature and ability to serve her during those years; the skills he had acquired in mastery of life and the world's affairs were brought to bear on the issues of state in patriotic service. An old hand at presenting "causes" in the public press, he presented the case for America in British newspapers and magazines—under various pseudonyms, just as he had done at home in his *Pennsylvania Gazette*. His knowledge of America was extraordinary and he answered statements made against his country by a display of statistics on population, agriculture, manufacturing and trade that was overwhelming. He knew that false claims and allegations could often be best answered by satire and that at other times a reasoned argument would be more effective. As colonial agent in England, he was at once lobbyist, propagandist, witness and the voice of America. In France, too, he used the press to the advantage of his country and he

225

understood how the self-interest of France could be harnessed to aid America. He knew that the French government would never help America for purely altruistic reasons, and he therefore played on the traditional rivalry between France and England and on the ambitions of France in the New World to enlist French arms and ammunition, capital, men and ships, and military engineers to serve American independence. A similarity, therefore, exists between the know-how Franklin displayed in the game of diplomacy and in the design of good works for the benefit of the community.

As early as the time of the Albany Plan of Union in 1754, Franklin had made clear that government must be grounded in the will of the people, and he put forth the view that taxation without representation is unjust and that restraints upon American manufacturing should be lifted. In his "generalization about opinion and government" and his "doctrine that government should promote the general welfare," Verner Crane (the greatest living student of Franklin's political thought) finds the basic elements of Franklin's outlook. His political thinking was "based upon observation, . . . a reading of history, and from observation of societies that he knew—including an especially acute analysis of the dynamics of growth in American society. . . . " Most of the thinking men in America, on the eve of the Revolution, thought in terms of the natural-rights philosophy, but although Franklin reached the same conclusions they did, he "rarely appealed to Locke, seldom used the conventional language of natural law, compact, and fundamental right." No student of the law, and having a distrust and dislike of lawyers, he grounded his principles on experience illuminated by reason.

Franklin's style of being American encompassed a respect for human dignity transcending the limitations of color (although in his early days he expressed a sentimental regard for his own Anglo-Saxon kind of English stock), a defense of the rights of the press and of freedom of speech and conscience, a concern for the liberty of every man to worship God in his own way, a regard for education and learning and for arts and letters, a sincere belief in equality of opportunity and condition that expressed itself in a concern to prevent excessive wealth and extreme poverty, and a passionate belief in the future greatness of America. The first acknowledged master of American literary expression, Franklin is also in the heroic tradition of American humor. Franklin's humor and wit—the gentle touch that won men's hearts and affections and the bite of satire that disconcerted the enemies of America and the opponents of freedom and progress—reveal him in his most creative aspect as a pioneer of the American personality. His spirit of fair play, tolerance and compromise for the better good of all have elicited, over the years, the respectful admiration of Americans and the love of the whole world.

I. DEMOCRATIC GOVERNMENT

Since Franklin's writings on political subjects were addressed to immediate issues, his principles of general welfare, respect for public opinion and democratic foundations of government must be discovered from an analysis of the arguments he made in his *ad hoc* compositions. But, although he was not a systematic political philosopher, he did—on occasion—express his ideas in a suffi-

ciently general form to enable the modern reader to gain
a measure of his principles: as in the series of three letters
to Governor Shirley, written at the time of the Albany
convention in 1754, and published by Franklin in the
London Chronicle, Feb. 8, 1766, as a part of his campaign
for the repeal of the Stamp Act. These letters were widely
reprinted in England and in America; they were the subject of much friendly and hostile comment and came to
be considered as the "point of departure" in the "advance of American claims toward the full claim of legislative independence."

Three Letters to Governor Shirley

LETTER I.

*Concerning the voice of the people in choosing the
rulers by whom taxes are imposed.*

Tuesday Morning. [December 17, 1754.]
Sir,

I return you the loose sheets of the plan, with thanks
to your Excellency for communicating them.

I apprehend, that excluding the *people* of the colonies
from all share in the choice of the grand council will give
extreme dissatisfaction, as well as the taxing them by act
of Parliament, where they have no representative. It is
very possible, that this general government might be as
well and faithfully administered without the people, as
with them; but where heavy burthens have been laid on
them, it has been found useful to make it, as much as
possible, their own act. . . .

LETTER II.

*On the imposition of direct taxes upon the colonies
without their consent.*

Wednesday Morning. [December 18, 1754.]

Sir,

I mentioned it yesterday to your Excellency as my opinion, that excluding the *people* of the colonies from all share in the choice of the grand council, would probably give extreme dissatisfaction, as well as the taxing them by act of Parliament, where they have no representative. In matters of general concern to the people, and especially where burthens are to be laid upon them, it is of use to consider, as well what they will be apt to think and say, as what they ought to think; I shall therefore, as your Excellency requires it of me, briefly mention what of either kind occurs to me on this occasion. . . .

LETTER III.

*On the subject of uniting the colonies more intimately
with Great Britain, by allowing them representatives
in Parliament.*

Boston, Dec. 22, 1754.

Sir,

Since the conversation your Excellency was pleased to honour me with, on the subject of *uniting the colonies* more intimately with Great Britain, by allowing them *representatives in Parliament*, I have something further considered that matter, and am of opinion, that such a

union would be very acceptable to the colonies, provided
they had a reasonable number of representatives allowed
them; and that all the old acts of Parliament restraining
the trade or cramping the manufactures of the colonies
be at the same time repealed, and the British subjects
on this side the water put, in those respects, on the same
footing with those in Great Britain, till the new Parliament, representing the whole, shall think it for the interest of the whole to reënact some or all of them. It is
not that I imagine so many representatives will be allowed the colonies, as to have any great weight by their
numbers; but I think there might be sufficient to occasion
those laws to be better and more impartially considered,
and perhaps to overcome the interest of a petty corporation, or of any particular set of artificers or traders in
England, who heretofore seem, in some instances, to
have been more regarded than all the colonies, or than
was consistent with the general interest, or best national
good. . . .

Now I look on the colonies as so many counties gained
to Great Britain, and more advantageous to it than if they
had been gained out of the seas around its coasts, and
joined to its land: For being in different climates, they
afford greater variety of produce, and being separated
by the ocean, they increase much more its shipping and
seamen; and since they are all included in the British
empire, which has only extended itself by their means;
and the strength and wealth of the parts are the strength
and wealth of the whole; what imports it to the general
state, whether a merchant, a smith, or a hatter, grow
rich in Old or New England? And if, through increase
of people, two smiths are wanted for one employed before, why may not the *new* smith be allowed to live and

thrive in the *new* country, as well as the *old* one in the *old?* In fine, why should the countenance of a state be *partially* afforded to its people, unless it be most in favour of those who have most merit? And if there be any difference, those who have most contributed to enlarge Britain's empire and commerce, increase her strength, her wealth, and the numbers of her people, at the risk of their own lives and private fortunes in new and strange countries, methinks ought rather to expect some preference. With the greatest respect and esteem, I have the honour to be

Your Excellency's most obedient
and most humble servant,
B. Franklin.

Franklin believed that the form of government that would be best for America would be a more direct kind of democracy than we know today. The legislature was to have a single chamber of elected representatives elected annually; the executive was to be plural, so that there would be no possibility of concentration of power in a single individual. These principles were the foundation of the first constitution of Pennsylvania. The single chamber expressed the will of the people in that there was no "upper house" to exert a conservative brake; furthermore, annual elections of representatives allowed for changes in popular sentiment to become immediately effective in government. Rather than a governor, there was an executive chosen by the assembly who presided over an executive council elected by the people. Franklin not only approved of the unicameral legislature, but objected to property qualifications for voters.

QUERIES AND REMARKS

Respecting Alterations in the Constitution of Pennsylvania

[The following "Queries and Remarks" are Franklin's marginal comments in reply to an article, "Hints for the Members of the Convention," published in the *Federal Gazette*, Nov. 3, 1789, when a revision of the Pennsylvania constitution was in view. Franklin's comments are printed in *roman type*, following extracts from the *Gazette* article which are printed in *italic type*.]

I. OF THE EXECUTIVE BRANCH.

"Your executive should consist of a single Person."

On this I would ask, Is he to have no council? How is he to be informed of the state and circumstances of the different counties, their wants, their abilities, their dispositions, and the characters of the principal people, respecting their integrity, capacities, and qualifications for offices? Does not the present construction of our executive provide well for these particulars? And, during the number of years it has existed, have its errors or failures in answering the end of its appointment been more or greater than might have been expected from a single person?

"But an individual is more easily watched and controlled than any greater number."

On this I would ask, Who is to watch and controul him? and by what means is he to be controuled? Will not those means, whatever they are, and in whatever body vested, be subject to the same inconveniencies of expence, delay, obstruction of good intentions, etc., which are objected to the present executive?

II. THE DURATION OF THE APPOINTMENT.

"This should be governed by the following principles, the independency of the magistrate, and the stability of his administration; neither of which can be secured but by putting both beyond the reach of every annual gust of folly and of faction."

On this it may be asked, Ought it not also to be put beyond the reach of every triennial, quinquennial, or septennial gust of folly and of faction, and, in short, beyond the reach of folly and of faction at any period whatever? Does not this reasoning aim at establishing a monarchy at least for life, like that of Poland? or to prevent the inconveniencies such as that kingdom is subject to in a new election on every decease, does it not point to an hereditary succession? Are the freemen of Pennsylvania convinced, from a view of the history of such governments, that it will be for their advantage to submit themselves to a government of such construction?

III. ON THE LEGISLATIVE BRANCH.

"A plural legislature is as necessary to good government as a single executive. It is not enough that your legislature should be numerous; it should also be divided.

Numbers alone are not a sufficient barrier against the impulses of passion, the combinations of interest, the intrigues of faction, the haste of folly, or the spirit of encroachment. One division should watch over and controul the other, supply its wants, correct its blunders, and cross its designs, should they be criminal or erroneous. Wisdom is the specific quality of the legislature, grows out of the number of the body, and is made up of the portions of sense and knowledge which each member brings to it."

On this it may be asked, May not the wisdom brought to the legislature by each member be as effectual a barrier against the impulses of passion, etc., when the members are united in one body, as when they are divided? If one part of the legislature may controul the operations of the other, may not the impulses of passion, the combinations of interest, the intrigues of faction, the haste of folly, or the spirit of encroachment in one of those bodies obstruct the good proposed by the other, and frustrate its advantages to the public? Have we not experienced in this colony, when a province under the government of the proprietors, the mischiefs of a second branch existing in the proprietary family, countenanced and aided by an aristocratic council? How many delays and what great expences were occasioned in carrying on the public business; and what a train of mischiefs, even to the preventing of the defence of the province during several years, when distressed by an Indian war, by the iniquitous demand that the proprietary property should be exempt from taxation! The wisdom of a few members in one single legislative body, may it not frequently stifle bad motions in their infancy, and so prevent their being adopted? whereas, if those wise men, in case of a double

legislature, should happen to be in that branch wherein
the motion did not arise, may it not, after being adopted
by the other, occasion lengthy disputes and contentions
between the two bodies, expensive to the public, obstructing the public business, and promoting factions
among the people, many tempers naturally adhering ob-
stinately to measures they have once publicly adopted?
Have we not seen, in one of our neighbouring states, a
bad measure, adopted by one branch of the legislature
for want of the assistance of some more intelligent members who had been packed into the other, occasion many
debates, conducted with much asperity, which could not
be settled but by an expensive general appeal to the
people? And have we not seen, in another neighbouring
state, a similar difference between the two branches
occasioning long debates and contentions, whereby the
state was prevented for many months enjoying the advantage of having senators in the Congress of the United
States? And has our present legislative in one assembly
committed any errors of importance, which they have
not remedied, or may not easily remedy; more easily,
probably, than if divided into two branches? And if
the wisdom brought by the members to the Assembly
is divided into two branches, may it not be too weak
in each to support a good measure, or obstruct a bad
one? The division of the legislature into two or three
branches in England, was it the product of wisdom, or
the effect of necessity, arising from the preëxisting preva-
lence of an odious feudal system? which government,
notwithstanding this division, is now become in fact an
absolute monarchy; since the King, by bribing the representatives with the people's money, carries, by his ministers, all the measures that please him; which is equiva-

lent to governing without a parliament, and renders the machine of government much more complex and expensive, and, from its being more complex, more easily put out of order.

Has not the famous political fable of the snake, with two heads and one body, some useful instruction contained in it? She was going to a brook to drink, and in her way was to pass thro' a hedge, a twig of which opposed her direct course; one head chose to go on the right side of the twig, the other on the left; so that time was spent in the contest, and, before the decision was completed, the poor snake died with thirst.

"Hence it is that the two branches should be elected by persons differently qualified; and in short, that, as far as possible, they should be made to represent different interests. Under this reasoning I would establish a legislature of two houses. The upper should represent the property; the lower the population of the state. The upper should be chosen by freemen possessing in lands and houses one thousand pounds; the lower by all such as had resided four years in the country, and paid taxes. The first should be chosen for four, the last for two years. They should in authority be coequal."

Several questions may arise upon this proposition. 1st. What is the proportion of freemen possessing lands and houses of one thousand pounds' value, compared to that of freemen whose possessions are inferior? Are they as one to ten? Are they even as one to twenty? I should doubt whether they are as one to fifty. If this minority is to chuse a body expressly to controul that which is to be chosen by the great majority of the freemen, what have this great majority done to forfeit so great a portion of their right in elections? Why is this power of controul, contrary to the spirit of all democracies, to be vested in a minority, instead of a majority? Then is it intended, or is it not, that the rich should have a vote in the choice of members for the lower house, while those of inferior property are deprived of the right of voting for members of the upper house? And why should the upper house, chosen by a minority, have equal power with the lower chosen by a majority? Is it supposed that wisdom is the necessary concomitant of riches, and that one man worth a thousand pounds must have as much wisdom as twenty who have each only 999; and why is property to be represented at all?

Suppose one of our Indian nations should now agree to form a civil society; each individual would bring into the stock of the society little more property than his gun and his blanket, for at present he has no other. We know that when one of them has attempted to keep a few swine, he has not been able to maintain a property in them, his neighbours thinking they have a right to kill and eat them whenever they want provision, it being one of their maxims that hunting is free for all; the accumulation therefore of property in such a society, and its security to individuals in every society, must be an effect of the protection afforded to it by the joint strength of the society, in the execution of its laws. Private property therefore is a creature of society, and is subject to the calls of that society, whenever its necessities shall require it, even to its last farthing; its contributions therefore to the public exigencies are not to be considered as conferring a benefit on the publick, entitling the contributors to the distinctions of honour and power, but as the return of an obligation previously received, or the payment of a just debt. The combinations of civil society are not like those of a set of merchants, who club their property in different proportions for building and freighting a ship, and may therefore have some right to vote in the disposition of the voyage in a greater or less degree according to their respective contributions; but the important ends of civil society, and the personal securities of life and liberty, these remain the same in every member of the society; and the poorest continues to have an equal claim to them with the most opulent, whatever difference time, chance, or industry may occasion in their circumstances. On these considerations, I am sorry to see the signs this paper I have been considering affords, of a disposition among some of our people to commence an aristocracy, by giving the rich a predominancy in government, a choice peculiar to themselves in one half the legislature to be proudly called the UPPER house, and the other branch, chosen by the majority of the people, degraded by the denomination of the LOWER; and giving to this upper house a permanency of four years, and but two to the lower. I hope, therefore, that our representatives in the convention will not hastily go into these innovations, but take the advice of the prophet, *"Stand in the old ways, view the ancient paths, consider them well, and be not among those that are given to change."*

II. IN DEFENSE OF AMERICA

Franklin's letters to the press in England prior to the Revolution show the different levels of address of which he was capable in defense of America. The first of these is a rollicking piece of sport in which Franklin put the enemy to rout by derision—one of the finest exercises of humor he ever published; it was a forerunner of generations of tall stories about nature to come from Americans and is worthy of a great tradition. (Except for this letter and the one immediately following it, all of the letters to the press printed below are not to be found in any edition of Franklin's writings. They were identified as Franklin's by the patient scholarship of Verner W. Crane and have been selected from the latter's volume, *Benjamin Franklin's Letters to the Press*, published in 1950 by the University of North Carolina Press.)

One of the Finest Spectacles in Nature
(Printed in the London *Public Advertiser*, May 22, 1765)
Sir,

In your paper of Wednesday last, an ingenious correspondent that calls himself THE SPECTATOR, and dates from Pimlico, under the guise of good will to the newswriters, whom he calls, an "useful body of men in this great city," has, in my opinion, artfully attempted to turn them & their works into ridicule, wherein if he could succeed, great injury might be done to the public as well as to those good people.

Supposing, sir, that the *"We hears"* they give us of this & t'other intended voyage or tour of this & t'other great personage, were mere inventions, yet they at least offer us an innocent amusement while we read, and useful matter of conversation when we are disposed to converse.

Englishmen, sir, are too apt to be silent when they have nothing to say; too apt to be sullen when they are silent; and, when they are sullen, to hang themselves. But, by these *We hears*, we are supplied with abundant

funds of discourse, we discuss the motives for such voyages, the probability of their being undertaken, and the
practicability of their execution. Here we display our
judgment in politics, our knowledge of the interests of
princes, and our skill in geography, and (if we have it)
show our dexterity moreover in argumentation. In the
mean time, the tedious hour is killed, we go home pleased
with the applauses we have received from others, or at
least with those we secretly give to ourselves. We sleep
soundly, & live on, to the comfort of our families. But,
sir, I beg leave to say, that all the articles of news that
seem improbable are not mere inventions. Some of them,
I can assure you on the faith of a traveller, are serious
truths. And here, quitting Mr. Spectator of Pimlico, give
me leave to instance the various numberless accounts the
newswriters have given us, with so much honest zeal for
the welfare of *poor old England,* of the establishing manufactures in the colonies to the prejudice of those of this
kingdom. It is objected by superficial readers, who yet
pretend to some knowledge of those countries, that such
establishments are not only improbable, but impossible,
for that their sheep have but little wooll, not in the whole
sufficient for a pair of stockings a year to each inhabitant;
and that, from the universal dearness of labour among
them, the working of iron and other materials, except
in some few coarse instances, is impracticable to any
advantage.

Dear Sir, do not let us suffer ourselves to be amused
with such groundless objections. The very tails of the
American sheep are so laden with wooll, that each has
a little car or waggon on four little wheels, to support
& keep it from trailing on the ground. Would they caulk
their ships, would they fill their beds, would they even

litter their horses with wooll, if it were not both plenty and cheap? And what signifies dearness of labour, when an English shilling passes for five and twenty? Their engaging 300 silk throwsters here in one week, for New York, was treated as a fable, because, forsooth, they have "no silk there to throw." Those who made this objection perhaps did not know that at the same time the agents from the King of Spain were at Quebec to contract for 1,000 pieces of cannon to be made there for the fortification of Mexico, and at N. York engaging the annual supply of woven floor-carpets for their West India houses, other agents from the Emperor of China were at Boston treating about an exchange of raw silk for wooll, to be carried in Chinese junks through the Straits of Magellan.

And yet all this is as certainly true, as the account said to be from Quebec, in all the papers of last week, that the inhabitants of Canada are making preparations for a cod and whale fishery this "summer in the upper lakes." Ignorant people may object that the upper lakes are fresh, and that cod and whale are salt water fish. But let them know, sir, that cod, like other fish when attacked by their enemies, fly into any water where they can be safest; that whales, when they have a mind to eat cod, pursue them wherever they fly; and that the grand leap of the whale in that chase up the Fall of Niagara is esteemed, by all who have seen it, as one of the finest spectacles in nature. Really, sir, the world is grown too incredulous. It is like the pendulum ever swinging from one extream to another. Formerly every thing printed was believed, because it was in print. Now things seem to be disbelieved for just the very same reason. Wise men wonder at the present growth of infidelity. They should have considered, when they taught people to doubt the authority of newspapers and the truth of predictions in almanacks, that the next step might be a disbelief in the well vouched accounts of ghosts, witches, and doubts even of the truths of the Creed!

Thus much I thought it necessary to say in favour of an honest set of writers, whose comfortable living depends on collecting & supplying the printers with news at the small price of sixpence an article, and who always show their regard to truth by contradicting in a subsequent article such as are wrong,—for another sixpence,—to the great satisfaction & improvement of us coffee-house students in history & politics, and the infinite advantage of all future Livies, Rapins, Robertsons, Humes, and McAulays, who may be sincerely inclined to furnish the world with that *rara avis,* a true history.

I am, sir, your humble servant,

A Traveller.

Indian Corn and Tea

(Printed in the London *Gazetteer,* JAN. 2, 1766)

VINDEX PATRIÆ, a writer in your paper, comforts himself, and the India Company, with the fancy, that the Americans, should they resolve to drink no more tea, can by no means keep that resolution, their Indian corn not affording "an agreeable, or easy digestible breakfast." Pray let me, an American, inform the gentleman, who seems ignorant of the matter, that Indian corn, take it for all in all, is one of the most agreeable and wholesome grains in the world; that its green leaves roasted are a

delicacy beyond expression; that samp, hominy, succa-
tash, and nokehock, made of it, are so many pleasing
varieties; and that johny or hoecake, hot from the fire,
is better than a Yorkshire muffin. But if Indian corn
were as disagreeable and indigestible as the Stamp Act,
does he imagine we can get nothing else for breakfast?—
Did he never hear that we have oatmeal in plenty, for
water gruel or burgoo; as good wheat, rye and barley
as the world affords, to make frumenty; or toast and ale;
that there is every where plenty of milk, butter and cheese;
that rice is one of our staple commodities; that for tea,
we have sage and bawm in our gardens, the young leaves
of the sweet white hickery or walnut, and, above all, the
buds of our pine, infinitely preferable to any tea from
the Indies; while the islands yield us plenty of coffee and
chocolate?—Let the gentleman do us the honour of a
visit in America, and I will engage to breakfast him every
day in the month with a fresh variety, without offering
him either tea or Indian corn.—As to the Americans using
no more of the former, I am not sure they will take such
a resolution; but if they do, I fancy they will not lightly
break it. I question whether the army proposed to be
sent among them, would oblige them to swallow a drop
more of tea than they chuse to swallow; for, as the proverb says, though one man may *lead* a horse to the water,
ten *can't make him drink*. Their resolutions have hitherto been pretty steadily kept. They resolved to wear no
more mourning;—and it is now totally out of fashion
with near two millions of people; and yet nobody sighs
for Norwich crapes, or any other of the expensive, flimsey,
rotten, black stuffs and cloths you used to send us for
that purpose, with the frippery gauses, loves, ribands,
gloves, etc., thereunto belonging.—They resolved last

spring to eat no more lamb; and not a joint of lamb has
since been seen on any of their tables, throughout a
country of 1500 miles extent, but the sweet little creatures
are all alive to this day, with the prettiest fleeces on their
backs imaginable. Mr. VINDEX's very civil letter will, I
dare say, be printed in all our provincial news-papers,
from Nova-Scotia to Georgia; and together with the other
kind, polite and humane epistles of your correspondents
PACIFICUS, TOM HINT, etc., etc. contribute not a little to
strengthen us in every resolution that may be of advantage, to *our* country at least, if not to *yours*.

Homespun.

One Word More about Indian Corn

(Printed in the London *Gazetteer,* JAN. 15, 1766)

To the Printer.

John Bull shews in nothing more his great veneration
for good eating, and how much he is always thinking of
his belly, than in his making it the constant topic of his
contempt for other nations, that *they do not eat so well
as himself.* The *roast beef of Old England* he is always
exulting in, as if no other country had beef to roast;—
reproaching, on every occasion, the Welsh with their
leeks and toasted cheese, the Irish with their potatoes,
and the Scotch with their oatmeal. And now that we
are a little out of favour with him, he has begun, by his
attorney VINDEX PATRIÆ, to examine our eating and drinking, in order, I apprehend, to fix some horrible scandal
of the same kind upon us poor Americans.

I did but say a word or two in favour of Indian corn,

which he had treated as "disagreable and indigestible," and this vindictive gentleman grows angry. "Let him tell the world, if he dares (says he) that the Americans prefer it to a place at their own tables." Ah, Sir, I see the dilemma you have prepared for me. If I should not *dare* to say that we do prefer it to a place at our tables, then you demonstrate that we must come to England for tea, or go without our breakfasts: and if I do *dare* say it, you fix upon me and my countrymen for ever, the indelible disgrace of being Indian corn-eaters.

I am afraid, Mr. Printer, that you will think this too trifling a dispute to deserve a place in your paper: but, pray, good Sir, consider, as you are yourself an Englishman, that we Americans, who are allowed even by Mr. Vindex to have some English blood in our veins, may think it a very serious thing to have the honour of our eating impeached in any particular whatsoever.

"Why doth he not deny the fact (says Vindex) that it is assigned to the slaves for their food? To proclaim the *wholesomeness* of this corn, without assigning a reason why white men give it to their slaves, when they can get other food, is only satirizing the good sense of their brethren in America." In truth I cannot deny the fact, though it should reflect ever so much on the *good sense* of my countrymen. I own we do give food made of Indian corn to our slaves, as well as eat it ourselves; not, as you suppose, because it is "*indigestible* and *unwholesome*"; but because it keeps them healthy, strong and hearty, and fit to go through all the labour we require of them. Our slaves, Sir, cost us money, and we buy them to make money by their labour. If they are sick, they are not only unprofitable, but expensive. Where

then was your *English good sense*, when you imagined
we gave our slaves our Indian corn because we knew it
to be *unwholesome?*

In short, this is only another of Mr. VINDEX's paradoxes,
in which he is a great dealer. The first endeavoured to
persuade us, that we were represented in the British
Parliament *virtually*, and by *fiction:*—Then that we were
really represented there, because the Manor of East Greenwich in Kent is represented there, and all the Americans
live in East Greenwich. And now he undertakes to prove
to us that taxes are the most profitable things in the
world to those that pay them; for that Scotland is grown
rich since the Union by paying English taxes. I wish he
would accommodate himself a little better to our dull
capacities. We Americans have a great many heavy taxes
of our own, to support our several governments and pay
off the enormous debt contracted by the war; we never
conceived ourselves the richer for paying taxes and are
willing to leave all new ones to those that like them.
At least, if we must with Scotland participate in your
taxes, let us likewise with Scotland participate in the
Union, and in all the privileges and advantages of commerce that accompanied it.

VINDEX, however, will never consent to this. He has
made us partakers in all the odium with which he thinks
fit to load Scotland:—"They resemble the Scots in sentiments, (says he) their religion is Scottish; their customs
and *laws* are Scottish; like the Scotch they Judaically
observe what *they call* the Sabbath, persecute old women
for witches, are intolerant to other sects, etc." But we
must not, like the Scots, be admitted into Parliament;
for that, he thinks, would increase "the Scotch interest

in England, which is equally hostile to the cause of liberty, and the cause of our church."

Pray, Sir, who informed you that our "*laws* are Scottish?" The same, I suppose, that told you our Indian corn is unwholesome. Indeed, Sir, your information is very imperfect. The common law of England is, I assure you, the common law of the colonies: and if the civil law is what you mean by the Scottish law, we have none of it but which is forced upon us by England, in its courts of Admiralty, depriving us of that inestimable part of the common law, trials by juries. And do you look upon keeping the *Sabbath,* as part of the Scottish law? "The Americans, like the Scots, (you say) observe what *they call* the Sabbath." Pray, Sir, you who are so zealous for your church (in abusing other Christians) what *do you call* it? and where the harm of their *observing* it? If you look into your prayer-book, or over your altars, you will find these words written, *Remember to keep holy the* SABBATH *Day*. This law, tho' it may be observed in Scotland, and has been *countenanced* by some of your statutes, is, Sir, originally one of *God's Commandments:* a body of laws still in force in America, tho' they may have become *obsolete* in *some other* countries.

Give me leave, Master John Bull, to remind you, that you are *related to all mankind;* and therefore it less becomes you than any body, to affront and abuse other nations. But you have mixed with your many virtues, a pride, a haughtiness, and an insolent contempt for all but yourself, that, I am afraid, will, if not abated, procure you one day or other a handsome drubbing. Besides your rudeness to foreigners, you are far from being civil even to your own family. The Welsh you have al-

ways despised for submitting to your government: But
why despise your own English, who conquered and settled Ireland for you; who conquered and settled America for you? Yet these you now think you may treat as
you please, because, forsooth, they are a *conquered*
people. Why despise the Scotch, who fight and die for
you all over the world? Remember, you courted Scotland for one hundred years, and would fain have had
your *wicked will* of her. She virtuously resisted all your
importunities, but at length kindly consented to become
your lawful wife. You then solemnly promised to *love,
cherish,* and *honour* her, as long as you both should live;
and yet you have ever since treated her with the utmost
contumely, which you now begin to extend to your common children. But, pray, when your enemies are uniting in
a *Family Compact* against you, can it be discreet in you
to kick up in your own house a *Family Quarrel?* And at
the very time you are inviting foreigners to settle on your
lands, and when you have more to settle than ever you
had before, is it prudent to suffer your lawyer, VINDEX,
to abuse those who have settled there already, because
they cannot yet speak "Plain English?"—It is my opinion,
Master Bull, that the Scotch and Irish, as well as the colonists, are capable of speaking much *plainer English* than
they have ever yet spoke, but which I hope they will
never be provoked to speak.

To be brief, Mr. VINDEX, I pass over your other accusations of the Americans, and of the Scotch, that we
"Persecute old women for witches, and are intolerant to
other sects," observing only, that we were wise enough
to leave off both those foolish tricks, long before Old
England made the act of toleration, or repealed the stat-
ute against witchcraft; so that even *you yourself* may

safely travel through all Scotland and the Colonies, without the least danger of being persecuted as a churchman, or taken (up) for a conjurer. And yet I own myself so far of an intolerant spirit, that though I thank you for the box-in-the-ear you have given TOM HINT, as being, what you justly call him, "a futile calumniator," I cannot but wish he would give you another—for the same reason.

One word more, however, about the Indian corn, which I began and must end with, even though I should hazard your remarking that it is certainly "indigestible," as it plainly appears to *stick in my stomach.* "Let him tell the world, if he dares, (you say) that the Americans prefer it to a place at their tables."—And, pray, if I should dare,—what then?—why then—"You would enter upon a discussion of its salubrity and pleasant taste."—Really?—Would you venture to write on the salubrity and *pleasant taste* of Indian corn, when you never in your life have tasted a *single grain* of it?—But why should that hinder you writing on it? Have you not written even on *politics?*

Yours,

Homespun.

George Grenville's Debit Account with Great Britain

(From the London *Public Advertiser,* Jan. 17, 1769)

To the Printer of the Public Advertiser.
Sir,

I thank you for the information you so readily gave at the request of the *Manufacturer of London,* relating to the agreement *going forward* in America not to use more

of our manufactures. The memorial you published in
your paper of the 13th inst. from the Merchants of Philadelphia, addressed to the Merchants and Manufacturers
of Great Britain, makes the point sufficiently clear. And
as, by what I can otherways learn, there is not the smallest probability of an accommodation while the present
A——n M——r* continues in that department, nor the
least prospect of his being removed; but on the contrary
all his rash ill-judged measures are to be approved, confirmed and pursued; and even the first projector of the
mischief, Mr. G.G.† is to be brought in again, to assist
in compleating it, I think 'tis time to state an account,
in order to form some kind of estimate what we are like
to be gainers or losers by quarreling with our best friends
and greatest customers. For a quarrel I see it will be!—
Depriving them of their privileges for no offence, and
sending soldiers to insult them, strengthens their determination to take no more of our goods, and makes that
determination more general. *This* will provoke us to
use them with more severity; *that* more alienates and
exasperates *them;* till, driven to despair, an open rupture
becomes unavoidable, and the cordial amity so much
to the advantage of both, which has hitherto subsisted
between the two countries, comes to be converted into
the most implacable mutual hatred, such as we see at
this day between the Spaniards and Portuguese, the Gen-
oese and the Corsicans, which arose originally from the
very same misconduct in the governing countries. By
this we are to lose a greatly growing trade, at present
worth five millions a year, which our enemies will gain

---

* [American Minister.]
† [George Grenville.]

sooner or later, and so to us make the difference double; and we are to turn three million of friends into so many mortal enemies, another double diminution of our comparative strength. And what is all this for? Is it that we may obtain *by force* much *less* than we might have had from them by *voluntary grant?*

And how comes it about? A wrong-headed, short-sighted financier imagined that he should make a great figure in opening his budget, and appear to have wonderful abilities, if he could shew how a new tax might be raised which none who heard him should either pay or feel. America was then no longer to *give;* but what we wanted was to be *taken* from her by our almighty power. The measure was found impracticable, and therefore soon dropt. An inconsiderate successor, from the same motives, renewed the attempt in another shape. Just or unjust, politic or impolitic, constitutional or unconstitutional, are with such statemen points entirely out of the question. The first disappointed and displaced projector harbours inveterate malice to the Americans for murdering his child. He and his scribblers are thence continually endeavouring to exasperate the nation against them, and urging every step that may provoke them to such acts as may justify the character he gives of them.—We are told indeed sometimes that the people of America would generally be quiet if it were not for their factious demagogues, and that the whole mischief is owing only to two or three restless spirits there; that the contest really is between Messrs. Otis, Cushing and Adams on the one part, and the whole people of England on the other. This is merely to countenance the proposition of sending for these men in order to hang them, which some seem to have much at heart; though from the blood of those three, probably would spring three hundred more. But in truth, the parties are G.G., L——d H., and the D. of B.,* on the one side, and on the other all our fellow-subjects in America. The people of England have no other concern in the dispute but that of being immense losers by it's being started and persisted in, or infinite gainers by it's being dropt.

I talked of stating in account:—For distinctness sake, I will state two:—the first of what our stockholders *have lost already,* the second of what the nation will probably lose; in doing which I shall not pretend to mathematical precision, for the premises will scarce admit of it, they being partly assumed upon probable conjecture. I only put them into the Form of Accounts for the sake of more distinctly viewing the Subject.

Dr. The Right Hon. G.G. Esq; and Co. in Account with the Stockholders of Great Britain.

To the Loss of Five per Cent. on their
Capital Stock of 145 Millions by
the Fall occasioned by the late   £
American Measure, amounting to   7,250,000

Supra .... *Cr.*

By the Stockholders' Share of the neat
Duties received in America, in Al-
leviation of British Taxes........   3,500

Balance due from the said G.G. and
Co.   7,246,500
                                7,250,000

In this I have stated the loss of five per cent. as so much loss to the stockholders only; and this already incurred. What their future loss will be, if the rupture

---

* [George Grenville, Lord Hillsborough, and the Duke of Bedford.]

hitherto only apprehended shall take place, is impossible to estimate, as no one can foresee how low the stocks will then fall. If it should be, as probably it may be, thirty per cent more, their loss will exceed FORTY MIL-LIONS. But it will besides be accompanied with a pro-portionate loss to the nation by the fall of public credit, since the state must of course give so much more for money wanted.

Now to form my other account, I will make several immediate suppositions. First, I will suppose no other nation shall take advantage of our embroil in America, to fall upon us while we are subduing her. Secondly, that a war of ten years, in which twenty-five thousand of land forces only are to be kept up and employed, with twenty frigates, and five thousand seamen, shall be sufficient to finish the business by reducing the whole fifteen colonies; though it cost us five years in the last war to reduce but one of them, with the help of all the rest, and double the number of men. Thirdly, that after they are reduced, they shall be in the most perfect good-humour with us, retain no resentment of the injuries we have done them, be as fond of us, and of our fashions and manufactures as ever they were, and that it will be therefore quite unnecessary to keep up an equal or indeed any army to continue and secure the subjection we have reduced them to. The account will then stand thus:

Dr. The Hon. G. G. Esq; and Co. in Account with Great-Britain.

For the Transport Service in carry-
    ing over 25,000 men, with the
    Stores, etc., at the Rate of £10   £
    per Man, including all Charges   250,000

The above to be repeated three
Times more in the ten Years to
keep up the Number; an Army
in actual Service always require-
ing a Number of Recruits equal
to the whole in every three Years   750,000
For the Recruiting Service and
Bounty Money of 100,000 Men
to be spent in this War.......   500,000
For the Pay, Cloathing and Subsistence of 25,000 Men ten
Years at £20 per Man, including
also Arms, Ammunition, etc....   5,000,000
For the Sea Service, 5000 Men,
their Pay, Subsistence, Wear and
Tear of Ships, etc. etc. etc. at
£200,000 per Ann.   2,000,000
For the Loss of our Trade with
those Countries during the ten
Years, at 5,000,000 per Ann....   50,000,000
For weakening the British Em-
pire by all the Damage done its
Subjects, in obstructing or de-
stroying their Improvements,
Buildings, Ships, Trade with
Foreigners, etc. and throwing all
the Commerce they used to carry
on for us into the Hands of our
Rivals or Enemies...........   50,000,000
For the Blood spilt on both Sides,
we charge   000
                                      ─────────
                                    108,500,000
                                      ─────────

Supra .... *Cr.*
By the Honour and Glory of having made Slaves of Three Millions of Freeman.............   ___ooo___

Thus stand the accounts; and yet this same G.G. the
root of the whole evil, sets up for an economist.

I am, SIR,

Your humble Servant,

Another Manufacturer of London.

(The optimism of reconciliation that marked the 1760s
gave way to a bitterness in the '70s, as affairs did not
mend but became worse. Franklin's letters became
sharper and the editors found it necessary to tone them
down. One editor, he observed, "has drawn the teeth
and pared the nails of my paper so that it can neither
scratch nor bite"; in print it could only "paw and mum-
ble." But two letters to the press on the eve of the Revolution bit deeply and they indicate the intensity of Franklin's feelings in the face of British military arrogance.
The occasion was a meeting with General Clarke at the
house of Sir John Pringle; the general, Franklin wrote,
"had the folly to say in my hearing . . . that with a thousand British grenadiers, he would undertake to go from
one end of America to the other, and geld all the males,
partly by force and partly by a little coaxing. It is plain
he took us for a species of animals little superior to brutes.
The Parliament too believed the stories of another foolish
general, I forget his name, that the Yankeys never *felt
bold*. Yankee was understood to be a sort of Yahoo, and
the Parliament did not think the petitions of such creatures were fit to be received and read in so wise an
assembly.")

A Proposal to Quiet the Disturbances in America
(From the London *Public Advertiser*, April 15, 1774)

To Lord North.
My Lord,

All your small politicians who are very numerous in
the English nation, from the patriotic barber to the patriotic peer, when big with their schemes for the good of
poor old England, imagine they have a right to give
advice to the minister, and condemn administration if
they do not adopt their plan. I, my Lord, who have no
mean opinion of my abilities, . . . have a proposal to make
to your Lordship, which I flatter myself will be approved
by the ministry, and if carried into execution, will quiet
all the disturbances in America, procure a decent revenue
from our colonies, make our royal master (at least there)
a King *de facto,* as well as *de jure;* and finally, as it may
be managed, procure a round sum towards discharging
the national debt.

My scheme is, without delay to introduce into North
America a government absolutely and entirely military.
The opposition which some people suspect would be
made by the colonies, is a mere bugbear. The sight of
a few regiments of bold Britons, appearing with ensigns
displayed, and in all the pomp of war, a specimen of
which may be seen every summer at the Grand Review
on Wimbledon Common, with that great Commander
G——l G——e* at their head, accompanied with a detach-
ment from the artillery, and half a dozen short sixes, would
so intimidate the Americans, that the general might march
through the whole continent of North America, and would
have little else to do but to accept of the submission of
the several towns as he passed. . . .

---

* [General Gage.]

Those who served in America the last war, know that
the colonists are a dastardly set of poltroons; and though
they are descended from British ancestors, they are de-
generated to such a degree that one born in Britain is
equal to twenty Americans. The Yankey Doodles have
a phrase when they are not in a humour for fighting,
which is become proverbial, *I don't feel bould to-day.*
When they make this declaration, there is no prevailing
on them to attack the enemy or defend themselves. If
contrary to expectation they should attempt an opposition, procure intelligence when it happens not to be their
fighting day, attack them and they will fly like sheep
pursued by a wolf.

When all North America have thus bent their neck to
the yoke designed for them, . . . [let] all the colonists be
enrolled in the militia, subject of course to martial law.
. . . Let no other courts be allowed through the whole
continent but courts martial. An inhabitant who dis-
obeys an order may by a court martial be sentenced to
receive from one hundred to a thousand lashes in a frosty
morning, according to the nature of his offence. Where
punishment is thus secure, this advantage will accrue,
that there will not be the same necessity of hanging up
so many poor devils as in this free country; by which
means the service of many an able man is lost to the community. I humbly propose that the general and commander in chief be vested with the power, and called
by the name of the King's Viceroy of all North America.
This will serve to impress the Americans with greater
respect for the first magistrate, and have a tendency to
secure their submission. All orders issuing from this supreme authority to have the force of laws. After this
happy change of government, how easy to collect what
taxes you please in North America. When the colonists

are drained of their last shilling, suppose they should be sold to the best bidder. As they lie convenient for France or Spain, it may be reasonably expected one of those little powers would be a purchaser. I think Spain is to be preferred, as their power hath more of the ready than France. I will venture a conjecture that the ministry might get at least two millions for the soil, and the people upon it. With such a sum what glorious things might he not atchieve! Suppose it should be applied towards the payment of one hundredth part of the national debt, it would give him an opportunity of drawing down upon him the blessing of the poor by making him to take off the halfpenny duty on porter. Considering the probable stability of the present ministry, this honour may be reserved for your Lordship.

My Lord, excuse the crudity of these indigested hints, which your wisdom is so capable of improving; and believe me, with infinite respect,

Your Lordship's
Most obedient
Humble Servant,
A Friend to Military Government.
Smyrna Coffee-House, April 5.

The Most Feasible Method of Humbling our Rebellious Vassals of North America
(From the London *Public Advertiser*, May 21, 1774)

To the Printer of the Public Advertiser.
Sir,

Permit me, thro' the channel of your paper, to convey to the Premier, by him to be laid before his mercenaries, our constituents, my own opinion, and that of many of

my brethren, freeholders of this imperial kingdom, of
the most feasible method of humbling our rebellious vas-
sals of North America. As we have declared by our representatives that we are the supreme lords of their persons and property, and their occupying our territory at
such a remote distance without a proper controul from
us, except at a very great expence, encourages a muti-
nous disposition, and may, if not timely prevented, dis-
pose them in perhaps less than a century to deny our
authority, slip their necks out of the collar, and from being
slaves set up for masters, more especially when it is considered that they are a robust, hardy people, encourage
early marriages, and their women being amazingly pro-
lific, they must of consequence in 100 years be very numerous, and of course be able to set us at defiance. Effectually to prevent which, as we have an undoubted right
to do, it is humbly proposed, and we do hereby give it
as part of our instructions to our representatives, that a
bill be brought in and passed, and orders immediately
transmitted to G——l G——e, our Commander in Chief in
North America, in consequence of it, that all the males
there be c—st—ed. He may make a progress thro' the
several towns of North America at the head of five bat-
talions, which we hear our experienced generals, who
have been consulted, think sufficient to subdue America
if they were in open rebellion; for who can resist the
intrepid sons of Britain, the terror of France and Spain,
and the conquerors of America in Germany. Let a company of sow-gelders, consisting of 100 men, accompany
the army. On their arrival at any town or village, let orders be given that on the blowing of the horn all the
males be assembled in the market place. If the corps
are men of skill and ability in their profession, they will

make great dispatch, and retard but very little the progress of the army. There may be a clause in the bill to
be left at the discretion of the general, whose powers
ought to be very extensive, that the most notorious offenders, such as Hancock, Adams, etc., who have been
the ringleaders in the rebellion of our servants, should
be shaved quite close. But that none of the offenders
may escape in the town of Boston, let all the males there
suffer the latter operation, as it will be conformable to
the modern maxim that is now generally adopted by our
worthy constituents, that it is better that ten innocent
persons should suffer than one guilty should escape. It
is true, blood will be shed, but probably not many lives
lost. Bleeding to a certain degree is salutary. The English, whose humanity is celebrated by all the world, but
particularly by themselves, do not desire the death of the
delinquent, but his reformation.

The advantages arising from this scheme being carried
into execution are obvious. In the course of fifty years
it is probable we shall not have one rebellious subject
in North America. This will be laying the axe to the root
of the tree. In the mean time a considerable expence may
be saved to the managers of the opera, and our nobility
and gentry be entertained at a cheaper rate by the fine
voices of our own c—st—i, and the specie remain in the
kingdom, which now, to an enormous amount, is carried
every year to Italy. It might likewise be of service to
our Levant trade, as we could supply the Grand Signor's
seraglio, and the harams of the grandees of the Turkish
dominions with cargos of eunuchs, as also with handsome
women, for which America is as famous as Circassia. I
could enumerate many other advantages. I shall mention
but one. It would effectually put a stop to the emigra-

tions from this country now grown so very fashionable.

No doubt you will esteem it expedient that this useful project shall have an early insertion, that no time may be lost in carrying it into execution.

I am, Mr. Printer,

(For myself and in Behalf of a Number of
independent Freeholders of Great Britain)

Your humble Servant,

A Freeholder of Old Sarum.

III. Appearance in Parliament

In addition to his publications in the London press, and his private conversations with gentlemen of influence, Franklin advocated the American cause in Parliament itself. On February 3, 1766, he was ordered to present himself at the House of Commons, sitting as a "committee of the whole," as one of the many witnesses to testify for the repeal of the Stamp Act. The merchants and their representatives were anxious for repeal and Franklin wrote out a kind of rehearsal of their probable questions and his answers; the adversaries of repeal would be met on their own grounds. On February 13, "Benjamin Franklin, having passed through his examination, was excepted from farther attendance," and repeal was assured. Two years later, Franklin had the questions and answers printed as a pamphlet; portions appeared in various newspapers and magazines and the whole piece was many times reprinted.

The following excerpts will give the reader some idea of Franklin's assurance that the cause he pleaded was just and his conviction that committees of inquiry should be

given straight answers without reservation. He replied
to each question with sincerity, and as one member of
Parliament after the other interrogated him, he patiently
set forth the American position as he saw it. Some of
the questioners, especially those representing the merchants who saw a loss of American trade in the Stamp Act,
were friendly but others, of the administration, were not.
Both those questions which had been rehearsed before
the hearing, and those others which were unexpected,
were turned by Franklin to his own and his country's
advantage. As Franklin's able replies to friend and foe
continued, the "examination" became a ringing demonstration in favor of American rights. When it was over,
Americans knew that they were represented by a man
whose stature was proportional to the justice of their
claims. All the world learned that the same might which
characterized the Philadelphia sage in the investigation
of nature had been applied in the affairs of man.

*The Examination of Doctor Benjamin Franklin, etc. in the
British House of Commons, Relative to the Repeal of
the American Stamp Act, in 1766*

Q. What is your name, and place of abode?

A. Franklin, of Philadelphia.

Q. Do the Americans pay any considerable taxes among
themselves?

A. Certainly many, and very heavy taxes.

Q. What are the present taxes in Pennsylvania, laid by
the laws of the colony?

A. There are taxes on all estates real and personal, a
poll tax, a tax on all offices, professions, trades and busi-
nesses, according to their profits; an excise on all wine,

rum, and other spirits; and a duty of ten pounds per head
on all Negroes imported, with some other duties.

Q. For what purposes are those taxes laid?

A. For the support of the civil and military establishments of the country, and to discharge the heavy debt
contracted in the last war.

Q. How long are those taxes to continue?

A. Those for discharging the debt are to continue till
1772, and longer, if the debt should not be then all discharged. The others must always continue.

. . . .

Q. Do you think it right that America should be protected by this country and pay no part of the expence?

A. That is not the case. The Colonies raised, cloathed
and payed, during the last war, near 25000 men, and
spent many millions.

Q. Were you not reimbursed by parliament?

A. We were only reimbursed what, in your opinion, we
had advanced beyond our proportion, or beyond what
might reasonably be expected from us; and it was a very
small part of what we spent. Pennsylvania, in particular,
disbursed about 500,000 pounds, and the reimbursements,
in the whole, did not exceed 60,000 pounds.

. . . .

Q. Do not you think the people of America would submit to pay the stamp duty, if it was moderated?

A. No, never, unless compelled by force of arms.

. . . .

Q. What was the temper of America towards Great
Britain before the year 1763?

A. The best in the world. They submitted willingly
to the government of the Crown, and paid, in all their
courts, obedience to acts of parliament. Numerous as the

people are in the several provinces, they cost you nothing in forts, citadels, garrisons, or armies, to keep them in subjection. They were governed by this country at the expence only of a little pen, ink and paper. They were lead by a thread. They had not only a respect, but an affection for Great-Britain; for its laws, its customs and manners, and even a fondness for its fashions, that greatly increased the commerce. Natives of Britain were always treated with particular regard; to be an Old-England man was, of itself, a character of some respect, and gave a kind of rank among us.

Q. And what is their temper now?

A. O, very much altered.

Q. Did you ever hear the authority of parliament to make laws for America questioned till lately?

A. The authority of parliament was allowed to be valid in all laws, except such as should lay internal taxes. It was never disputed in laying duties to regulate commerce.

Q. In what proportion hath population increased in America?

A. I think the inhabitants of all the provinces together, taken at a medium, double in about 25 years. But their demand for British manufactures increases much faster, as the consumption is not merely in proportion to their numbers, but grows with the growing abilities of the same numbers to pay for them. In 1723, the whole importation from Britain to Pennsylvania was about 15,000 pounds sterling; it is now near half a million.

Q. In what light did the people of America use to consider the parliament of Great-Britain?

A. They considered the parliament as the great bulwark and security of their liberties and privileges, and always spoke of it with the utmost respect and veneration. Arbitrary ministers, they thought, might possibly, at times, attempt to oppress them; but they relied on it, that the parliament, on application, would always give redress. They remembered, with gratitude, a strong instance of this, when a bill was brought into parliament, with a clause, to make royal instructions laws in the colonies, which the House of Commons would not pass, and it was thrown out.

Q. And have they not still the same respect for parliament?

A. No, it is greatly lessened.

Q. To what cause is that owing?

A. To a concurrence of causes; the restraints lately laid on their trade, by which the bringing of foreign gold and silver into the Colonies was prevented; the prohibition of making paper money among themselves; and then demanding a new and heavy tax by stamps; taking away, at the same time, trials by juries, and refusing to receive and hear their humble petitions.

Q. Don't you think they would submit to the stamp-act, if it was modified, the obnoxious parts taken out, and the duty reduced to some particulars, of small moment?

A. No; they will never submit to it.

. . . .

Q. What is your opinion of a future tax, imposed on the same principle with that of the stamp-act? How would the Americans receive it?

A. Just as they do this. They would not pay it.

Q. Have not you heard the resolutions of this House, and of the House of Lords, asserting the right of parliament relating to America, including a power to tax the people there?

A. Yes, I have heard of such resolutions.

Q. What will be the opinion of the Americans on those resolutions?

A. They will think them unconstitutional and unjust.

. . . .

Q. If the stamp act should be repealed, would not the Americans think they could oblige the parliament to repeal every external tax-law now in force?

A. It is hard to answer questions of what people at such a distance will think.

Q. But what do you imagine they will think were the motives of repealing the act?

A. I suppose they will think that it was repealed from a conviction of its inexpediency; and they will rely upon it, that while the same inexpediency subsists, you will never attempt to make such another.

. . . .

Q. Before there was any thought of the stamp act, did they wish for a representation in parliament?

A. No.

Q. Don't you know, that there is, in the Pennsylvania charter, an express reservation of the right of parliament to lay taxes there?

A. I know there is a clause in the charter, by which the King grants, that he will levy no taxes on the inhabitants, unless it be with the consent of the assembly, or by act of parliament.

Q. How, then, could the assembly of Pennsylvania assert, that laying a tax on them by the stamp act was an infringement of their rights?

A. They understand it thus; by the same charter, and otherwise, they are entitled to all the privileges and liberties of Englishmen; they find in the great charters, and the petition and declaration of rights, that one of the privileges of English subjects is, that they are not to be taxed but by their common consent; they have therefore relied upon it, from the first settlement of the province, that the parliament never would, nor could, by colour of that clause in the charter, assume a right of taxing them, till it had qualified itself to exercise such right, by admitting representatives from the people to be taxed, who ought to make a part of that common consent.

Q. Are there any words in the charter that justify that construction?

A. "The common rights of Englishmen," as declared by Magna Charta, and the petition of right, all justify it.

Q. Does the distinction between internal and external taxes exist in the words of the charter?

A. No, I believe not.

Q. Then, may they not, by the same interpretation, object to the parliament's right of external taxation?

A. They never have hitherto. Many arguments have been lately used here to shew them, that there is no difference, and that, if you have no right to tax them internally, you have none to tax them externally, or make any other law to bind them. At present they do not reason so; but in time they may possibly be convinced by these arguments.

. . . .

Q. Is not the post-office rate an internal tax laid by act of parliament?

A. I have answered that.

Q. Are all parts of the Colonies equally able to pay taxes?

A. No, certainly; the frontier parts, which have been ravaged by the enemy, are greatly disabled by that means; and therefore, in such cases, are usually favoured in our tax laws.

Q. Can we, at this distance, be competent judges of what favours are necessary?

A. The parliament have supposed it, by claiming a right to make tax-laws for America; I think it impossible.

. . . .

Q. If the stamp act should be repealed, would it induce the assemblies of America to acknowledge the rights of parliament to tax them, and would they erase their resolutions?

A. No, never.

Q. Are there no means of obliging them to erase those resolutions?

A. None that I know of; they will never do it, unless compelled by force of arms.

Q. Is there a power on earth that can force them to erase them?

A. No power, how great soever, can force men to change their opinions.

. . . .

Q. What used to be the pride of the Americans?

A. To indulge in the fashions and manufactures of Great Britain.

Q. What is now their pride?

A. To wear their old cloaths over again, till they can make new ones.

withdrew.

IV. COMPROMISE

A trait Americans have always admired is an ability to see the best side of things, which is closely allied to that virtue which enables a leader to submit to the will of his group on matters of detail without compromising fundamental principles. Franklin failed to have his cherished ideas of a single-chambered legislature and a plural executive become a part of the Constitution of the United States. But that Constitution was a good one, a serviceable working pattern for a free America, and it permitted of amendment. America, he wrote to Jonathan Shipley in 1786, was on "the right road of improvement, for we are making experiments. I do not oppose all that seem wrong, for the multitude are more effectually set right by experience, than kept from going wrong by reasoning with them. And I think we are daily more and more enlightened; so that I have no doubt of our obtaining in a few years as much public felicity as good government is capable of affording." In this spirit, we may understand the speech he wrote for delivery on the final day of the Constitutional Convention, after the secretary had read the engrossed document. At the conclusion of his speech, he moved that the Constitution be signed as: "Done in Convention by the unanimous consent of the states present"—a motion put into Franklin's hands, as recorded by Madison, "that it might have a better chance of success."

Speech on the Final Day of the Constitutional Convention, Moving the Unanimous Acceptance of the Constitution by the States
(Delivered September 17, 1787)

Mr. President: I confess that I do not entirely approve of this Constitution at present; but, sir, I am not sure I shall never approve it; for, having lived long, I have experienced many instances of being obliged, by better information or fuller consideration, to change my opinions even on important subjects, which I once thought right, but found to be otherwise. It is therefore that, the older I grow, the more apt I am to doubt my own judgment of others. Most men, indeed, as well as most sects in religion, think themselves in possession of all truth. . . . But though many private persons think almost as highly of their own infallibility as that of their sect, few express it so naturally as a certain French lady, who, in a little dispute with her sister, said: "But I meet with nobody but myself that is always in the right." "*Je ne trouve que moi qui aie toujours raison.*"

In these sentiments, sir, I agree to this Constitution, with all its faults—if they are such; because I think a general government necessary for us, and there is no *form* of government but what may be a blessing to the people, if well administered; and I believe, farther, that this is likely to be well administered for a course of years, and can only end in despotism, as other forms have done before it, when the people shall become so corrupted as to need despotic government, being incapable of any other. I doubt, too, whether any other convention we can obtain, may be able to make a better Constitution; for, when you assemble a number of men, to have the advantage of their joint wisdom, you inevitably assemble with those men all their prejudices, their passions, their errors of opinion, their local interests, and their selfish views. From such an assembly can a *perfect* production be expected? It therefore astonishes me, sir, to find this system approaching so near to perfection as it does; and I think it will astonish our enemies, who are waiting with confidence to hear that our counsils are confounded like those of the builders of Babel, and that our States are on the point of separation, only to meet hereafter for the purpose of cutting one another's throats. Thus

I consent, sir, to this Constitution, because I expect no better, and because I am not sure that it is not the best. The opinions I have had of its *errors* I sacrifice to the public good. I have never whispered a syllable of them abroad. Within these walls they were born, and here they shall die. If every one of us, in returning to our constituents, were to report the objections he has had to it, and endeavour to gain partisans in support of them, we might prevent its being generally received, and thereby lose all the salutary effects and great advantages resulting naturally in our favor among foreign nations, as well as among ourselves, from our real or apparent unanimity. Much of the strength and efficiency of any government in procuring and securing happiness to the people, depends on *opinion*, on the general opinion of the goodness of that government, as well as of the wisdom and integrity of its governors. I hope, therefore, for our own sakes, as a part of the people, and for the sake of our posterity, that we shall act heartily and unanimously in recommending this Constitution, wherever our influence may extend, and turn our future thoughts and endeavours to the means of having it *well administered.*

On the whole, sir, I cannot help expressing a wish, that every member of the Convention who may still have objections to it, would with me on this occasion doubt a little of his own infallibility, and, to make *manifest* our *unanimity*, put his name to this instrument.

V. FREEDOM OF SPEECH AND PRESS

At the age of sixteen, Franklin wrote an anonymous article which he slipped under the door of his brother's printing shop—the first of the "Dogood Papers," marking the beginning of Franklin's career as a journalist. One of these communications (July 1722) from "Mrs. Silence Dogood," as Franklin called himself, was devoted to "freedom of thought" and "liberty of speech"; it took the form of an "abstract from the London journal" which Mrs. Dogood said she preferred "to any thing of my own." Whether from an "abstract" or an original composition, the principles expressed were held by Franklin for the remainder of his life.

Silence Dogood to the Author of the New-England Courant

Without freedom of thought, there can be no such thing as wisdom; and no such thing as publick liberty, without freedom of speech; which is the right of every man, as far as by it, he does not hurt or controul the right of another: and this is the only check it ought to suffer, and the only bounds it ought to know.

This sacred privilege is so essential to free governments that the security of property and the freedom of speech always go together; and in those wretched countries where a man cannot call his tongue his own, he can scarce call any thing else his own. Whoever would overthrow the liberty of a nation must begin by subduing the freeness of speech; a thing terrible to publick traytors. . . .

That men ought to speak well of their governours is true, while their governours deserve to be well spoken of; but to do publick mischief without hearing of it, is only the prerogative and felicity of tyranny. A free people will be shewing that they are so by their freedom of speech.

The administration of government is nothing else but the attendance of the trustees of the people upon the interest and affairs of the people. And as it is the part and business of the people, for whose sake alone all publick matters are, or ought to be transacted, to see whether they be well or ill transacted; so it is the interest, and ought to be the ambition, of all honest magistrates to have their deeds openly examined, and publickly scanned: only the wicked governours of men dread what is said of them. . . .

Freedom of speech is ever the symptom, as well as the effect of a good government. In old Rome, all was left to the judgment and pleasure of the people, who examined the publick proceedings with such discretion, & censured those who administred them with such equity and mildness, that in the space of three hundred years, not five publick ministers suffered unjustly. Indeed whenever the commons proceeded to violence, the great ones had been the agressors.

Guilt, only, dreads liberty of speech, which drags it out of its lurking holes, and exposes its deformity and horrour to day-light. Horatius, Valerius, Cincinnatus, and other vertuous and undesigning magistrates of the Roman commonwealth, had nothing to fear from liberty of speech. Their virtuous administration, the more it was examined, the more it brightned and gained by enquiry. . . .

But things afterwards took another turn. Rome with the loss of its liberty, lost also its freedom of speech; then men's words began to be feared and watched; and then first began the poysonous race of informers banished indeed under the righteous administration of Titus, Narva, Trajan, Aurelius, etc. but encouraged and enriched under the vile ministry of Sejanus, Tigillinus, Pallas, and Cleander: *Queri libet, quod in secreta nostra non inquirant principes, nisi quos odimus,* says Pliny to Trajan.

The best princes have ever encouraged and promoted freedom of speech; they know that upright measures would defend themselves, and that all upright men would defend them. Tacitus, speaking of the reign of some of the princes abovementioned, says with extasy, *Rara temporum felicitate, ubi sentire quæ velis, & quæ sentias dicere licet:* a blessed time when you might think what you would, and speak what you thought.

I doubt not but old Spencer and his son, who were the chief ministers and betrayers of Edward the Second, would have been very glad to have stopped the mouths of all the honest men in England. They dreaded to be called traytors, because they were traytors. And I dare say, Queen Elizabeth's Walsingham, who deserved no reproaches, feared none. Misrepresentation of publick measures is easily overthrown, by representing publick measures truly; when they are honest, they ought to be publickly known, that they may be publickly commended; but if they are knavish or pernicious, they ought to be publickly detested.

[On June 10, 1731, Franklin published in his *Pennsylvania Gazette* a masterly defense of the freedom of the printer to print anything of worth, subject only to the restriction that nothing should issue from the press that might "countenance vice, or promote immorality." This "Apology for Printers" was based on the fundamental postulate that men hold differing opinions and that, therefore, the printer is obliged to give a hearing to each, to allow truth to combat error in public.]

An Apology For Printers

Being frequently censured and condemned by different persons for printing things which they say ought not to be printed, I have sometimes thought it might be necessary to make a standing apology for my self, and publish it once a year, to be read upon all occasions of that nature.

Much business has hitherto hindered the execution of this design; but having very lately given extraordinary offence by printing an advertisement with a certain *N. B.* at the end of it, I find an apology more particularly requisite at this juncture, tho' it happens when I have not yet leisure to write such a thing in the proper form, and can only in a loose manner throw those considerations together which should have been the substance of it.

I request all who are angry with me on the account of printing things they don't like, calmly to consider these following particulars.

1. That the opinions of men are almost as various as their faces; an observation general enough to become a common proverb, *So many men, so many minds.*

2. That the business of printing has chiefly to do with men's opinions; most things that are printed tending to promote some, or oppose others.

3. That hence arises the peculiar unhappiness of that business, which other callings are no way liable to; they who follow printing being scarce able to do any thing in their way of getting a living, which shall not probably give offence to some, and perhaps to many; whereas the smith, the shoemaker, the carpenter, or the man of any other trade, may work indifferently for people of all persuasions, without offending any of them: and the merchant may buy and sell with Jews, Turks, hereticks and infidels of all sorts, and get money by every one of them, without giving offence to the most orthodox, of any sort; or suffering the least censure or ill will on the account from any man whatever.

4. That it is as unreasonable in any one man or set of men to expect to be pleased with every thing that is printed, as to think that nobody ought to be pleased but themselves.

5. Printers are educated in the belief, that when men differ in opinion, both sides ought equally to have the advantage of being heard by the publick; and that when truth and error have fair play, the former is always an overmatch for the latter. Hence they chearfully serve all contending writers that pay them well, without regarding on which side they are of the question in dispute.

6. Being thus continually employed in serving both parties, printers naturally acquire a vast unconcernedness as to the right or wrong opinions contained in what they print, regarding it only as the matter of their daily labour. They print things full of spleen and animosity, with the utmost calmness and indifference, and without the least ill will to the persons reflected on, who nevertheless unjustly think the printer as much their enemy as the author, and join both together in their resentment.

7. That it is unreasonable to imagine printers approve of every thing they print, and to censure them on any particular thing accordingly, since in the way of their business they print such great variety of things opposite and contradictory. It is likewise as unreasonable what some assert, "That printers ought not to print any thing but what they approve"; since if all of that business should make such a resolution, and abide by it, an end would thereby be put to free writing, and the world would afterwards have nothing to read but what happened to be the opinions of printers.

8. That if all printers were determined not to print any thing till they were sure it would offend no body, there would be very little printed.

9. That if they sometimes print vicious or silly things not worth reading, it may not be because they approve such things themselves, but because the people are so viciously and corruptly educated that good things are not

encouraged. I have known a very numerous impression
of Robin Hood's Songs go off in this province at 2s. per
book, in less than a twelvemonth, when a small quantity
of David's Psalms (an excellent version) have lain upon
my hands above twice the time.

10. That notwithstanding what might be urged in behalf of a man's being allowed to do in the way of his business whatever he is paid for, yet printers do continually
discourage the printing of great numbers of bad things,
and stifle them in the birth. I myself have constantly
refused to print anything that might countenance vice,
or promote immorality, tho' by complying in such cases
with the corrupt taste of the majority I might have got
much money. I have also always refused to print such
things as might do real injury to any person, how much
soever I have been solicited, and tempted with offers of
great pay, and how much soever I have by refusing got
the ill will of those who would have employed me. I have
hitherto fallen under the resentment of large bodies of
men, for refusing absolutely to print any of their party or
personal reflections. In this manner I have made myself
many enemies, and the constant fatigue of denying is almost insupportable. But the publick being unacquainted
with all this, whenever the poor printer happens either
through ignorance or much persuasion to do any thing
that is generally thought worthy of blame, he meets with
no more friendship or favour on the above account, than
if there were no merit in't at all. Thus, as Waller says,

> Poets lose half the praise they would have got
> Were it but known what they discreetly blot,

yet are censured for every bad line found in their works
with the utmost severity.

I come now to the particular case of the *N. B.* above mentioned, about which there has been more clamour against me, than ever before on any other account.—In the hurry of other business an advertisement was brought to me to be printed; it signified that such a ship lying at such a wharff, would sail for Barbadoes in such a time, and that freighters and passengers might agree with the captain at such a place; so far is what's common. But at the bottom this odd thing was added, "*N. B.* No Sea Hens nor Black Gowns will be admitted on any terms." I printed it, and received my money; and the advertisement was stuck up round the town as usual. I had not so much curiosity at that time as to enquire the meaning of it, nor did I in the least imagine it would give so much offence. Several good men are very angry with me on this occasion; they are pleased to say I have too much sense to do such things ignorantly; that if they were printers they would not have done such a thing on any consideration; that it could proceed from nothing but my abundant malice against religion and the clergy. They therefore declare they will not take any more of my papers, nor have any farther dealings with me, but will hinder me of all the custom they can. All this is very hard!

I believe it had been better if I had refused to print the said advertisement. However, 'tis done, and cannot be revoked. I have only the following few particulars to offer, some of them in my behalf, by way of mitigation, and some not much to the purpose; but I desire none of them may be read when the reader is not in a very good humour.

1. That I really did it without the least malice, and imagined the *N. B.* was placed there only to make the advertisement stared at, and more generally read.

2. That I never saw the word *Sea-Hens* before in my

life; nor have I yet asked the meaning of it; and tho' I had certainly known that *Black Gowns* in that place signified the clergy of the Church of England, yet I have that confidence in the generous good temper of such of them as I know, as to be well satisfied such a trifling mention of their habit gives them no disturbance.

3. That most of the clergy in this and the neighbouring provinces, are my customers, and some of them my very good friends; and I must be very malicious indeed, or very stupid, to print this thing for a small profit, if I had thought it would have given them just cause of offence.

4. That if I had much malice against the clergy, and withal much sense, 'tis strange I never write or talk against the clergy myself. Some have observed that 'tis a fruitful topic, and the easiest to be witty upon of all others; yet I appeal to the publick that I am never guilty this way, and to all my acquaintances as to my conversation.

5. That if a man of sense had malice enough to desire to injure the clergy, this is the foolishest thing he could possibly contrive for that purpose.

6. That I got five shillings by it.

7. That none who are angry with me would have given me so much to let it alone.

8. That if all the people of different opinions in this province would engage to give me as much for not printing things they don't like, as I can get by printing them, I should probably live a very easy life; and if all printers were everywhere so dealt by, there would be very little printed.

9. That I am obliged to all who take my paper, and am willing to think they do it out of meer friendship. I only desire they would think the same when I deal with them. I thank those who leave off, that they have taken it so

long. But I beg they would not endeavour to dissuade others, for that will look like malice.

10. That 'tis impossible any man should know what he would do if he was a printer.

11. That notwithstanding the rashness and inexperience of youth, which is most likely to be prevailed with to do things that ought not to be done, yet I have avoided printing such things as usually give offence either to Church or State, more than any printer that has followed the business in this Province before.

12. And lastly, that I have printed above a thousand advertisements which made not the least mention of *Sea-Hens* or *Black Gowns;* and this being the first offence, I have the more reason to expect forgiveness.

I take leave to conclude with an old fable, which some of my readers have heard before, and some have not.

"A certain well meaning man and his son were travelling towards a market town, with an ass which they had to sell. The road was bad, and the old man therefore rid, but the son went a-foot. The first passenger they met, asked the father if he was not ashamed to ride by himself, and suffer the poor lad to wade along thro' the mire; this induced him to take up his son behind him. He had not travelled far, when he met others, who said, they are two unmerciful lubbers to get both on the back of that poor ass in such a deep road. Upon this the old man gets off, and let his son ride alone. The next they met called the lad a graceless, rascally young jackanapes, to ride in that manner thro' the dirt, while his aged father trudged along on foot; and they said the old man was a fool, for suffering it. He then bid his son come down, and walk with him, and they travelled on leading the ass by the halter 'till they

met another company, who called them a couple of sense-
less blockheads, for going both on foot in such a dirty way,
when they had an empty ass with them which they might
ride upon. The old man could bear no longer. My son,
said he, it grieves me much that we cannot please all these
people. Let me throw the ass over the next bridge, and be
no further troubled with him."

Had the old man been seen acting this last resolution,
he would probably have been called a fool for troubling
himself about the different opinions of all that were
pleased to find fault with him. Therefore, tho' I have a
temper almost as complying as his, I intend not to imitate
him in this last particular. I consider the variety of humors
among men, and despair of pleasing everybody; yet I shall
not therefore leave off printing. I shall continue my business. I shall not burn my press and melt my letters.

A Second Apology for Printers

(The following extract is reprinted from the
"postscript" to the *Pennsylvania Gazette*, July 24, 1740.)

It is a principle among printers, that when truth has fair
play, it will always prevail over falshood; therefore, though
they have an undoubted property in their own press, yet
they willingly allow, that any one is entitled to the use
of it, who thinks it necessary to offer his sentiments on
disputable points to the publick, and will be at the expence of it. If what is thus published be good, mankind
has the benefit of it: if it be bad (I speak now in general
without any designed application to any particular piece

whatever) the more 'tis made publick, the more its weakness is exposed and the greater disgrace falls upon the author, whoever he be; who is at the same time deprived of an advantage he would otherwise without fail make use of, *viz.* of complaining that truth is suppressed, and that he could say mighty matters, had he but the opportunity of being heard.

The printers of this city have been unjustly reflected on, as if they were under some undue influence, and guilty of great partiality in favour of the preaching lately admired among us, so as to refuse printing anything in opposition to it, how just or necessary soever. A reflection entirely false and groundless, and without the least colour of fact to support it; which all will be convinced of when they see the following piece from one press, and the Rev. Mr. Cummings's sermons against the doctrines themselves, from the other.

English men thought it an intolerable hardship, when (tho' by an act of their own Parliament) thoughts, which should be free, were fettered and confined and an officer was erected over the nation, called a licenser of the press, without whose consent no writing could be published. Care might indeed be taken in the choice of this officer, that he should be a man of great understanding, profound learning and extraordinary piety; yet, as the greatest and best of men may have some errors, and have been often found averse to some truths, it was justly esteemed a national grievance, that the people should have nothing to read but the opinions, or what was agreeable to the opinions of one man. But should every petty printer (who, if he can read his hornbook, may be thought to have learning enough to qualify him for his own sphere) presume to erect himself into an officer of this kind, and arbitrarily decide what ought and what ought not to be published, much more justly might the world complain. 'Tis true, where invectives are contained in any piece, there is no good-natured printer but had much rather be employed in work of another kind: however, tho' many personal reflections be interwoven in the following performance, yet as the author (who has subscribed his name*) thought then necessary, to vindicate his own conduct and character it is therefore hoped, on that consideration the reader will excuse the printer in publishing them.

VI. RESPONSIBILITIES OF THE PRESS

One of the functions of a newspaper, as Franklin tells us, is to educate the public. A newspaper publisher and editor had, in Franklin's view, to be scrupulous in avoiding character assassination or an endorsement of either party in private altercations. Franklin's policy was not to follow a safe middle ground and avoid controversy, but rather to advance private unorthodoxies and "causes" chiefly in pamphlets and not in newspapers, except in a few cases where the issue was of general interest.

(The first of the following two extracts comes from Franklin's autobiography. The second is a letter written by Franklin to the editors of the *Pennsylvania Gazette* in

---

* *I.e.*, Ebenezer Kinnersley, a Baptist preacher, Professor of the English Tongue and of Oratory in the College of Pennsylvania: one of Franklin's co-experimenters in electricity. Franklin's article, unsigned, was followed by a letter from Kinnersley "to a friend in the country," dated Philadelphia, July 15, 1740, explaining his opposition to the preaching of the revivalist George Whitefield and defending his own character.

1788, long after he had ceased to edit and publish it; Franklin's style is shown here in a letter to the editor enclosing one just received—both written by Franklin for the occasion.)

No Abuse of Persons by the Press

In the conduct of my newspaper, I carefully excluded all libelling and personal abuse, which is of late years become so disgraceful to our country. Whenever I was solicited to insert any thing of that kind, and the writers pleaded, as they generally did, the liberty of the press, and that a newspaper was like a stage-coach, in which any one who would pay had a right to a place, my answer was, that I would print the piece separately if desired, and the author might have as many copies as he pleased to distribute himself, but that I would not take upon me to spread his detraction; and that, having contracted with my subscribers to furnish them with what might be either useful or entertaining, I could not fill their papers with private altercation, in which they had no concern, without doing them manifest injustice. Now, many of our printers make no scruple of gratifying the malice of individuals by false accusations of the fairest characters among ourselves, augmenting animosity even to the producing of duels; and are, moreover, so indiscreet as to print scurrilous reflections on the government of neighboring states, and even on the conduct of our best national allies, which may be attended with the most pernicious consequences. These things I mention as a caution to young printers, and that they may be encouraged not to pollute their presses and disgrace their profession by such infamous practices, but refuse steadily, as they may see by my example that such a course of conduct will not, on the whole, be injurious to their interests. . . .

To the Editors of the Pennsylvania Gazette

Messrs. Hall and Sellers,

I lately heard a remark, that on examination of *The Pennsylvania Gazette* for fifty years, from its commencement, it appeared, that, during that long period, scarce one libellous piece had ever appeared in it. This generally chaste conduct of your paper is much to its reputation; for it has long been the opinion of sober, judicious people, that nothing is more likely to endanger the liberty of the press, than the abuse of that liberty, by employing it in personal accusation, detraction, and calumny. The excesses some of our papers have been guilty of in this particular, have set this State in a bad light abroad, as appears by the following letter, which I wish you to publish, not merely to show your own disapprobation of the practice, but as a caution to others of the profession throughout the United States. For I have seen a European newspaper, in which the editor, who had been charged with frequently calumniating the Americans, justifies himself by saying, "that he had published nothing disgraceful to us, which he had not taken from our own printed papers." I am, etc.   *A. B.*

"New York, March 30, 1788.
"Dear Friend,
    "My gout has at length left me, after five months' painful confinement. It afforded me, however, the leisure to

read, or hear read, all the packets of your various newspapers, which you so kindly sent for my amusement.

"Mrs. W. has partaken of it; she likes to read the advertisements; but she remarks some kind of inconsistency in
the announcing so many diversions for almost every evening of the week, and such quantities to be sold of expensive superfluities, fineries, and luxuries just imported,
in a country, that at the same time fills its papers with
complaints of hard times, and want of money. I tell her,
that such complaints are common to all times and all
countries, and were made even in Solomon's time; when
as we are told, silver was as plenty in Jerusalem as the
stones in the street; and yet, even then, there were people
who grumbled, so as to incur this censure from that knowing prince. 'Say not thou that the former times were
better than these; for thou dost not enquire rightly concerning that matter.'

"But the inconsistence that strikes me the most is, that
between the name of your city, Philadelphia, (Brotherly
Love,) and the spirit of rancour, malice, and hatred that
breathes in its newspapers. For I learn from those papers,
that your state is divided into parties, that each party
ascribes all the public operations of the other to vicious
motives; that they do not even suspect one another of the
smallest degree of honesty; that the antifederalists are
such, merely from the fear of losing power, places, or
emoluments, which they have in possession or in expectation; that the federalists are a set of conspirators, who aim
at establishing a tyranny over the persons and property of
their countrymen, and to live in splendor on the plunder
of the people. I learn, too, that your justices of the peace,
tho' chosen by their neighbours, make a villainous trade of
their office, and promote discord to augment fees, and

fleece their electors; and that this would not be mended by placing the choice in the executive council, who, with interested or party views, are continually making as improper appointments; witness a 'petty fidler, sycophant, and scoundrel,' appointed judge of the Admiralty; 'an old woman and fomenter of sedition' to be another of the judges, and 'a Jeffries' Chief Justice, etc., etc.; with 'two Harpies' the comptroller and naval officers, to prey upon the merchants and deprive them of their property by force of arms, etc.

"I am informed also by these papers, that your General Assembly, tho' the annual choice of the people, shows no regard to their rights, but from sinister views or ignorance makes laws in direct violation of the Constitution, to divest the inhabitants of their property and give it to strangers and intruders; and that the Council, either fearing the resentment of their constituents, or plotting to enslave them, had projected to disarm them, and given orders for that purpose; and finally, that your president, the unanimous joint choice of the Council and Assembly, is 'an old rogue,' who gave his assent to the federal Constitution merely to avoid refunding money he had purloined from the United States.

"There is, indeed, a good deal of manifest inconsistency in all this, and yet a stranger, seeing it in your own prints, tho' he does not believe it all, may probably believe enough of it to conclude, that Pennsylvania is peopled by a set of the most unprincipled, wicked, rascally, and quarrelsome scoundrels upon the face of the globe. I have sometimes, indeed, suspected, that those papers are the manufacture of foreign enemies among you, who write with a view of disgracing your country, and making you appear contemptible and detestable all the world over;

but then I wonder at the indiscretion of your printers in publishing such writings! There is, however, one of your inconsistencies that consoles me a little, which is, that tho' living, you give one another the characters of devils; dead, you are all angels! It is delightful, when any of you die, to read what good husbands, good fathers, good friends, good citizens, and good Christians you were, concluding with a scrap of poetry that places you, with certainty, every one in heaven. So that I think Pennsylvania a good country to dye in, though a very bad one to live in."

VII. Humor in the Pennsylvania Gazette

As a skilled writer, a well-informed student of international affairs and a keen observer of life around him, Franklin made of his newspaper—the *Pennsylvania Gazette*—one of the foremost papers in the land. Like all good editors, Franklin did not limit himself to the presentation of information; the pages of the *Gazette* were a forum for the debate of public issues, and the editorial policy was to advance useful projects for the betterment of the community. But over and above such qualities, the one consistent feature of delight to its readers was the stream of good fun that flowed from Franklin's pen—often at his own expense—satirical essays, humorous poems and amusing letters, and sometimes burlesques of the news, riddles and the annual "carrier's address." Here is a news item about a local "p——r" [printer]:

Thursday last, a certain p——r ('tis not customary to give names at length on these occasions) walking carefully in clean clothes over some barrels of tar on Carpenter's Wharff, the head of one of them unluckily gave

way, and let a leg of him in above the knee. Whether he
was upon the catch at that time, we cannot say, but 'tis
certain he caught a Tar-tar. 'Twas observed he sprang
out again right briskly, verifying the common saying, as
nimble as a bee in a tarbarrel. You must know there are
several sorts of bees: 'tis true he was no honey bee, nor yet
a humble bee; but a boo-bee he may be allowed to be,
namely B. F.

No wonder Philadelphians in the mid-eighteenth century looked forward to each issue of the *Gazette!* Report-
ing how a Bucks County farmer had had the pewter but-
tons of his "waistband" melted off by a stroke of lightning,
Franklin observed, " 'Tis well nothing else thereabouts
was made of pewter." He had a "correspondent" write
that he was "courting a girl" with whom he was not well
acquainted; "How shall I come to a knowledge of her
faults, and whether she has the virtues I imagine she has?"
The answer given by the editor was: "Commend her
among her female acquaintances." Readers of the *Gazette*
learned in 1729:

This week two young fellows, taylors, near Hungerford
Market, who made love to the same young damsel (she
not knowing which to chuse), resolved to decide the affair
by single combat. Accordingly they went into the fields,
attended by a great crowd of spectators, and fought man-
fully 'till at length one of them was beat, and it is supposed the other will be married; so that it is a dispute
which gets the worst of it.

[This paragraph, the one quoted just above, and the
selection immediately below are taken from Paul Leicester
Ford's *The Many-Sided Franklin* (New York: The Century Co., 1899).]

Printerum est errare

Sir,

As your last paper was reading in some company where I was present, these words were taken notice of in the article concerning Governor Belcher, "after which his Excellency, with the gentlemen trading to New England, died elegantly at Pontack's." The word died should doubtless have been dined, Pontack's being a noted tavern and eating-house in London for gentlemen of condition; but this omission of the letter *n* in that word, gave us as much entertainment as any part of your paper. One took the opportunity of telling us that in a certain edition of the Bible, the printer had, where David says I am fearfully and wonderfully made, omitted the letter *e* in the last word, so that it was, I am fearfully and wonderfully mad; which occasioned an ignorant preacher, who took that text, to harangue his audience for half an hour on the subject of spiritual madness. Another related to us, that when the Company of Stationers in England had the printing of the Bible in their hands, the word *not* was left out in the Seventh Commandment, and the whole edition was printed off with Thou shalt commit adultery, instead of Thou shalt not, etc. This material erratum induced the Crown to take the patent from them which is now held by the King's printer. The Spectator's remark upon this story is, that he doubts many of our modern gentlemen have this faulty edition by 'em, and are not made sensible of the mistake. A third person in the company acquainted us with an unlucky fault that went through a whole impression of common-prayerbooks; in the funeral service, where these words are, We shall all be changed in a moment, in the twinkling of an eye, etc., the printer had omitted the *c* in changed, and it read thus, We shall all be hanged, etc. And lastly, a mistake of your brother news-printer was mentioned in the speech of James Prouse written the night before he was to have been executed, instead of I die a Protestant, he has put it, I died a Protestant. Upon the whole you came off with the more favourable censure, because your paper is most commonly very correct, and yet you were never known to triumph upon it, by publickly ridiculing and exposing the continual blunders of your contemporary. Which observation was concluded by a good old gentlemen in company, with this general just remark, that whoever accustoms himself to pass over in silence the faults of his neighbours, shall meet with much better quarter from the world when he happens to fall into a mistake himself; for the satyrical and censorious, whose hand is against every man, shall upon such occasions have every man's hand against him.

The Drinker's Dictionary*

A.

He is Addled.
He's casting up his
 Accounts.
Afflicted.
In his Airs.

B.

He's Biggy.
Bewitched.
Block and Block.

Boozy.
Bowz'd.
Been at Barbadoes.
Drunk as a Wheelbarrow.
Burdock'd.
Busky.
Buzzey.
Has stole a Manchet out of
 the Brewer's Basket.
His head is full of Bees.
Has been in the Bibbing
 Plot.

---

* Reprinted from James Parton's *Life and Times of Benjamin Franklin* (New York: Mason Brothers, 1864), vol. 1, pp. 222-225.

Drank more than he has Bled.
He's Bungey.
As drunk as a Beggar.
He sees the Bears.
He's kiss'd Black Betty.
Had a thump over the head with Sampson's Jawbone.
Bridgey.

C.

He's Cat.
Cagrin'd.
Capable.
Cramp'd.
He's Cherubimical.
Cherry Merry.
Wamble Crop'd.
Crack'd.
Concern'd.
Half way to Concord.
Has taken a Chirriping-Glass.
Got Corns in his head.
A Cup too much.
Coguy.
Copey.
He's heat his Copper.
Crocus.
Catch'd.
He cuts his Capers.
He's been in the Cellar.
In his Cups.
Non Compos.
Cock'd.
Curv'd.

Cut.
Chipper.
Chickery.
Loaded his Cart.
Been too free with the Creature.
Sir Richard has taken off his Considering Cap.
He's Chap-fallen.

D.

He's Disguiz'd.
Got a Dish.
Killed his Dog.
Took his Drops.
It is a Dark Day with him.
He's a Dead Man.
Has Dipp'd his Bill.
He's Dagg'd.
Seen the Devil.

E.

He's Prince Eugene.
Enter'd.
Wet both Eyes.
Cock Ey'd.
Got the Pole Evil.
Got a brass Eye.
Made an Example.
Eat a Load & a half for Breakfast.
In his Element.

F.

He's Fishey.
Fox'd.

Fuddled.
Sore Footed.
Frozen.
Well in for't.
Owes no man a Farthing.
Fears no Man.
Crump Footed.
Been to France.
Flush'd.
Froze his Mouth.
Fetter'd.
Been to a Funeral.
His Flag is out.
He's Fuzl'd.
  Spoke with his Friend.
  Been at an Indian Feast.

G.

He's Glad.
He's Groatable.
  Gold-headed.
  Glaiz'd.
  Generous.
  Booz'd the Gage.
  As Dizzy as a Goose.
  Been before George.
  Got the Gout.
  Had a Kick in the Guts.
  Been with Sir John Goa.
  Been at Geneva.
  Globular.
  Got the Glanders.

H.

He's Half and Half.
  Hardy.

Top Heavy.
Got by the Head.
Hiddey.
  Got on his little Hat.
  Hammerish.
  Loose in the Hilts.
  Knows not the way
    Home.
  Got the Hornson.
  Haunted with Evil
    Spirits.
Has taken Hippocrates'
  Grand Elixir.

I., J.

He's Intoxicated.
Jolly.
Jagg'd.
Jambl'd.
  Going to Jerusalem.
  Jocular.
  Been to Jerico.
  Juicy.

K.

He's a King.
  Clips the King's English.
  Seen the French King.
  The King is his Cousin.
  Got Kib'd Heels.
  Knapt.
  Het his Kettle.

L.

He's in Liquor.
  Lordly.

He makes Indentures
  with his Leggs.
Well to Live.
Light.
Lappy.
Limber.

M.

He sees two Moons.
Merry.
Middling.
Moon-eyed.
Muddled.
Seen a Flock of Moons.
Maudlin.
Mountous.
Muddy.
Rais'd his Monuments.
Mellow.

N.

He's Eat the Cocoa Nut.
Nimptopsical.
Got the Night Mare.

O.

He's Oil'd.
  Eat Opium.
  Smelt of an Onion.
  Oxycrocium.
He's Overset.

P.

He drank till he gave up his
  Half Penny.
Pidgeon Ey'd.

Pungey.
Priddy.
As good conditioned as a
  Puppy.
Has Scalt his Head Pan.
Been among the
  Philistines.
In his Prosperity.
He's been among the
  Philippians.
Contending with
  Pharaoh.
Wasted his Paunch.
Polite.
Eat a Pudding Bag.

Q.

He's Quarrelsome.

R.

He's Rocky.
  Raddled.
  Rich.
  Religious.
  Lost his Rudder.
  Ragged.
  Rais'd.
  Been too free with Sir
    Richard.
  Like a Rat in Trouble.

S.

He's Stitch'd.
  Seafaring.
  In the Sudds.
  Strong.

Been in the Sun.
He's as Drunk as David's
  Sow.
Swampt.
His Skin is full.
He's Steady.
He's Stiff.
He's burnt his Shoulder.
He's got his Top Gallant
  Sails out.
Seen the yellow Star.
As Stiff as a Ringbolt.
Half Seas over.
His Shoe pinches him.
Staggerish.
It is Star-light with him.
He carries too much Sail.
Stew'd.
Stubb'd.
Soak'd.
Soft.
Been too free with Sir
  John Strawberry.
He's right before the wind
  with all his Studding
  Sails out.
Has sold his Senses.

T.

He's Top'd.
Tongue-ty'd.
Tann'd.
Tipium Grove.
Double Tongu'd.
Topsy-Turvey.
Tipsey.
He's swallowed a Tavern
  Token.
He's Thaw'd.
He's in a Trance.
He's Trammel'd.

V.

He makes Virginia Fence.
Valiant.
Got the Indian Vapours.

W.

The Malt is above the
  Water.
He's Wise.
He's Wet.
He's been to the Salt Water.
He's Water Soaken.
He's very Weary.
Out of the Way.

VIII. Last Acts

Characteristically, the last public act Franklin performed
was in the service of his fellow men and the last letter he
wrote was in the service of his country. In 1787, he had
become president of the Pennsylvania Society for Promoting the Abolition of Slavery, and the Relief of Free Ne-

groes, Unlawfully Held in Bondage. Franklin signed "An Address to the Public" (which he may even have written) on November 9, 1789.

An Address to the Public

It is with peculiar satisfaction we assure the friends of humanity, that, in prosecuting the design of our association, our endeavours have proved successful, far beyond our most sanguine expectations.

Encouraged by this success, and by the daily progress of that luminous and benign spirit of liberty, which is diffusing itself throughout the world, and humbly hoping for the continuance of the divine blessing on our labours, we have ventured to make an important addition to our original plan, and do therefore earnestly solicit the support and assistance of all who can feel the tender emotions of sympathy and compassion, or relish the exalted pleasure of beneficence.

Slavery is such an atrocious debasement of human nature, that its very extirpation, if not performed with solicitous care, may sometimes open a source of serious evils.

The unhappy man, who has long been treated as a brute animal, too frequently sinks beneath the common standard of the human species. The galling chains, that bind his body, do also fetter his intellectual faculties, and impair the social affections of his heart. Accustomed to move like a mere machine, by the will of a master, reflection is suspended; he has not the power of choice; and reason and conscience have but little influence over his conduct, because he is chiefly governed by the passion of fear. He is poor and friendless; perhaps worn out by extreme labour, age, and disease.

Under such circumstances, freedom may often prove a misfortune to himself, and prejudicial to society.

Attention to emancipated black people, it is therefore to be hoped, will become a branch of our national policy; but, as far as we contribute to promote this emancipation, so far that attention is evidently a serious duty incumbent on us, and which we mean to discharge to the best of our judgment and abilities.

To instruct, to advise, to qualify those, who have been restored to freedom, for the exercise and enjoyment of civil liberty, to promote in them habits of industry, to furnish them with employments suited to their age, sex, talents, and other circumstances, and to procure their children an education calculated for their future situation in life; these are the great outlines of the annexed plan, which we have adopted, and which we conceive will essentially promote the public good, and the happiness of these our hitherto too much neglected fellow-creatures.

A plan so extensive cannot be carried into execution without considerable pecuniary resources, beyond the present ordinary funds of the Society. We hope much from the generosity of enlightened and benevolent freemen, and will gratefully receive any donations or subscriptions for this purpose, which may be made to our treasurer, James Starr, or to James Pemberton, chairman of our committee of correspondence.

Signed, by order of the Society,

B. Franklin, President.

Philadelphia, 9th of
November, 1789.

Franklin also signed the Society's memorial (of February 12, 1789) to the first Congress, in which the new government was urged to do everything within its power to dis-

courage the traffic in human beings; following debate, the
memorial went to a committee which reported that the
Congress could not interfere in any way in the internal
affairs of the several states. In his Last Will and Testament, Franklin bequeathed his Ohio lands to his son-in-
law Richard Bache, and forgave him a debt of over two
thousand pounds—"in consideration thereof he would immediately after my decease manumit and set free his Negro man Bob." Just three months before his death, Franklin wrote a spirited hoax "On the Slave Trade" for the
Federal Gazette in reply to a speech of James Jackson of
Georgia, who had in Congress opposed any "meddling
with the affair of slavery, or attempting to mend the condition of slaves." It was a brilliant parody in the form
of a defense by Sidi Mehemet Ibrahim of Algiers of the
right and duty of the Algerians to have and to sell Christian slaves, despite "the petition of the sect called Erika,
or Purists, who prayed for the abolition of piracy and
slavery, as unjust."

To the Editor of the Federal Gazette

March 23d, 1790

Sir,

Reading last night in your excellent paper the speech
of Mr. Jackson in Congress against their meddling with
the affair of slavery, or attempting to mend the condition
of the slaves, it put me in mind of a similar one made
about 100 years since by Sidi Mehemet Ibrahim, a member of the Divan of Algiers, which may be seen in Martin's
Account of his Consulship, anno 1687. It was against
granting the petition of the sect called *Erika*, or Purists,

who prayed for the abolition of piracy and slavery as
being unjust. Mr. Jackson does not quote it; perhaps he
has not seen it. If, therefore, some of its reasonings are to
be found in his eloquent speech, it may only show that
men's interests and intellects operate and are operated
on with surprising similarity in all countries and climates,
when under similar circumstances. The African's speech,
as translated, is as follows.

"Allah Bismillah, etc. God is great, and Mahomet is his
Prophet.

"Have these *Erika* considered the consequences of
granting their petition? If we cease our cruises against
the Christians, how shall we be furnished with the commodities their countries produce, and which are so necessary for us? If we forbear to make slaves of their people,
who in this hot climate are to cultivate our lands? Who
are to perform the common labours of our city, and in our
families? Must we not then be our own slaves? And is
there not more compassion and more favour due to us
as Mussulmen, than to these Christian dogs? We have
now above 50,000 slaves in and near Algiers. This number,
if not kept up by fresh supplies, will soon diminish, and
be gradually annihilated. If we then cease taking and
plundering the infidel ships, and making slaves of the
seamen and passengers, our lands will become of no value
for want of cultivation; the rents of houses in the city
will sink one half; and the revenues of government arising
from its share of prizes be totally destroyed! And for
what? To gratify the whims of a whimsical sect, who
would have us not only forbear making more slaves, but
even to manumit those we have.

"But who is to indemnify their masters for the loss?

Will the state do it? Is our treasury sufficient? Will the
Erika do it? Can they do it? Or would they, to do what
they think justice to the slaves, do a greater injustice to
the owners? And if we set our slaves free, what is to be
done with them? Few of them will return to their countries; they know too well the greater hardships they must
there be subject to; they will not embrace our holy religion; they will not adopt our manners; our people will
not pollute themselves by intermarrying with them. Must
we maintain them as beggars in our streets, or suffer our
properties to be the prey of their pillage? For men long
accustomed to slavery will not work for a livelihood when
not compelled. And what is there so pitiable in their
present condition? Were they not slaves in their own
countries?

"Are not Spain, Portugal, France, and the Italian states
governed by despots, who hold all their subjects in slavery, without exception? Even England treats its sailors
as slaves; for they are, whenever the government pleases,
seized and confined in ships of war, condemned not only
to work, but to fight, for small wages, or a mere subsistence, not better than our slaves are allowed by us. Is
their condition then made worse by their falling into our
hands? No; they have only exchanged one slavery for another, and I may say a better; for here they are brought
into a land where the sun of Islamism gives forth its light,
and shines in full splendor, and they have an opportunity
of making themselves acquainted with the true doctrine,
and thereby saving their immortal souls. Those who remain at home have not that happiness. Sending the slaves
home then would be sending them out of light into dark-
ness.

"I repeat the question: What is to be done with them?

I have heard it suggested that they may be planted in the wilderness, where there is plenty of land for them to subsist on, and where they may flourish as a free state; but they are, I doubt, too little disposed to labour without compulsion, as well as too ignorant to establish a good government, and the wild Arabs would soon molest and destroy or again enslave them. While serving us, we take care to provide them with every thing, and they are treated with humanity. The labourers in their own country are, as I am well informed, worse fed, lodged, and cloathed. The condition of most of them is therefore already mended, and requires no further improvement. Here their lives are in safety. They are not liable to be impressed for soldiers, and forced to cut one another's Christian throats, as in the wars of their own countries. If some of the religious mad bigots, who now teaze us with their silly petitions, have in a fit of blind zeal freed their slaves, it was not generosity, it was not humanity, that moved them to the action; it was from the conscious burthen of a load of sins, and hope, from the supposed merits of so good a work, to be excused damnation.

"How grossly are they mistaken in imagining slavery to be disallowed by the *Alcoran!* Are not the two precepts, to quote no more, '*Masters, treat your slaves with kindness; Slaves, serve your masters with cheerfulness and fidelity,*' clear proofs to the contrary? Nor can the plundering of infidels be in that sacred book forbidden, since it is well known from it that God has given the world, and all that it contains, to his faithful Mussulmen, who are to enjoy it of right as fast as they conquer it. Let us then hear no more of this detestable proposition, the manumission of Christian slaves, the adoption of which would, by depreciating our lands and houses, and thereby depriving

so many good citizens of their properties, create universal
discontent, and provoke insurrections, to the endangering
of government and producing general confusion. I have
therefore no doubt, but this wise council will prefer the
comfort and happiness of a whole nation of true believers
to the whim of a few *Erika*, and dismiss their petition."

The result was, as Martin tells us, that the Divan came
to this resolution; "The doctrine, that plundering and en-
slaving the Christians is unjust, is at best *problematical;*
but that it is the interest of this state to continue the
practice, is clear; therefore let the petition be rejected."

And it was rejected accordingly.

And since like motives are apt to produce in the minds
of men like opinions and resolutions, may we not, Mr.
Brown, venture to predict, from this account, that the
petitions to the Parliament of England for abolishing the
slave-trade, to say nothing of other legislatures, and the
debates upon them, will have a similar conclusion? I am,
Sir, your constant reader and humble servant,

Historicus.

Franklin's last letter, written just nine days before his
death, was addressed to Thomas Jefferson—an association
of two great democrats which has a symbolic fitness in
a great American tradition. This letter, dated April 8,
1790, represents Franklin's last service to his country,
which called on him to the very end. Jefferson had written
him a request for any facts which his "memory or papers"
might enable him to recollect concerning the eastern
boundary of the United States, between Maine and Nova
Scotia: was it the *western* or the *eastern* "river of the Bay
of Passamaquoddy which was designated by the name of
St. Croix in the treaty of peace"? Franklin still had the

map used by the commissioners, the one published by his old friend John Mitchell twenty years earlier; he sent along to Jefferson "that sheet which contains the Bay of Passamaquoddy, where you will see that part of the boundary traced." He was then eighty-four years of age and "under a severe fit of my malady"; he had not, therefore, been able to answer the letter immediately, nor attend "to any kind of business." When at last he found himself able to write to Jefferson, his mind was sharp and his memory precise, and he supplied the needed data to the accompaniment of these magnificent words: "I am perfectly clear in the remembrance."

BIBLIOGRAPHY AND INDEX

BIBLIOGRAPHY

Readers interested in the life of Benjamin Franklin may consult Carl Van Doren's biography, *Benjamin Franklin* (New York: The Viking Press, 1938), and the companion volume, *Benjamin Franklin's Autobiographical Writings* (New York: The Viking Press, 1945), and Paul Leicester Ford's *The Many-Sided Franklin* (New York: The Century Co., 1899). Various aspects of Franklin's career are discussed in *Meet Dr. Franklin* (Philadelphia: The Franklin Institute, 1943). Carl L. Becker's stimulating essay on Franklin, first published in the *Dictionary of American Biography*, has been reprinted by the Cornell University Press. The conflicting views held about Franklin during the nineteenth and twentieth centuries are ably presented by Dixon Wecter in "Poor Richard: The boy who made good," Chapter 4 of his book *The Hero in America, a chronicle of hero-worship* (New York: Charles Scribner's Sons, 1941).

Franklin's political views prior to the Revolution may best be studied in Verner W. Crane's *Benjamin Franklin, Englishman and American* (Baltimore: Williams and Wilkins, 1936) and his edition of *Benjamin Franklin's Letters to the Press 1758-1775* (Chapel Hill: University of North Carolina Press, 1950). Franklin's scientific writings are available in I. Bernard Cohen, *Benjamin Franklin's Experiments: a new edition of Franklin's "Experiments and Observations on Electricity,"* edited with a critical and historical introduction (Cambridge: Harvard University Press, 1941); a monograph on Franklin's science is being completed for publication by the American Philosophical Society and the Princeton University Press.

Franklin's writings on education have been edited by Thomas Woody, *Educational Views of Benjamin Franklin* (New York: McGraw-Hill, 1931), and his writings on economics have been summarized in Lewis J. Carey, *Franklin's Economic Views* (Garden City, N. Y.: Doubleday, Doran, 1928). Benjamin Smith has edited material from the almanacs, *Poor Richard's Almanack . . . Selections from the prefaces, apothegms, and rimes* (New York: The Century Co., 1926); a similar collection was made by Paul Leicester Ford, *The Sayings of Poor Richard, The prefaces, proverbs, and poems of Benjamin Franklin, originally printed in Poor Richard Almanacs for 1733-1758* (Brooklyn, N. Y.: privately printed, 1890).

The most recent edition of Franklin's writings was edited by Albert H. Smyth, *The Writings of Benjamin Franklin* (10 vols.; New York: The Macmillan Co., 1910); it does not contain all the works printed in earlier collections by John Bigelow, Jared Sparks and others; several important volumes of Franklin correspondence (with his sister Jane Mecom, with Richard Jackson and with Catherine Ray) have been published under the sponsorship of the American Philosophical Society. Franklin's manuscript version of his autobiography, in the Huntington Library, was edited by Max Farrand and printed in *Benjamin Franklin's Memoirs, parallel text edition, comprising the texts of Franklin's original manuscript, the French translation by Louis Guillaume le Veillard, the French translation published by Buisson, and the version edited by William Temple Franklin, his grandson* (Berkeley: University of California Press, 1949). Several uncollected writings have been made available in Nathan G. Goodman's *A Benjamin Franklin Reader* (New York: Thomas Y. Crowell Company, 1945); Frank Luther Mott and Chester E. Jorgenson, *Benjamin Franklin, Representative Selections, with Introduction, Bibliography, and Notes* (New York: American Book Company, 1936) contains a notable bibliography of primary and secondary material. Paul Leicester Ford's *Franklin Bibliography: A list of books written by or relating to Benjamin Franklin* (Brooklyn, N. Y.: no publisher, 1889), although faulty and incomplete, is still valuable.

INDEX

A

Abraham, 28
Adams, Matthew, 75
Addison, Joseph, *Cato*, quoted, 127-128
Adult education, 44, 149
Albany Plan of Union (1754), 37, 144-145, 226, 228
Allen, Judge, 99
American Philosophical Society, 171
Archer, Dr., 197

B

Bache, Richard, son-in-law of Franklin, 156, 298
Bacon, Francis, 52, 56
Bailey, Francis, 163
Baird, Dr., 102
Balzac, Honoré de, 38
Becker, Carl, on Franklin, 39
Bedford, Duke of, 252, 252 n.
Belcher, Gov. Jonathan, 290
Bond, Thomas, 177
Boston
    Franklin's birthplace, 71; Franklin leaves, 82; bequest to free schools of, 157-158, 158 n.; small pox and practice of inoculation in, 193-

Boston—*cont.*
    195, 196, 198; Franklin's trust fund to, provisions of, 158-163
Boston News Letter, The, 79
Boyle's Lectures, 100
Boylston, Dr. Zabdiel, 195
Bradford, Andrew, printer, 83, 85, 98, 102, 103, 104, 108-109
Bradford, William, printer, 82-83, 85
Brientnal, Joseph, 102, 103, 107
Brockden, Charles, 165
Brownell, George, 72
Bunyan, John, *Pilgrim's Progress*, 74
Burlington, N. J., Franklin visits on business, 98-99
Burnet, Governor William, 104
Burton, R., *Historical Collections*, 74
Bustill, Samuel, 99

C

Carlyle, Thomas, 38
Carnegie, Andrew, 115
Carroll, John, 46
Catholic Church, 46
Cicero, quoted, 128
Clark, Gen., 255